Scott Walker and the Song of the One-All-Alone

ex:centrics

Series Editors
Greg Hainge and Paul Hegarty

Books in the Series

Philippe Grandrieux: Sonic Cinema by Greg Hainge
Gallery Sound by Caleb Kelly

Scott Walker and the Song of the One-All-Alone

Scott Wilson

BLOOMSBURY ACADEMIC
NEW YORK · LONDON · OXFORD · NEW DELHI · SYDNEY

BLOOMSBURY ACADEMIC
Bloomsbury Publishing Inc
1385 Broadway, New York, NY 10018, USA
50 Bedford Square, London, WC1B 3DP, UK

BLOOMSBURY, BLOOMSBURY ACADEMIC and the Diana logo are trademarks
of Bloomsbury Publishing Plc

First published in the United States of America 2020
Reprinted 2020 (twice)

Cover image: Scott Walker of the Walker Brothers
© Mick Ratman / Topfoto / The Image Works

Library of Congress Cataloging-in-Publication Data
Names: Wilson, Scott, 1962- author.
Title: Scott Walker and the song of the one-all-alone / Scott Wilson.
Description: New York, NY: Bloomsbury Academic, 2019. | Series: Ex:centrics
Includes bibliographical references and index.
Identifiers: LCCN 2019013193 | ISBN 9781501332593 (hardback: alk. paper) |
ISBN 9781501332555 (pbk. : alk. paper)
Subjects: LCSH: Walker, Scott, 1943—Criticism and interpretation. | Popular
music—History and criticism. | Music and literature.
Classification: LCC ML420.W1725 W55 2019 | DDC 782.42164092—dc23
LC record available at https://lccn.loc.gov/2019013193

ISBN: HB: 978-1-5013-3259-3
PB: 978-1-5013-3255-5
ePDF: 978-1-5013-3257-9
eBook: 978-1-5013-3258-6

Typeset by Deanta Global Publishing Services, Chennai, India
Printed and bound in the United States of America

Series: ex:centrics

To find out more about our authors and books visit www.bloomsbury.com and
sign up for our newsletters.

For Jacqueline

CONTENTS

INTRODUCTION

The existentialist pop star

'Scott Walker, experimental pop hero, dies', announced the headline in *The Guardian* on March 26 2019. Though not front page, the piece heralded a number of tribute-pieces from Alex Petrides, Rob Young and Eimear MacBride, alongside soundbites from a range of mainstream and avant-garde figures such as Thom Yorke, Damon Albarn, Cosey Fanni Tutti and Agnes Obel. Super fan Marc Almond's *Instagram* account was quoted, hailing Walker as 'an absolute musical genius, existential and intellectual and a star right from the days of the Walker Brothers' (*The Guardian*, 2019). While at first sight Scott Walker might seem a perfect artist to fit the brief of the Ex:Centrics series that sets out to examine non-mainstream artists, he has not been overlooked. Walker remains a significant if perplexing figure in the UK and elsewhere in Europe. Indeed, his death was reported by all the mainstream newspapers in the UK. Every rare new album over the last 20 years of his life was widely reviewed and generated online comment.

But as *The Guardian* headline suggests, with its contradictory conjunction of 'pop' and the 'experimental', Walker's career is difficult if not impossible for many commentators to fathom. 'Andy Williams re-inventing himself as Stockhausen' (*The Times*, 2019: 59). The lead singer of the 1960s pop group the Walker Brothers was, after many tribulations, destined to become 'a composer of some of the most serious and uncompromising music of his time' (Young, 2013: 2). But how? This trajectory towards 'serious' art continued to attract suspicion; the experimental diminished the pop, disappointing fans, guaranteeing the commercial failure that impeaches the value of a work in an era when popularity is the main measure of legitimacy. 'Scott Walker contrived a brooding mystique of philosophical angst' writes *The Times*, disapprovingly, the word 'contrived' underscoring the journalistic cliché of the superficial nature of philosophical reflection (*The Times*, 2019: 59). To indulge in the latter is to kill the instinctive, natural genius of pop: the English version of bad faith. It is a view that has informed every mainstream review of Walker's later work, but not altogether convincingly because Walker's cultural ambition was evident from the start. To cite just one example from a review of *Soused* (2014) by Neil McCormack of *The Daily Telegraph*. While McCormack initially approves of Walker's 'sublime quasi-orchestral Sixties pop', the 'series of fabulously inventive solo recordings he made on his wayward path from pin-up to serious artist', he then goes on to lament the 'sonically and structurally challenging albums that are easier to appreciate intellectually than listen to'. Regarding his latest effort as 'too self-absorbed for any but the most masochistic listener', McCormick gives *Soused* one star out of five and suggests that a 'beating would do him good', inevitably quoting a line from 'Brando', the first song on the album (which is as far as he seems to have got) (Neil McCormick, 2014).

While any hint of pretention in a pop or rock star immediately brings out the violence in a critic, the problem is also that people are still discovering and falling in love with Walker's 'sublime quasi-orchestral pop', particularly the four solo albums of the late 1960s. These were celebrated on 2017 at the Royal Albert Hall when Prom 15 was dedicated to 'The Songs of Scott Walker (1967-70)' (25.07.17). While the Heritage Orchestra did justice to Walker's imagination, Wally Stott's arrangements and John Frantz's production of the originals, the vocal efforts of Jarvis Cocker, John Grant, Suzanne Sandfør and Richard Hawley more than demonstrated the unsurpassed quality and skill of Walker's singing. With this embrace from the heart of the musical establishment, fifty years after the fact, and now following his death, Scott Walker seems set to become a kind of national treasure – or at least in the shape of a particular romantic image, a cameo from the 1960s set in amber. It seems a strange circuitous route that closes off the journey that Walker actually takes throughout the end of the twentieth century and into the twenty-first, producing songs that I would wager may take at least another fifty years to return in tribute to the Royal Albert Hall.

The 22-year-old Scott Walker arrived in the UK as the bass player of the Walker Brothers in February 1965; the band's calling-card a new single called 'Love Her' produced by Jack Nitzsche. Nitzsche was at the time Phil Spector's arranger and co-creator of the famous 'wall of sound' associated with hits by girl groups such as the Crystals and the Ronettes. The song features Scott on lead vocal for the first time, the bassist's baritone more suited to the sound-template that Nitzsche wanted to employ, the one he and Spector had perfected with the Righteous Brothers' hit 'You've Lost That Lovin' Feeling', a few months earlier. Penned by the same writers, Barry Mann and Cynthia Weil, 'Love Her' was recorded in America but the band promoted it in Europe because they wanted to re-locate to the UK, apparently in order to avoid the draft to fight in Vietnam. London was also supposed to be swinging of course but Walker found that it resembled more the drab if quaint, black-and-white world of the Ealing Comedies. He was familiar with these and other weightier European art films from his days at the Chouinard Art Institute in Los Angeles (LA). Like John Lennon, Pete Townshend and others in the UK pop and rock scene, Scott Walker was an art school alumnus whose cultural horizons were extended at college as much if not more than his illustrious British contemporaries. While Scott is overlooked by Mike Roberts in his history of the powerful link between art and pop from the 1950s to the present, Walker unquestionably shared the 'burning desire to be outside the ordinary' that Roberts suggests characterizes so many of the 'art-school-educated artists/musicians' that he discusses (Roberts, 2018: 12).

After college in LA, Walker gigged with various bands playing bass until hooking up with John Maus. Renaming themselves Walker Brothers, John and Scott played the Sunset Strip, bringing beat music to the supper clubs: young lounge lizards among the go-go girls and film stars, visually if not musically at this time aping the swinging sophistication of Jack Jones and Frank Sinatra. They would achieve a six months residency at the famous Whisky A Go Go club, preceding the Doors' occupancy as house band by two years. Both LA groups eschewed the burgeoning LA 'jingle-jangle' folk-rock associated with the Byrds, and the Walker Brothers' development paralleled the Doors' use of jazz-inflected motifs. When Scott took on lead vocal duties, both bands were fronted by the two greatest baritone voices in pop and rock. It was at the Whisky that Gary Leeds, who had been drumming for P.J. Proby, joined the band and suggested they seek their fortune in London.

In the UK the Walker Brothers produced three hit albums, *Take It Easy With The Walker Brothers* (1965), *Portrait* (1966) and *Images* (1967), alongside a series of unforgettable pop songs such as 'Take It Easy on Yourself', 'My Ship Is Coming In' and 'The Sun Ain't Gonna Shine Anymore' that rank among the best recordings of the 1960s.

Instantly recognizable, these are the songs for which the Walker Brothers are remembered. Always slightly awkward in his persona as a pop heartthrob, eyebrows were raised and lips curled when a sleeve note from *Portrait* (1966) claimed that Scott was 'the existentialist who knows what [it] means and reads Jean-Paul Sartre'. For sure, by the late 1950s and early 1960s, existentialism had become associated with a certain style adopted by 'modernist' hipsters into jazz, American beat culture, European fashion and cinema. Mike Roberts argues that this was the style that the young German artists Astrid Kirchherr and Klaus Vormann encouraged the Beatles to adopt as they became in Hamburg part of 'a clique of Euro-beatniks whom Lennon would refer to as "the Exies" – short for existentialists' (Roberts, 2018: 25). For Walker, however, existentialism was not simply 'a stylistic, lifestyle aspiration' and a set of fashion clichés (Roberts: 24); it remained throughout his life a touchstone of his commitment to his art. This first flourished in the series of eponymous, numbered solo albums that Walker produced from 1967 to 1970. European bohemianism and the dramatic appeal of youthful angst provides the *mise-en-scene* for the startling ambition of these existentialist pop records. The inspired use of orchestral arrangements and lyrical themes drawn from the European avant-garde, *Chanson française*, the cinema of Ingmar Bergman, French New Wave cinema and British social realism make these albums unique. Significantly, Walker's distinctive cover versions of Jacques Brel's songs were partly responsible for introducing the Belgian *chanteur* to the English-speaking world.

According to Sarah Bakewell's best-selling re-evaluation of the philosophical movement, *At the Existentialist Café* (2016), 'existentialism is more of a mood than a philosophy' (1). An indefinable unity of thought and feeling, mood is best conveyed in sound, and Walker has suggested that it is just such a mood that provides continuity throughout the work of his long career (Graham-Dixon, 2006). Existentialism is most closely associated with French philosophers, such as Jean-Paul Sartre, Simone de Beauvoir, Albert Camus and Maurice Merleau-Ponty, whose interpretation of German phenomenologists Edmund Husserl, Karl Jaspers and Martin Heidegger captured the intellectual scene of the late 1930s and 1940s. Rather than construct theories of knowledge around metaphysical ideas that are necessarily detached from the world they seek to conceptualize, phenomenology attempts to ground knowledge in perception and lived experience. Locating itself in a broad tradition that included Søren Kierkegaard, Friedrich Nietzsche and aspects of

Romanticism, existentialism poses the question of existence and how one might take up the responsibility and burden of 'freedom': in particular the freedom to 'become who you are' in the paradoxical formulation of Nietzsche. Accordingly, the vicissitudes of everyday life – and the death that defines it for the one living – took on for these writers more significance than abstract concepts and mathematical formulae. The philosophy thus leant itself to forms of expression found in novels, plays, film and music rather than to academic theses. The struggle to take up the challenge of becoming oneself in contradistinction to an identity that is socially expected and conventional – or even successful – provides the animating focus of much of the literature. The importance of the 'for-itself', however, is for Sartre not at all the basis for hedonistic pleasures or solipsistic self-regard. It is the basis for an *'engagement'*, a commitment that calls upon one's very life. To give up on the desire to commit oneself in this way constitutes for Sartre *mauvaise foi* or 'bad faith'. In the 1950s Sartre sought to evade the tentacles of bad faith by becoming fully committed to Marxism. While Scott Walker retained a strong interest in politics, the goal to become 'for-himself' meant a Camusian 'revolt' against the pop spotlight and a renewed commitment to his art that eventually produced work of an extraordinary, uncompromising quality.

But not before his own collapse into what he has described as his years of bad faith (Kijak, 2006) – and serious 'imbibing'. With the surprising commercial failure of *Scott 4* – a dip that was not arrested by the follow-up *Til the Band Comes In* (1970) – Walker suffered a sudden loss of confidence that left him drifting in an early 1970s hinterland of easy listening covers albums. He defaulted to a middle-of-the-road milieu supposed to generate commercial success in a genre that was already becoming, as Ian Penman notes, 'something of a lost world' (Penman in Young, 2013: 98). Languishing in the radiogram lounge of crooning kitsch, albums like *The Moviegoer* (1973), *Any day Now* (1973) and *Stretch* (1973) failed to generate the sales that might have restored the financial credit and creative drive for more innovative work. A brief moment of commercial success did arrive with the Walker Brothers reunion in 1975, but by 1978 both the band and their record company were facing dissolution. With nothing to lose, the Brothers released an album of their own material rather than the country-rock covers of the previous two. Scott's songs are drawn from a dark, solitary period of his life in the mid-70s following the break-up of his marriage. They constitute a new beginning in which Walker would disappear into the darkness in order to discover his own cavernous and disturbing sound world. The mining of this world would take a long time: new albums came along on average only every ten years. But when they did they were like nothing else in the world of rock and pop, even as they drew from that world in combination with other elements from classical music to modern jazz, *musique concrète* and industrial noise.

As I have suggested, there is an ethic in existentialism that one should not take the conventional or popular path, an ethic that was transformed into a style that informed pop and rock rebellion, the desire for authenticity and the demand to 'keep it real'. It is a style that has been indelibly associated with both artistic and commercial success, the imbalance between the two often marking degrees of 'sell out'. I am going to argue that this familiar logic does not apply to Scott Walker. Certainly, Walker has not followed either the mainstream or 'alternative' path, with the result that he has frequently produced work that is a commercial failure. Neither pop nor punk, Walker has implacably followed his own path, gone his own way – there being, as Nietzsche insists, no correct or right way. As such, it is difficult, if not impossible, to judge whether such uncompromising work is an artistic success; there are no significant comparators. In that regard the existentialism of the work's 'for-itself' is profound. The unfamiliarity of the work means that unpopularity is guaranteed, the rule rather than the exception. Consequently, his fans and listeners are required to show the same commitment to his art as he does; many do not. Yet, in following the ethical path of the unpopular, Walker has arrived at a unique sound according to his own method that has produced a genuinely new form of song. In the phrase of Devin William Daniels, an online enthusiast, 'he may be not only one of the truly strangest musicians of our time, but one of the truly incommensurable' (Daniels, 2012). If you are strange and incommensurable then you are neither mainstream nor extreme, nor are you anywhere in between. You are one all alone.

This poses a problem for anyone wishing to write about Walker's late albums because they can only be defined in the light of his own *savoir-faire* or know-how. *Scott Walker and the Song of the One-all-Alone* is accordingly not a work of criticism where I attempt to evaluate Walker's songs from a position of supposed mastery authorized by my knowledge of something like a 'rock' or even literary canon. Instead, what I propose is to follow Walker's lead, and the brief of this series, by producing my own 'ex-centric' commentary on his work, the nature of which I will come to shortly. First, I will distinguish my approach from the main journalistic and academic forms of writing on contemporary culture, particularly popular music. While apparently opposite both approaches are similar in that they seek to ground their authority in the authenticity of either the artist or the audience – measuring the work's artistic or social value subjectively or according to a quasi-scientific standard of objectivity.

Scott Walker's voice merits a brief mention in Nick Coleman's recent book *Voices: How A Great Singer Can Change Your Life* (2017) where its quality is nicely described as an 'esoteric boom' (200). However, this brief mention comes in the context of a general discussion about the influence of Frank Sinatra, whom Coleman does not like. He does not like Sinatra nor the tradition of the crooner, the mode of singing enabled by the invention of the microphone in the 1920s. Sinatra means nothing to Coleman, and he is therefore 'suspicious' of him. This is because Coleman cannot identify with Sinatra. He cannot put himself in his place. 'I can admire his technical assurance. I can be awed by his éclat. ... But I can't identify. It just isn't in me to be that man, even for a second' (207). I see what Coleman means. I can even identify with it, but I doubt if we can get very far in a discussion of song when it is circumscribed by this highly subjective and ultimately imaginary measure. While identification is inevitable and important, its frustration and problematization is precisely what is at stake in Walker's work. This is particularly the case with the albums from the late 1970s onward where he seeks to strip his famous voice of all 'personality', all soul inflections with which one might identify. Worse, if one were to seek to identify with the various personae in his songs one would be likely to be identifying with a dictator, torturer or child murderer. This is not impossible, of course, and the success and relative popularity of a song like 'The Electrician' (1978) precisely does rely, in an equivocal way, on identification with Sadean and masochistic fantasies. In the late work, Walker's voice will often convey someone in extreme emotional agony. But the problem is that this is sometimes rendered in such a formal, a-tonal manner that it fails to arouse a listener's sympathy or, as with 'The Electrician', cause anything to resonate with his or her darkest desires. It is 'the voice', as Walker says in Stephen Kijak's indispensable documentary *30th Century Man*, 'of just a man singing', (2006) but voided of the usual predicates. As such, the question now concerns not so much what is sung, or how it is sung, but *that* it is sung, and why. The question devolves to the unrepresentable cause of enunciation that is occluded by a voice that Walker always felt was 'a beast all on its own' (*The Times*, 2019). We will return to this.

Since pop and rock music are normally regarded as too simple to interest most musicologists, and pop lyrics not thought worthy of the attention of literary scholars, academic writing on popular music and culture has been left to social scientists interested in the social dimension of music and the ways of life that it promotes. Such work tends to concentrate on audiences, fans and subcultures. It is not much interested in the work as such, but in how it is 'consumed' and what the different modes of consumption can tell us about the effects of such work. Generally by means of questionnaires and more recently by the monitoring of online data, statistics are generated and patterns discerned indicating levels of viewer or listener engagement, orientation and their demographic and diversity profiles. Usually of particular interest are the presumed effects of representations of sex and violence, and the representation of women and other categories of identification. The danger with this approach, as ever, is that responses are conditioned by the framework of the questions and the issues, priorities and world view that inform them. It is nevertheless increasingly the only type of research that is valued by universities because it generates data and purports to be useful. Since this book does not take this approach, I hope, perhaps in vain, that researchers will nevertheless take an interest in Walker's own understanding of the use of questionnaires, attention to audience demand and indeed scientific method generally in songs like 'The Day the Conducator Died (An Xmas Song)' (2012), 'Hand Me Ups' (2005) and 'Pilgrim' (2012) discussed in detail later in the book.

Method and meditation: Tilting Camus

I propose instead to use two methods that are now largely out of favour in academic discourse: interpretation and commentary.[1] This is because I think they are still valuable, and because Walker's work demands them and is incomplete without them. Which is not to say that interpretation and commentary could ever complete them, but their meaning and affect – which can only be registered in a listener – is enhanced through careful engagement with them. Here I seek to elaborate and extend the work through interpretation while acknowledging that such a process is potentially inexhaustible and delusional. Which is why it requires a principle of limitation.

In interviews about his work, Walker would always indicate that 'the idea of listening to [my songs] is that you bring your own interpretation'. Clearly aware of what those in literary studies used to call the 'intentionalist fallacy' (if not 'the death of the author'), he would also allow that an attentive listener's interpretation will 'nine times out of ten [be] probably better' than his own (Young, 2013: 249). However, in this book, I do not intend to go as far as David Bowie recommends in Kijak's documentary. While Bowie commends Walker's song writing, he admits that 'I have no idea what he is singing about, no idea, and I never bothered to find out, and I'm not really interested. I'm quite happy to take the songs that he sings and make something of them myself and read my own reasoning into the images' (Kijak, 2006). Since I am not Bowie, what I make of Walker's lyrics purely for myself will be of no interest to anyone. If it is not to be entirely delusional, interpretation must be organized around a point of orientation external to the work that is both derived from the origin of the work, its references, and which adds something to the half-saying of the lyrics. Some shared sense can then be produced in relation to that point of orientation. Walker himself never fails in interviews to offer these points of orientation. This is as true of the 1960s as it is of the later work. While perhaps not as oblique as some of the later lyrics, the vignettes in the earlier songs are just as seriously engaged with ideas. Lyrics can be deceptively simple, just as they can be deceptively complex.

Supremely, Walker gave over the whole of the back cover of *Scott 4* (1969), the album that some consider to be his best, to a quotation from Albert Camus: 'A man's work is nothing but his slow trek to discover through the detours of art, those two or three great and simple images in whose presence his heart first opened.' This will be the starting principle of the book along with the philosophical tradition with which Camus is associated. As I have already noted, from his early career to the present, Walker has referenced existentialist thought in a variety of ways in relation to different writers. These writers are not exclusively existentialist, of course, but this relation is something that will be emphasized here and used as a centre of gravitation in discussion of Walker's work.

Another indication of how to listen to the records from the 1990s on, following the lyrics which Walker regards as the central governing element to his songs, comes with the album titles. In two instances they even suggest that this has been their method of production, and thus also a legitimate approach to their reception and interpretation. The idea of the album *The Drift* (2006) is that 'it starts with something we know – a political issue, and then it drifts into another world, and into something else. So, all kinds of disparate elements take place'. Ultimately, most of the songs zero into 'an existential moment – the self' (Young, 2013: 249, 251). What constitutes this existential moment, or indeed the self, and how it is lyrically conveyed develops in intensity and complexity over the various albums. *Tilt* (1995), the album that preceded *The Drift*, invites listeners to 'tilt' a theme or object of meditation, following his own practice, thereby bringing to it the light of a different perspective, to the point where it moves or captures you. This manipulation of language and thematic elements also occurs sonically. Speaking of his 'psychological sound', Walker suggests that he and his musicians 'grope around' for sounds until he catches 'this terrifying moment ... the impact of feeling' (Young, 2013: 22).

In her introduction to *Sundog*, Faber's edition of Walker's lyrics, Eimear McBride argues that Walker's method is closer to 'the more Medieval tradition of "artist as conduit" rather than that of a Modernist or Postmodernist' (McBride, 2018: xxi). A Medieval artist would be the conduit of the word of God, of course. But since the early 1960s when, according to fellow Walker Brother Gary Leeds, Scott spent most of his time 'reading Nietzsche and going to Bergman movies' (Woods, 2013: 45), Walker has been the glorifying conduit of the divine inexistence of God. This is why, in this book, interpretation – which has its roots in medieval biblical exegesis – will be supplemented by commentary. While interpretation can provide an orientation that may contract an object (song-text, poetic image, sonic event) around certain points of sense-affect, a commentary or 'gloss', in contrast, tends to magnify and multiply productive syntheses of meanings, ideas and references following the medieval principles of 'dilation', 'copia' and 'proliferation'. In accordance with this practice, I will add other pertinent historical facts and anecdotes in order to illuminate Walker's texts. The book is thus built around interpretative commentaries that will operate a double movement of contraction and dilation in which meanings are both amplified and reduced to points of fixation that bear the pitch and tonal traces of singular events that orient artistic and critical practice. Interpretations will therefore sometimes be tilted in relation to the political and philosophical questions that are raised in the songs, just as the commentaries will drift into broader discussions in relation to the relevant thinkers of the existentialist tradition and some of their contemporaries. In the chapters that follow, Walker's work is read with Albert Camus, Jean-Paul Sartre, Friedrich Nietzsche, Søren Kierkegaard, Maurice Blanchot, Georges Bataille, Simone de Beauvoir, Hannah Arendt, Pier Paolo Pasolini, Martin Heidegger, Franz Kafka, Samuel Beckett and Clarice Lispector. In passing, I will of course also mention other musicians, film makers, artists and writers who have influenced or have an affinity with Walker. But I am not concerned with ranking Walker or the Walker Brothers in the history of pop, or of comparing him with other rock singers. Nor am I taking a biographical approach, although I will refer to events and biographical statements where I think they are pertinent. Readers interested in Walker's biography could consult Paul Woods's *The Curious Life and Work of Scott Walker* (2013). For an attempt at an exhaustive itemization and description of Walker's complete back catalogue up to and including *The Drift*, there is Lewis Williams, *Scott Walker: The Rhymes of Goodbye* (2006). Both these books have been useful in the writing of this one. Another important book is *No Regrets: Writings on Scott Walker* (2013) edited by Rob Young. This book contains an extremely important interview with Walker by Young himself (there is also an extended version available online, see Young, 2006). I make no attempt to give an exhaustive account of Walker's life and work. This book is selective, the principle of selection being driven by the orientation I bring to the work. While some songs will be read out of sequence, the book takes a broadly chronological approach.

By way of example, and to introduce my method and some of the themes in this book, I want to look at Walker's song 'Clara (Benito's Dream)' from *The Drift* (2006). I should note that throughout his career Walker has credited different names to his work. As is oft repeated, none of the Walker Brothers were called Walker nor were they brothers. Their given names are John Maus, Gary Leeds and Noel Scott Engel. For the most part, Scott Walker credits his own compositions to that name, specifically 'N. S. Engel', or 'Scott Engel'. More recently, in the case of *The Drift* (2006), *Bish Bosch* (2012) and *Soused* (2014), the songs are credited to 'Scott Walker'. Throughout the commentaries I refer to the name of the composer that is given in the song credits. When I am referring to the performer of these songs, I refer to 'Scott Walker'. As may well be imagined, the various gaps indicated by the difference in names between writer and performer, private man and public persona becomes an important theme in the work.

Clara (Benito's Dream) (2006)

(Scott Walker)

Track two on *The Drift* (2006), 'Clara (Benito's Dream)', is named after Claretta Petacci, lover of Italian fascist dictator Benito Mussolini. The song is related from the perspective of Mussolini (or his ghost) in a dream that anticipates (or recalls) their death. This is one of Walker's most remarkable songs and it is singled out for special attention here because its origin can be found in one of those defining images mentioned by Camus in the quotation that Walker placed prominently on the back cover of *Scott 4* (1969). It might be assumed that such an image would concern an experience of wonder or awe in nature, perhaps, or a moment of human

FIGURE 1 The dead bodies of Benito Mussolini and Claretta Petacci on display in Milan on 29 April 1945 in Piazzale Loreto. Photograph by Vincenzo Carrese.

kindness. But Walker's image is authentically 'Camusian'. An example of what Camus means occurs in his novel *The Plague* (1982), written in 1942 as an allegory of the Nazi occupation of France, but set in Algeria. In the novel, the character Jean Tarrou is the mouthpiece for much of Camus's philosophy, and in particular his horror of the death penalty, a topic which also features in his most famous novel *The Outsider* (2012). Camus's philosophical reflections here are drawn in part from Martin Heidegger's notion of being-for-death, wherein awareness of the imminence of death can provide the impetus to free oneself from adherence to established social conventions. The image 'at which his heart first opened' occurs when Camus's character is a child and is taken by his father, the Director of Public Prosecutions, to see a murder trial. Tarrou watches in fascinated disgust as his father clamours for the defendant's head. 'The only picture I carried away with me of that day's proceedings was a picture of the criminal … he looked like a yellow owl scared blind by too much light' (Camus, 1982: 202–3). The sudden 'flash of understanding' that this was 'a living human being' who was to be routinely executed provides the cue for Tarrou to dedicate his life to the abolition of the death penalty and to the refusal to kill. The image of death becomes the bedrock of the character's commitment for which he too will have to risk his life.

It was another picture of death to which the young Noel Scott Engel was exposed at the tender age of five or six that becomes the basis for 'Clara', and for Walker's commitment to his art that this and other songs of this period represent. It may also be the basis for his fascination with Europe, its cinema and politics. In various interviews including the one filmed by Kijak in *30th Century Man* (2006), Walker recalls that he was taken to the cinema by his aunt and that before the main feature a documentary newsreel was shown about the aftermath of the Second World War. 'And there they were, hanging upside down, these two mutilated bodies surrounded by a large jeering crowd' (see also Woods, 2013: 294). 'It was quite shocking for me to see it, and I asked about it but nobody really wanted to explain it to me' (294). Subsequently the image of the man and woman, brutalized and dead, became the source of repeated nightmares (294), nightmares becoming much later the basis for some of his most powerful songs. For Walker, the dream is the creative work of an unconscious desire that continually evokes and conceals itself through the production of nightmarish images. As a song that itself relates a fascist nightmare, 'Clara' is related to a number of Walker's songs, notably 'The Cockfighter' (1995), that conjoin sexual transgression with Nazism.

The occasion for Walker to revisit this image through writing the song was, he says, his concern about the rise of neo-fascism during the last decade of the twentieth century, including the emergence of Alessandra Mussolini, the grand-daughter of the former dictator, and the 'post-fascist' parties *Movimento Sociale Italiano* (MSI) and *Destra Nazionale* (National Right). A fervent anti-fascist, yet clearly fascinated by the phenomenon and the grotesque characters it attracts, Walker wanted to engage with the topic, but in a different manner to that of a conventional protest song. The result is what Walker describes as 'a fascist love song' that offers different and oscillating points of identification as it examines the power of fatal attraction in love and politics. In his research, Walker was interested and amused to discover that Claretta Petacci was essentially a fan. 'She was like someone today, a celebrity-obsessed person, posters all over her walls and mainly of him' (Weidel, 2006; see also Young: 2006). If she lived today she could be filling in questionnaires for social scientists and algorithms using the data to enhance the presentations of *Il Duce* in his appeal to women. But she went further than this, she went to her death for him. 'In the end she turned out to be someone of some kind of real quality because she could have gotten away, he offered her a chance that she could have left, but she actually went all the way with him' (Weidel, 2006; see also Young, 2006).

On the one hand, then, Claretta Petacci proves herself to be an exemplary existentialist in her choice of death for her commitment to her lover. This for Walker exhibits her 'real quality'. But in dying for Mussolini, she also dies for fascism and the *Repubblica Sociale Italiana* (RSI: Italian Social Republic). Consequently, her death haunts Italian fascism, lending it the glamour of a fatal love affair. Indeed, there were reports in 2011-12 that Petacci's ghost had appeared on the lakeside at Salò, capital of the RSI (and title of Pasolini's notorious last film, a re-telling of the Marquis de Sade's *One Hundred Days of Sodom* set in the last days of fascism). In April 2012, the ghost of Petacci, 'dressed in a flowing 1930s-style gown, tall and beautiful' was reported speaking 'to condemn rightist infighting and leftist temptations' as the Berlusconi era appeared to be coming to an end (Bosworth, 2017: 4). While Walker wrote 'Clara' seven or eight years before these sightings, they testify to the continuing power that the myth of the doomed lovers has on the continuing flirtation with fascism. Indeed, it lends it an erotic charge. For years, it has been possible to visit the Villa Fiordaliso in the RSI where Petacci lived in 1943-4 protected by an SS guard. It is even possible to sleep in the bed she shared on occasion with Mussolini, still furnished as it was in 1944. Those who have enjoyed the facilities and signed the visitors' book include 'Laurence Olivier, Monica Vitti, Claudia Cardinale, 'Stormin' Norman Schwarzkopf' and of course Silvio Berlusconi along with one or two guests (Bosworth, 2017: 5).

In his concern with the rise of neofascism, Walker chooses to write a love song about the fascist couple with whom people remain entranced, including Walker himself. But while the song may concern love's sacrifice, it sounds nothing like 'Romeo and Juliet', in whatever version one cares to recall. It is a brutal song, difficult and unpleasant in parts, but also powerfully affecting. As Alexis Petridis notes of Walker's songs generally, 'the results frequently affect the listener's gut before their brain' (Petridis, November 2012). Even as multiple points of view are evoked in the song, there is a sonic fixation on the body. The centre of affect, the body becomes the basis for events with a political scope. In Walker's interrogation of the couple and the circumstances and legacy of their death, a different configuration of the political body emerges in the wake of the couple. This may well not be intentional, but it chimes with themes elsewhere on *The Drift* and later albums, as I will argue. This political body in its various iterations is also one of the themes of this book.

There are at least four 'voices' in the song and bodies that are related to them: two that are gendered and two that are not. The track begins curiously with the sound of electronic noise, as if a machine were being switched on, perhaps meant to evoke the reel of documentary film clicking in the cinema in Ohio where Engel first saw the images of the dead couple. The film, Engel's memory of the film and 'Benito's dream' are thus all superimposed. Immediately following the switch, a female voice and then a male voice say the word 'birds', indicating that, retrospectively, the electronic noise may also be taken to represent a flock of mechanical birds. To the melody of an ocarina above a funereal military drum beat, the Benito voice intones the first section of the song. Later, Claretta will be voiced by Vanessa Contenay-Quinones. Duets are quite rare in Walker – he usually sings the female parts himself – so it was evidently important for him to explicitly signal her femininity. Politically, these two bodies can be correlated: first, the *fascist* body that, like Mussolini's familiar image, is, as Walker underscored in interviews, both grotesque and 'puffed up'. It is the body of a certain fascist-phallic sublimation in a political will bound to destruction. By contrast but also in a sympathetic way, Claretta's *feminine* body is associated, as is traditionally the case, with the mystical ecstasies of love's sacrifice bound in its own way to destruction in the form of martyrdom. The song's starting premise is that these two bodies are already dead. They are battered, mutilated and strung-up by the heels like meat-hooked pigs. Indeed, 'Clara' is famous for the way this battering is rendered percussively through Alastair Malloy's 'meat punching' of a side of pork. This occurs prominently in three sections of the song, first when a voice (presumably still Benito's) declaims, in a negative blazon, all of Claretta's imperfections: heavy breasts, short upper lip, small teeth and so on, as the meat is punched in the midst of the deep, lurching, almost nauseating sound of bowed bass strings. This is repeated later in a third iteration, but rather than furious, random punching, Malloy provides a steady yet sickening beat over the blazon. In between, meat-punching occurs a second time when Contenay-Quinones sings a cappella lines about a swallow who has trapped herself in an attic by mistake to the sound of the flock of mechanical birds. The single swallow is juxtaposed to the sound of the flock; the one to the many.

The 'voice' represented by the meat-punching is not that of the poor dead pig, but the collective body of the mob ably conveyed first by Malloy's frenzied, non-rhythmic punch-beats. This is the body that Sartre, in *Critique of Dialectical Reason* (1976), calls the 'group-in-fusion'. This mob has no essential identity; for Sartre, in one instance it can be progressive, in another fascistic. Perhaps the mechanical birds are another example of this group-in-fusion, in contrast to the violent gang. But certainly, in 'Clara', the punching is itself ambiguous: it is indefinably the fascist mob, the anti-fascist mob and, as the song also acknowledges, the American democratic mob. Indeed, it is also America where the fourth body in the song is identified. This is the 'cornhusk doll' that is brought into negative equivalence with the bodies of Claretta and Benito by the latter in the song's opening lines.

The inclusion of the cornhusk doll is curious. On the one hand it links the image of the couple's corpses to an American childhood, and perhaps therefore to Walker's formative exposure to it. On the other, the picture of Petacci hanging upside down with her skirt pinned-up for modesty's sake above her battered and bloody chest, could be seen to resemble a cornhusk doll shaped out of the twisted dry leaves of a corn cob. At the end of each 'cornhusk' section of the song, the sound intensifies in a disturbing way as Walker's anguished voice cries 'still coming through', perhaps attesting to the continuing traumatic insistence of the images of these dead bodies.

In America, cornhusk dolls are children's toys associated with Native American culture. The dolls are faceless. According to the Legend of the Corn Husk Doll of the Oneida Nation of Wisconsin, the doll that was made to entertain children neglected them, spending all her time contemplating her beauty; consequently, her face was erased. The cornhusk doll sections of the song are also linked to other references to America which seems to be the site of a different, perhaps non-fascist way of life, but one that remains brutal nevertheless; it is a place where rabbits are skinned and the shells of terrapins torn off. For the young Engel in Ohio, perhaps such country cruelty provided the basis for his recognition of the violence of the newsreel image. The final reference to the doll directly symbolizes the figure of Claretta. Her hanging, twisting body now just a cornhusk. Like the faceless doll, her corpse is without identity, even as it remains the object over which identifications and fantasies rotate. This is illustrated in the line immediately before when a single man, representative of the group, pokes the body with a stick.

This figure of the cornhusk doll, that is defined against both the fascist couple and the narcissistic body image, is the body prior to identification. I am going to call this the *one-all-alone*. It is all-alone because it is not defined by a locus of signification, but lies outside it. The body prior to identification is the erased basis of signification: not the start of the chain but its excised condition: the one become zero. The body of the 'group-in-fusion' I am going to call the *one-among-many*. This group is another form of the 'one' since it essentially acts as one. This is illustrated in 'Clara' when the mob is reduced to the 'one' the second time it is juxtaposed to Petacci's battered corpse when Malloy punches one beat at a time, and then in the shape of the man who pokes her twisted body. Elsewhere on *The Drift* and *Bish Bosch*, Walker uses the figure of the one in the shape of the swarm that moves in an in-human dimension. In 'Clara' this idea is also registered in the sound of the mechanical birds that swarm around Claretta's song of the swallow.

Like the swallow, the faceless body of the cornhusk doll at the very beginning of the song can structurally be connected to the fourth voice that speaks (it does not sing) the final section. 'The song ends', as Walker told Rob Young, 'with me, or you, or anyone else talking at the end' (Young, 2006). This is the voice – explicitly *not* that of Benito, as Walker states – that attempts to free the trapped swallow, the other figure for the one-all-alone that, along with the one-among-many, displaces the couple. It represents freedom, progress perhaps and – unusually for Walker – an optimistic ending. The hand of the voice carrying the swallow opens at an opened window, but the song stops there. The listener does not know if the swallow stayed where it was, if it took flight, if it fell or if it flew to a better or a worse place.

In sum, then, to push the song towards a more abstractly political conclusion. Benito Mussolini and Claretta Petacci are a doomed couple whose glamour and infamy can be taken to represent symbolically the general fatality of what Judith Butler has called the 'heterosexual matrix' that condemns couples to the repression of 'binary opposition'. As Jacques Derrida famously advanced, such binary oppositions determine meaning in the West in the form of 'violent hierarchies' in which 'one of the two terms governs the other' (Derrida, 1981: 41). The act of deconstruction, Derrida further advances, involves inverting the opposition in order to displace it (43). In the inverted image of the strung-up Italian couple, the structure of the European cult of heterosexual romance is disclosed as fascist and abject: Romeo and Juliet, Tristan and Iseult, Abelard and Heloise … Benito and Claretta. While this would no doubt be pushing Walker's song towards a meaning beyond any intention he may have, I am going to suggest that 'Clara', the fascist love song, is the dream (or nightmare) of the last heterosexual couple. While there are, of course, still heterosexual couples, the 'matrix' that defined them in the West is now a heritage site like Petacci's bedroom in Villa Fiordaliso. As psychoanalyst Francois Ansermet notes, in the post-Butlerian world 'we are living in a time that is defined by disruptions in gender. … Everyone constructs their own gender. … To each their own creativity, to each their own solution. A new world is being invented' (Ansermet, 2019). In 'Clara', as we have seen, the voices of the traditional heterosexual couple are displaced by the voice of the mob and the voice of the cornhusk doll. They belong to bodies that are not gendered or even 'sexed', but which can take on multiple significations, some of which may be taken as the idiosyncratic basis of what might be called the *singular couple* that is predicated upon the solitude of the one-all-alone.

If one were to generalize, on the basis of his songs, about Scott Walker's view of the traditional heterosexual couple, it would not be positive. The albums of the Walker Brothers and the solo records are full of the tears of loss, betrayal, incompatibility, promiscuous ennui and depression. When they occur, traditional heterosexual couples tend to represent repressive or totalitarian regimes – Nicolae and Elena Ceausescu being another example from *Bish Bosch* (2012). Walker seems to have taken to heart Simone de Beauvoir's view, propounded in *The Second Sex* (2009), that the 'patriarchal' couple relegates 'Woman' to the position of the 'Other', the negative 'Symptom of Man'. In contrast, couples in Walker's solo work can also be highly idiosyncratic, as if the partner provided a non-binary, singular solution to the problem of desire. One of the most sympathetic characters is the trans-sexual 'Big Louise' from *Scott 3* (1969). Further, as we shall see, from 'Sleepwalkers woman' (1984), the partner is pre-eminently the choice of unconscious processes (the effect of one's dreams or nightmares), or a homosexual couple such as Pasolini and Nino Davetti, whose voices alternate in 'Farmer in the City' from *Tilt* (1995), or the flatulent anally-erotic Sachem and Sagamore sharing wine and cornflakes to 'sphincters tooting our tune' ('Corps de Blah', 2012), or perverse couples such as the phantasmatic pair in 'The Electrician' (1978), or the masochistic Marlon Brando (allegedly) demanding beatings from all his movies in a fetishism encapsulated by Elizabeth Taylor's whip ('Brando', 2014). From Elvis haunted by the imaginary corpse of his dead twin 'Jesse' (2005) to the glaucoma-clouded eyes that are beloved of 'A Lover Loves' from *The Drift* (2006), Walker's idiosyncratic couples exemplify what psychoanalysis calls the 'symptom-partner'. While the symptom can indicate a malfunctioning, in another register it can be a solution, 'a means of jouissance that enables one to secure oneself in the world' (Miller in Guéguen, 2017: 33).[2] The choice of partner here is not determined by how well he or she performs the traditional role of Man or Woman, but how far the other, found by chance or accident, satisfies the unique requirements of the one. Colette Soler writes, 'a symptom is always singular, one-by-one. As for symptoms that make up for the absence of the sexual rapport – symptoms capable of producing a relation to a partner, man or woman – there are many and various' (Soler, 2018: 65). Scott Walker is the chronicler par excellence of 'the absence of the sexual rapport' that renders everyone one-all-alone.

The song of the one-all-alone

I must now come to my enigmatic subtitle. At first sight there should be no mystery. If anyone knows anything about Scott Walker, it is that his songs and his persona are defined by solitude and loneliness. Moreover, as far as the former is concerned, this is not always a negative thing. 'I'm good at solitary, always have been', Walker confirmed to Andrew Graham-Dixon of BBC TV's *The Culture Show* in 2006. 'I can spend lots of time on my own, I'm fine'. Indeed, in the 1960s, he would regularly be seen at *Ronnie Scott's* enjoying the jazz night after night, alone at his own table. Even *The Times* obituary ended on Walker's claim that he 'craved solitude', implying that at last he had definitively found it (2019: 59). Yet there is a strange – if quite lovely – statement by Ady Semel that nuances this claim somewhat. Semel is credited with co-writing the songs of *Til the Band Comes In* (1970),[3] the record that came after the four famous eponymous albums, sometimes regarded as 'Scott 5'. On the sleevenotes Semel writes, 'I've known Scott for over a year now, but can't really tell whether we think alike. We tend to respect, though, each other's idea of solitude and suspect, each in his own way, that "it might be lonelier without the loneliness"'. Semel's further itemization of Walker's collection of solitary types and singular couples that feature on the songs of the album are characteristic of his oeuvre generally: 'an old age pensioner, a kept cowboy, a resigned girl lover, a telephone crank, a landlady's grasp of an unneighbourly stripper, an immigrant waiter'. Indeed, on the previous four Philips albums, Walker's original songs and Jacques Brel *chanson* covers generally take as their subject solitary figures such as abandoned lovers, lonely transvestites, spinsters and prostitutes. To which will be added loveless despots, Sadists, fetishists, addicts, psychopaths, prisoners, executioners, farmers lost in the city and flagpole sitters.

The political dimension of Walker's work is throughout concerned with the social isolation that Hannah Arendt argues is the pre-requisite of totalitarianism (Arendt, 2017: 627). An irony of the social goal to deconstruct the binary couple is that this isolation has become a formal condition of the social bond that is now established, through the development of cybernetics, between data subjects organized by ubiquitous predictive computing. While there may well be unending layers of exploitation, there are no longer masters or slaves in the old sense; while there may be multiple signs of gender, there are no more men or women; no parents or children, just a perpetual state of neoteny; no teachers or students, just partners in knowledge acquisition whose activities uploading and downloading information in virtual learning environments are essentially the same. In the world organized by cybernetics, there are no longer even 'individuals' in the old bourgeois sense, but subjects whose primary relation is to the various technical objects that 'dividuate' (divide, control and monitor) in a uniform way their numerous data trails in the so-called digital network. In the neat phrase of Sherry Turkle, these subjects are 'alone together' (Turkle, 2010). The contemporary data subject is uni-dividuated, both one-all-alone and one-among-many. Like the subject of science, however, the data subject has no substance, in contrast to the body that suffers in its own singular manner from the data that deploys, tracks and measures it. This suffering is recognized, of course, but the ever finer means developed to gauge and absorb bodily stress simply generates and exacerbates it like the anxiety-producing electronic tags that are worn to monitor anxiety.

The quotation in Semel's anecdote about his lonely yet companionable relationship with Scott suggests that this might be Walker's own phrase. Loneliness, here, becomes a kind of social bond within which there is another kernel of loneliness. This idea of two dimensions of loneliness, or aloneness, one of which is an effect of a certain formation of the social bond, while the other sits outside it, is an organizing principle in Walker's work and in this book. On the one hand, there is the social isolation of being that, for Arendt, provides the basis for totalitarianism and, for Turkle, the contemporary condition of online sociality. On the other hand, there is the inevitable solitude, at the level of existence, of a body that is born, lives and dies, the nature of whose existence is unquantifiable and therefore not reducible to data. This solitude is the basis precisely of an openness to the 'other' without predicates and pre-conditions, including the self-as-other. According to Semel, Walker suggests that the former, social isolation, would be much lonelier without the latter, existential solitude, implying further perhaps that care for the former is only possible on the basis of the latter.

The difference is articulated by the distinction, made variously in the tradition of existentialist philosophy, between being and existence. These are the two aspects of the philosophy that Walker highlighted even when he was in the Walker Brothers. Speaking to Keith Altham of the *NME* (Altham would later write some of the sleeve notes for the solo records), Walker explained that 'an existentialist is a person who needs no other people – a world in himself. He lives for the moment. A belief in existence rather than essence' (Altham, 1966). While the latter phrase comes from Sartre, the idea is already there in Heidegger, who also adds a third term *Ek-sistence*.

In brief and very crudely, the metaphysics of being, whose house is language, derives for Heidegger from the Platonic tradition and concerns the dimension of Ideas, essence, meaning and identity. Existence, in contrast, is the non-metaphysical condition of being, as its direct experience in *Dasein*, or being-there. Similarly, with Heidegger there is not the same sense of opposition as with Sartre – whose formula 'existence precedes essence' he regards as simply a reversal that remains metaphysical. The Lacanian psychoanalyst Jacques-Alain Miller has revisited this existentialist distinction between being and existence in his attempt to 'de-ontologize' analysis in the light of new symptoms that have emerged in the de-sublimated world of contemporary practice. This is a world in which the 'master signifiers' that once commanded the binary oppositions that structure signifying chains have been disclosed as 'semblants'. The (big) Other that once organized the order of being no longer exists in the sense that there is no recognized 'universal' (Law, God, meaning) valid for all. Rather than the 'all', Miller substitutes the perspective of the 'one'. In his last years throughout the 1970s, Jacques Lacan would repeatedly make the passionate utterance '*Yadl'un!*' suggesting thereby that existence, or the 'there is', is 'something of the One'.[4] (See Lacan, 2018) In his own seminar on 'Being and the One', Miller takes this statement as an invitation to 'sacrifice the totalitarianism of the universal for the singularity of the One' ['*Je la prend ici au niveau clinique comme une invitation à sacrifier le totalitarisme de l'universel à la singularité de l'Un*']. (From *L'orientation lacanienne, L'être et l'Un*, leçon du 4 avril 2011).

Accordingly, the phrase the 'one-all-alone' comes from the concept '*L'Un tout seul*' developed in the seminar *L'Orientation lacanienne: le corps de Jacques-Alain Miller* (2010-2011). This Lacanian One-all-alone (S_1) denotes the part of existence that cannot be negativized by the register of being that is articulated in the chain of signifiers (S_2). The One-all-alone is not to be confused with the master signifier that is given as the source and ground of the meaning and significance of the chain. Rather, it is outside the chain and therefore outside sense, marking nevertheless the body in an event that produces an enigmatic symptom that is beyond interpretation (for an excellent introduction to this concept with reference to popular culture, see Nancy Gillespie, 2018). It is interesting to note that Miller claims that in its non-clinical register, psychoanalysis 'is existentialism' (Miller, 2016: 28). He writes,

> It is existentialism, and I don't repudiate Jean-Paul Sartre's formula with which he decorated it, 'existence precedes essence.' I could very well give my Lacanian formulation of it, by saying that the real precedes meaning, except that an analysis implies that one must pass

through meaning in order to accede to the real, inasmuch as it could precede meaning. (Miller, 2016: 28)

I am not concerned here with psychoanalysis, but with the process of interpretation that is involved in the production and reception of Walker's songs which ultimately results in a commentary on its affects rather than meaning. When it comes to Walker, the 'S_1' therefore is not a signifier, but a sound that 'heralds the real'. (For the importance of the sonic register to the (missed) encounter with the real. see Wilson (2015).) Sound is not a signifier because the latter promises to denote meaning rather than sensation. However, even as sound escapes interpretation, it can retrospectively be seen to precede it and ground the commentary's supplementation of the song's reduction of meaning to a sound-affect – a sense-ation.

Structure

This book is also eccentric in that every chapter is numbered 'one' – in one or other of its various iterations: zero, the one-missing, the One, swarm and the one-all-alone. This is because its concern is not primarily how song brings into being an artist (or a listener), an individual or subject, but rather how Walker's song discloses the logic of singular existence. In *Being and Nothingness* (2003), Sartre famously distinguishes being from the nothingness that provides the 'nihilating' condition of consciousness (35-7). For Walker this is the 'zero' that is equivalent to the silence that is the basis for everything. It is not a general or cosmic silence, however, but *one* singular silence: a hole in being. While everyone of us may be a 'zero' or a 'nothing' in Sartre's terms, that nothingness is unique, as unique as one's own death. The chapter following 'Zero' addresses Walker's love songs where the figure of the 'other' is always an effect of the one-missing in both senses. The lover loves in lack and in solitude, conventionally longing for that special partner who would fill the lack, the fantasy partner who does not exist. Walker's songs examine the impossibility of the couple except as an affect or an emotion – or indeed a symptom – in which the 'symptom-partner' enables the one to manage the suffering-enjoyment of the body. Often in disturbing ways, the one cares for the other, and vice versa. Accordingly, Walker explores how it is through affect and the pain of loss that the experience of the other (and even the other's body) can be broached. In the next chapter, the One refers to the figure who would be exceptional, even *the* exception. For Walker this is the One who would live outside, above or even below the law, again as its condition: the political leader, despot or dictator, the artist, the buffoon. The One thus denotes the limit of the law in its inherent violence and absurdity. The swarm, in contrast, is the figure for the unlimited: lawlessness, or the absolute contingency that is a law unto itself; it marks the place where the teeming of undead life below the horizon of human being meets the divine inexistence of God. It should go without saying that all these ones are the Same but not Identical, to echo Heidegger (1996: 123). In Walker's work, the one is attuned to a specific mood and tonality that provides the principle of consistency to the song of the one-all-alone, that is addressed in more detail in the final chapter.

The logic of existence disclosed by Walker's song necessitates that its foundation is in-existence defined by a locus of ex-sistence, the nothingness that is both within and outside us, as Sartre writes (2003: 29). From where it is not, existence arises suddenly from a singular sonic event. It results in a sonic body that consists of a hole, a resonant surface and a vector of ex-sistence that links a site of enunciation (and audition) to the outside. Commenting on his practice, Walker says, 'all the honing down I've done in the lyric will lead me to just one sound that will tell me – and tell everyone – what the lyric is trying to say. Maybe two or three sounds' (Woods, 2013: xiii). The process of interpretation that is described here as 'honing down' produces the song as an 'S_1', a song of the one-all-alone, because it absorbs the context (historical or political anecdote) that once provided its meaning to the point where it is reduced to a personal residue of affective excess. This residue of meaning that points to the precedence of existence over essence is, ultimately, simply a sound or cluster of two or three sounds that encapsulate the lyric and conveys its sense in an affective rather than denotative manner. In the song of the one-all-alone, both meaning (outside of semantics) and affect are ultimately solitary affairs; they are hidden, unknown. That is what the lyric is paradoxically 'trying to say'. As Heidegger writes in his own commentary on Hölderlin, 'we never know a mystery by unveiling or analyzing it to death, but only in such a way that we preserve the mystery as mystery' (Heidegger, 2000: 43). As we shall see, there are various layers of enigma in Walker's work: the enigma of the meaning of the various textual allusions and fragmented lyrics, the enigma of the 'personal' elements that are withheld and the 'spiritual moments' that are lost. Ultimately there is the enigma of enunciation itself through which Walker's 'alien' voice represents the unsayable. The level of the listener's interpretation that is demanded by Walker's songs leads to the disclosure and preservation of the mystery-as-mystery announced in sound. It is the listener who is brought to the point of the enigma of the real in the affective experience of the sound in so far as this experience derives from and exceeds interpretation.

Frequently this sound is encapsulated in the form of what Pierre Schaeffer called a 'sound object'. By the latter, Schaeffer famously means 'sound itself, considered as *sound*, and not the material object (instrument or some sort of device) that produces it' (Schaeffer, 2017: 8). A sound object is, then, another kind of 'S_1' that has become detached from its 'S_2', the world of musical instruments or locus of recognizable sounds by which it can be identified. Schaeffer's example of how the sound object is isolated from its context and therefore meaning is a sound on a vinyl record that becomes caught in 'a groove [that is] closed in on itself, thereby isolating a fragment of recording, which can be listened to indefinitely' (7). While Walker's songs feature a good number of sound objects whose origin is difficult to discern, Schaeffer's example shows that the obscurity of the origin is not what is at stake. A sound becomes a sound object when, through the process of recording and repetition, it takes on a new sonic significance as an effect of its different context, or loses it entirely, just as a word that is endlessly repeated loses its meaning to become an estranged sound. It thereby becomes an 'S_1' whose isolation retrospectively echoes the sonic encounter with the real of existence that precedes meaning. In 'Clara', for example, the sound of the 'meat-punching' oscillates in the visceral imagination of the listener from the side of pork to the beaten body of Claretta Petacci. But it quickly becomes evident that in the context of the song, the sound is not that of an animal body (even less a biological body) nor even a sexual body, but an enunciation whose violence evinces the frustration of an impassable limit. No matter how hard it tries, the 'one' cannot penetrate or link with the 'other'. Malloy even emits a gasp of frustration at the end of one section of pummelling. In his interview with Rob Young, Walker remarks that 'most of my stuff is about frustration, of being unable to hold on to a spiritual moment, always losing it' (Young, 2006). The violent sound of this frustration reverberates throughout Walker's work, including in *Soused* (2014) as I discuss in the final chapter of this book.

It is by way of this sound (the sound of the absence of sexual rapport) that the song of the one-all-alone produces the intimacy of a sonic bond in a way that is exterior to both being and existence. Neither simply ontological nor ontic, there is a *sonic* dimension of ex-sistence that cannot be reduced to the second term of the metaphysical opposition between essence and existence. The sound that broaches the real has a relation of ex-sistence to language and, indeed, to music. The sound of the one-all-alone necessarily has a relation only to that which it is not: to the other that is missing, to non-sound or silence. This is the locus of ex-sistence that leads to the outside of what Walker calls his 'spiritual dimension'. As he has insisted throughout the latter part of his career, the idea of a spiritual dimension remains logically indispensable to his work even if it is materially untenable. It is through song, according to Walker, that the language of being can touch on the unspeakable nature of existence, or indeed of the in-existence that is its foundation. 'I've always done this [in my songs]. It's just a way to talk about the unsayable things of existence, the unnameable' (Walker in Young, 2006: 23). The unsayable is conveyed sonically in the many 'unnameable' (neither major nor minor) chords that feature in his songs. These 'impossible-to-play' chords, that lie 'outside the normal tuning space' (Kijak, bonus interview, 2006), locate Walker's songs in a strange position of exteriority that is, nevertheless, at the same time, the vehicle of the most intimate, somatic affect. It is an affect that is sometimes extreme, even ecstatic, including the sonic sublimation of agony. As such a vehicle, sound provides the pre-condition for the *resonance* of a knowledge that is grounded in the sonic experience of bodily substance, and the medium for its care.

ZERO

'SDSS14+13B (Zercon, A Flagpole Sitter)' (2012)

(Scott Walker)

This song, a mock-epic 22 minutes long, would appear to be an allegory of Scott Walker's life and work, fortelling his death. The song begins with a spectral voice, old doom-laden moan, echoing a cappella into a surrounding silence. In an Interview with Stuart Maconie promoting *Bish Bosch* (2012) on the BBC Radio 6 show *The Freak Zone* in January 2013, Walker described this silence at the opening of the album's centrepiece:

> At the beginning of the song [Zercon] is being heckled by silence. He has heckle responses to this. Silence is making him feel guilty … because silence is where everything starts from; it's the basis for everything. (Maconie, 2013)

Silence is the beginning of everything for two reasons. In one way, it is the basis of everything that can be known numerically or mathematically since it is the sonic equivalent of zero, which of course accounts for most of Zercon's name. Zero is the basis upon which the world of objects can be perceived and enumerated, the means by which the universe can be conceived mathematically and, through the practical application of scientific instruments, observed and heard. Every number follows from the silence of 0: 1, 2, 3, 4 (like Walker's eponymous albums of the late 1960s). The Romans famously failed to signify it, so as he reads aloud the Roman numerals graffitied on the latrine walls, Zercon finds himself, the embodiment of zero, both inside the lavatory and outside the Roman chain of being. The transposition of (non)number to language in the name Zercon emphasizes that the silence of zero is symbolic, but here the symbol is unconnected to the Roman numerical system which in anycase is signified in letters – the 'one' being pronounced 'I'. Zercon the zero is not an 'I', but he is singular. The silence of zero 'speaks' just to Zercon because it comes from him and him alone. It 'heckles' Zercon, surrounding him like a circle that marks his own unique, singular place, as intimate as the toilet bowl from deep within which his own heckling echoes back.

Zercon's voice is that of a quotidian ghost emerging from a dark hole to haunt the margins of history's barbarity and deepest space. It wants to escape, to be alone; it is alone, always, in this hole. This is the song of that solitary desire for solitude, a song that is always being written. But is it actually a song? It sounds like nothing else. It is not, or is no longer, a pop song. It is not a rock song, not even a prog rock song. Narratively, the song is much longer than twenty-two minutes, longer than a lifetime, many lifetimes. The song evokes the metamorphosis of a voice over millennia. Indeed, the timescale covers billions of years because it relates the transformation of one brown dwarf, Zercon, a Moorish jester in the court of Attila the Hun in the fifth century, into the coldest known sub-stellar astral body, also known as a brown dwarf, that was first perceived deep in the dark night sky in 2010 and given the name SDSS14+13B. The process of the metamorphosis is conveyed by an aged yet undead voice that unfolds its song along a path of ex-sistence, outside yet alongside the confines of historical being, on the basis of a singular a-tonality that has always defined its existence. As Walker himself describes:

> I was interested in this thing about someone trying to escape his situation – in this case Attila's wooden palace, which he regards as an immense toilet – and achieve a kind of spiritual sovereignty, and a height beyond calculation. As the song moves forward he imagines himself at different stages of height: he imagines first that he escapes and finds himself surrounded by eagles; then there's the mention of St Simon on his pillar; then he jumps to 1930s America where it's become a flagpole-sitter … Flagpole-sitting – trying to spend several days alone on a platform at the top of a pole – achieved a brief craze status in the 30s. At the end of the song he eventually becomes a Brown Dwarf, known as SDSS1416+13B. As with the majority of my songs, it ends in failure. Like a brown dwarf, he freezes to death. (Walker in Doyle, 2013)

Echoing around the toilet bowl of language and numbers, Zeron's voice emerges miraculously clear and strong – just like Walker's in 1965. After all, the latrine has excellent acoustics, conveying reverb like the natural echo chambers deployed by John Franz and Peter Olliff on the Walker Brothers' hit singles: a simple 'tiled room with a microphone in it, with a speaker in front of it' (Kijak, 2006, bonus interviews; see also Woods, 2013: 52–3). On the walls of the room alongside the Roman numerals are also messages and dedications. 'For Lavinia' who 'goes like a gynozoon', and 'for the citizen whose joke lays in their hand'. They are another singular couple slated for death: muse and poet de-sublimated as whore and masturbator, separated by sex and desire, by a fundamental non-relation that provokes an endless amorous commentary ceaselessly exacerbating the disunion. The toilet vocal booth is also an enormous library like the Library of Babel. Describing the genesis of the song to Maconie, Walker explained, 'I have a friend with an enormous library, and he lets me roam around and look at things, and I opened this book and found this character' (Maconie, 2013). In the library, Zercon is forever longing for a wife in an archive of amorous invention and cruelty, the peculiarity of desire staging different encounters and conjunctions, inscribing new relationships, challenging social norms, precipitating history as a twisted path of perversions from bestial Greeks and Gauls (bears and sheep, respectively), big pink mint-eating Norsemen to Barbata, bald Goddess of the double-sexed Venus. A gynozoon, for example, is a female animal who was trained by the Romans to copulate with humans. But whether or not she was also the fervid dream of transhuman animality, the Roman Lavinia is best known as the last wife of Aeneas, a woman who features briefly in Virgil's *Aeneid*, someone for whom, as the song goes on to note, cosmic sacrifices are made. This was, legend tells us, because of her ominous reputation as a herald of war and glory.

Walker's lyrics are as allusive and complex as modern poetry, and he and others like Brian Eno have suggested that they be read as such. Like the poetry of T.S. Eliot, they are filled with historical and mythical allusions, quotations, anachronisms, some of which are referenced, some not. *Lavinia* is also a novel by Ursula Le Guin, published in 2010, the same year as the discovery of the sub-stellar brown dwarf. Le Guin's novel re-tells the composition of Virgil's *Aeneid*, in which the historical Lavinia appears as an allegorical figure for poetry – or song – in the way she reflexively comments on the inter-dependence of verse and history, fact and legend. Her character in the novel holds conversations with the poet, her creator, who is himself a shade of Virgil, already dead. On the one hand, then, the suggestion of the shade of a dying poet resonates powerfully with one of the dominant themes of *Bish Bosch*, which is indeed of death and dying. The album was released in December 2012 by a man at the end of his seventieth year, an album that Walker assumed might be his last given the length of time that he had hitherto taken to produce new albums. Throughout *Bish Bosch* there are vivid contemplations of rancid decay, ageing old men, or, as here with Zercon and the brown dwarf, a body freezing to death. On the other hand, as a self-aware figure of textual reflexivity in conversation with a dying poet, Lavinia haunts Walker's voice at the beginning of 'Zercon' as it articulates the opening exchange of ripostes between himself and his echo, between the analogical masturbating whores, Lavinia and the citizen, exchanges that are punctuated by cold digital silences, emphasizing the absence of relation.

Silence must be produced through an at least minimal action of symbolization. In 'Zercon', silence is simulated through the use of digital recording. Throughout the song, and indeed the album, Walker's long-time producer Peter Walsh switches between the analogue and digital multi-tracks that he was recording simultaneously. 'I had two feeds', Walsh recalls, 'there's moments of the album that are so incredibly quiet, where the signal is so low, like string harmonics or vocal breathing. I wanted to have the option, if the tape hiss was getting in the way, of going to the digital, so that I could have complete silence' (Walsh in Doyle, 2013). Silence punctuates the dialogue, as if pregnant with meaning. But such silence is artificial in the sense that it has to be produced through digital technology. It is a remastered silence rather than simply a pause or relational element in a musical sequence. Everything comes from silence, Walker avers, but it is a de-natured silence. As is now widely acknowledged, even in deep space there is no natural silence. Since the discovery of cosmic background radiation, it has been known that the universe is noisy in the sense that it is filled with sound audible through scientific instruments that reveal the cosmos as a mathematical techno-verse. Of course, since Pythagoras discovered the natural proportionality of tuning ratios, music has been regarded in the West as the sonic form of mathematics and the cosmos thus understood as 'musical' in this broader sense. It is noise-music, however, an idea now common from the avant-garde tradition represented by Luigi Russolo's 'Art of Noises' and John Cage's seminal piece 4.33. The universe is not silent, but nor can it be said to be pure noise since the sounds it consists of are mathematically organized even if such organization requires technical instruments to perceive or theoretical speculation to conceive it. From the octave and the Perfect Fifth to the theory of resonant super strings, *natura* remains *musicans*.

Perhaps there is another silence that is not simply one of pause and erasure, the inescapably symbolic silence of mathematics, speech and song that Walker further suggests makes Zercon feel strangely 'guilty'. What is this obscure guilt that, as Zercon's responses make clear, is related to his very existence? In the Christian tradition, this guilt is conceptualized as original sin, the result of the inaugural transgression of God's prohibition concerning the knowledge of good and evil, the fall into the mortal world of the flesh that must be renounced. But Zercon is not a Christian, and the sins of the flesh should not be at issue. Rather, this guilt concerns the question of his very existence that silence tauntingly poses to him. Zercon is confronted with the fact of his existence, the result of immeasurably good or bad fortune, depending upon one's point of view. Or rather, since there is so much more likelihood of not existing than existing, the point of view is itself an effect of the unimaginably unlikely event of his conception. It is therefore already on an entirely contingent basis that he must choose whether his existence is a happy or unhappy accident. What is one supposed to make of it? To this question, there is only the empty response of the symbol that erases all memory of its birth. In its place is that obscure yet original feeling of guilt that is often recalled when one is the beneficiary of great good fortune or, even more significantly, the victim of great misfortune. Though the event might be entirely accidental, we still ask ourselves: 'What have I done to deserve this?' This existential question is impossible, but it is continually – and guiltily – posed. The existential guilt is related to what Sartre called 'facticity': the absence of a reason for existence. Since no one, no sage, saint, God or system of knowledge can give any kind of commensurate response to this fundamental question of existence, one must take it on oneself. There is no Other who can take account of it. Since I am one-all-alone, I can only put the blame on myself, consoling myself with the momentary and fragmentary compensations afforded by the flesh of which, inexplicably, I feel vaguely ashamed.

What's the matter, didn't you get enough attention at home?'

Silence

Zercon interprets the silence as ribald heckling, comparing his shit music to a brass band, suggesting he should stop pleasuring himself in solitude and get some artistic representation. In these lines, the poetic, extra-historical reflexivity of Lavinia summons the equally reflexive autobiographical concerns that sometimes lurk in Walker's oeuvre. Perhaps here can also be heard the bathos of the good fortune and the pathos of the misfortune of becoming a teen idol who now wants to be seen as a serious artist, even a poet in the manner of T.S. Eliot or Samuel Beckett. The shame of being a mere popular entertainer, or of being entirely forgotten; the concern with prostituting oneself, selling out, the days of bad faith. In the early part of Walker's career, agents and A&R representatives were plentiful, promising Noel Scott Engel the means to exchange his solitude for a world of wealth, fame and sensual pleasures. At the same time, this clearly wasn't enough. Another 'agent' provided the means of reflecting on the question of existence, Jean-Paul Sartre. For Sartre, in *Being and Nothingness*, the facticity of existence concerned the fact that the 'in-itself' of existence remained intrinsic to the reflective 'for-itself' that hollows out the 'nothingness' through which a being becomes conscious, pre-eminently, in that it is 'condemned to be free'. At the beginning of 'SDSS 1416+13B (Zercon, A Flagpole Sitter)', Zercon is driven to the awareness that it is he and he alone who can answer for his existence, thereby taking responsibility for it. He is guilty, without a doubt, but determines to make his escape in an act of rebellion. 'What is a rebel? A man who says no: but whose refusal does not imply a renunciation' (Camus, 1977b: 19). Walker continually sought to rebel through escape: escape from the Walker Brothers to the Quarr Abbey monastery on the Isle of Wight before being driven out after three weeks of solitude, silence and the study of Gregorian chant by fans. Escape into alcohol, into pubs to silently watch darts players, escape from the music business to go back into art school, escape from from the world of pop and rock – except none of this is entirely renounced. What are these 'songs' if not the strange, mutated residue of pop and rock?

The desire to escape his situation and, like Zercon, transform himself meant Scott Walker had to become a more remote and reclusive figure, producing work that, according to Jarvis Cocker, sounds like it comes from some dark and inhospitable place that no one would wish to visit, even if he admires anyone who does (Cocker in Kijak, 2006). But like St Simon stranded on his pillar, or a flagpole sitter from 1930s America atop a greased pole, this movement towards a solitary extremity continues to be paradoxical because it attracts the attention and the ridicule it hopes to escape. The desire to be exceptional, and indeed to make exceptional work, succeeds but continues to be greeted by accusations of 'pretention' and 'musical masturbation' from disappointed critics yearning for the 'Godlike Genius' celebrated by Julian Cope. The silent ripostes can no doubt be further read as the voice of someone with a dual identity, Noel Scott Engel, the writer, stuck with his celebrity alter ego, the singer Scott Walker, sunk in schizophrenic depression, handling himself in the dark, covered in his own shit. Is Walker's music shit, or is it 'Godlike genius'? It was after all from the position of number one in the charts that Walker continued to ascend away to who knows where, perhaps to a kind of spiritual sovereignty, beyond the aesthetic league tables of pop and critical enumeration. He fails and freezes to death in deep space at absolute zero in total solitude. It is a kind of suicide, like the career suicide Walker risked in rejecting the popularity and style of his orchestral pop classics, giving up the seductive power of his peerless voice.

Zercon is a man, Walker explained to Maconie, 'who is trying to achieve a kind of height but without a top or a bottom. He has a spiritual calling. Nothing can be calculated' (Maconie, 2013). But what is this spiritual sovereignty for which it is worth risking suicide? Albert Camus famously claimed in *The Myth of Sisyphus* that the question of suicide poses the only serious philosophical problem (Camus, 1977: 11). The absurdity of existence impeaches the semblance of being that obscures life's fundamental absence of meaning. *The Times* reported that at the height of his young fame, Walker was 'unable to deal with the maelstrom around him, he was … found unconscious in his gas-filled apartment in a presumed suicide attempt' (26 March, 2019). The quotation from Camus that Walker reproduced on the back of *Scott 4* comes from an early essay entitled 'Between a Yes and a No' in which existence, and the choice it implies, is poised between the two. Accordingly, Camus finds in the affirmation of the absurdity that might prompt suicide the three principles that enable him to choose existence: 'My revolt, my freedom and my passion' (1977: 62). Suicide remains as the mode of absolute revolt, the ultimate form of freedom and the incalculable measure of passion. Michel Foucault pinpoints how the historical shift from the classical to modern periods pivots on the problem of suicide. Once a crime, suicide was 'a way to usurp the power of death which the sovereign alone, whether the one here below or the Lord above, had the right to exercise' (Foucault, 1978: 138). Now the object of sociological analysis, suicide currently confounds 'a society in which political power [assigns] itself the task of administering life' (139). An interesting character who perhaps marks the transition between Foucault's two periods is cited by Camus in his absurdist pantheon: Kirilov from Fyodor Dostoevsky's novel *Demons* (1994). The absurdity of Kirilov's passionate revolt is that 'he wants to kill himself to become God' (1977: 97). While God is dead, the attributes of independence and freedom from the vicissitudes of life that defined God remain to be asserted. Kirilov contends that this requires an affirmative act of suicide in order to mark the exit to a sovereign outside in relation to which the servitude of being can be overcome.

Kirilov's theoretical contention might thus constitute one version in which Zercon's suicide constitutes spiritual sovereignty in the absence of God. And it is possible to see in Zercon's transformation into an astral body a parodic image of an abandoned God, turning his back on the horror of his creation, preferring to freeze to death in solitude rather than seek the love of Man. But while Walker's notion of the spiritual is similarly atheological, it is not certain that Zercon deliberately kills himself. His death is an effect of a desire which remains enigmatic. In this regard, he is closer to the sovereign indifference of Dostoevsky's character Stavrogin. Unlike Kirilov who simply theorizes about suicide, Stavrogin, the central character of Dostoevsky's novel does actually kill himself, but gives no reason. Russian scholar Jeff Love associates Stavrogin, whom he calls a 'hero of emptiness', with Nietzsche's aphorism from *Twilight of the Idols* that suggests 'those who are never understood have authority precisely for that reason – the authority of the enigmatic, mystery' (Love, 2018: 57).

Without top nor bottom, neither the authority of God and his representatives, nor that of the popular audience, Walker suggests that Zercon's spiritual sovereignty is not just enigmatic, but is to be located in the very enigma that his performances disclose to a listener sceptical, like the final heckling voice in the song, that there's anything there at all. Zercon drops into the darkness, into the emptiness that's the place he's always been in, and which he has always challenged the listener to find.

'The Sun Ain't Gonna Shine Anymore' (1966)
(Bob Crewe and Bob Gaudio)

'The Sun Ain't Gonna Shine Anymore' by the Walker Brothers was number one in the British charts for four weeks in 1966. It is their most successful single, and even now usually heads lists of Scott Walker's best songs. For example, Jon Dennis places it first in his top-ten list in *The Guardian* in 2014, noting that its longevity owes much to the way Walker brought his philosophical interests into his art. 'Scott was no witless pop idol: even in the 60s he'd quote Sartre in interviews. ... "The Sun Ain't Gonna Shine Anymore" is an all-or-nothing existential ballad ... it was about darkness, the void' (Dennis, 2014).

It is generally accepted that this early hit contains in mood and temper much of what was to come in Walker's career. It is not, of course, an original composition by Walker, but was written by Bob Crewe and Bob Gaudio, writers for Frankie Valli and the Four Seasons. Since Valli recorded it without much chart success in 1965, Crewe passed it on to John Walker and the Walker Brothers for whom Ivor Raymonde, alongside producer Jack Nitzsche, gave it the fashionable 'wall of sound' treatment associated with Phil Spector.

'The Sun Ain't Gonna Shine Anymore' begins with thickly layered acoustic guitars, the typical foundation of the wall of sound, over which floats a descending melancholic brass refrain even as portentous echoing bass guitar notes, propelled by a booming bass pedal and insistent tambourine, count down the doom of time to an impatient offbeat: 'Loneliness', Scott Walker's perfect baritone measures out the opening statement, 'is the cloak you wear'. There is something, then, more profound than the cloak of loneliness that it veils. The next verse reveals that, no, it is not something, it is nothing: 'Emptiness', Walker intones, 'is the place you're in'. The cloak of loneliness veils a place that is empty, but singularly so. It is your place; it is you, disclosed as a void so desolate it requires the objective correlative of a cosmic catastrophe to do it justice. Neither the sun nor the moon will rise again. For Lewis Williams, it is the almost in-human or more-than-human quality of emotion in Walker's voice that grants the hyperbole credibility. The climactic cry '"I can't go oo-oo-oo-oo-ooon" [*is*] more like the sound of the end of the world than a rainy day', he writes (Williams, 2006: 30). Walker turns a tale of lost love into an existential predicament. This is not sadness but anguish.

Many commentaries on 'The Sun Ain't Gonna Shine Anymore' re-tell the anecdote from the autobiography of Reggie Kray, the celebrity London gangster twin from the 1960s. There are always three groups of brothers in stories about this record: the Righteous Brothers, the Walkers and the Krays. The anecdote concerns Ronnie Kray's murder of rival gangster George Cornell in the Blind Beggar pub on 9 March 1966. Kray writes that

Ron and Ian [Barrie] walked into the saloon bar. Cornell was sitting at the end of the bar … a record was playing peculiarly enough entitled 'The Sun Ain't Gonna Shine Anymore'. … Ron drew a Luger gun out of his right hand overcoat pocket, levelled it at Cornell's head and fired … the record jammed at the same time as the bullet hit Cornell in the forehead, and it kept repeating, 'the sun ain't gonna shine any more … any more … any more … '. (Kray, 1991: 97)

It is the kind of historical detail that fascinates Walker, often providing the impetus to his songs. They are snippets of 'history' that Walker likes to detach from their source and context so that they function like Schaeffer's sound objects. They become not so much frozen in time as detached from time, circulating eternally in a groove closed in on itself like a destructive obsessive thought, a mind-worm repeatedly turning and tormenting the soul.

As such, Reggie Kray's story is a meta-anecdote since it contains the sound-image of its own obsessive circulation in the detail about the scratched record that uncannily comments on the scene of execution it has just witnessed, an act that will condemn Ronnie Kray to his own death sentence in a lifetime's imprisonment. The turntable drives the record on, but the needle is stuck at a moment of perfect paradox where the sun will eternally never shine any more. Cornell's death, and Kray's future, are arrested at the point where the sun will never stop no longer shining. The sonority of such an existential moment is worthy not only of Jack Nitzsche, but Friedrich Nietzsche.

At the conclusion of Book IV of *The Gay Science*, Nietzsche asks what might happen if one day or night

a demon were to steal upon you in your loneliest loneliness and say to you: 'you will have to live this life – as you are living it now and have lived it in the past – once again and countless times more; and there will be nothing new in it, but every pain and pleasure, every thought and sigh'. (Nietzsche, 1974: IV, 34)

It is possible to imagine this question posed to George Cornell. The demon evokes the taste of the drink at the bar of the Blind Beggar, the sound of the latest hit on the jukebox, the disturbance at the sinister appearance of Ronnie Kray and his henchman, and the glint of light on the Luger's smooth barrel, its muzzle-flash, and the sharp, deafening sound. The moment is reminiscent of Camus's decisive scene in *The Outsider* (2012). The manner in which one of the 'Arabs' repeatedly blows 'three musical notes' on a little flute, breaking the state of sun-drenched silence, first suggests the idea of killing one of them to Raymond and Meursault, the narrator (50–1). It is the sonic power of the sun that Meursault blames for his passage to the act: 'All I could feel was the sun crashing like cymbals against my forehead … my whole body tensed as I gripped the gun more tightly. It set off the trigger' (Camus, 2012: 54). The sun shines no more for the Arab, just as later for Meursault following his execution.

Back in the London pub, the demon scratches the record at the moment of Cornell's 'loneliest loneliness', lonelier even than the Blind Beggar whose environs are fast fading away to disclose a place of emptiness that is his and his alone. The demon scratches the record so that the second can recur to illuminate to Cornell in his death throes how this instance will return in the 'eternal hourglass of time turning over and over – and you with it, speck of dust!' Would Cornell cast himself down and 'gnash his teeth' at such a suggestion, or would he greet it with joy? This is the question that lies, for Nietzsche, at the heart of his doctrine of the Eternal Return, the hyperbolic experience of dread and anguish that lies at the basis of his re-evaluation of all values. Whether one responds with despair or joy to this demon becomes the test of one's refutation of nihilism and affirmation of life.

In his commentary on these lines from *The Gay Science*, Martin Heidegger lights specifically on this state of 'loneliest loneliness'. This is a loneliness that lies hidden beneath the cloak of loneliness, the loneliness similar to the one that, according to Ady Semel, Walker considered the basis of existence in common. For Heidegger, the distinction is used to differentiate his understanding of *Dasein* that subsists beneath the world of individuals among whom one stands in the midst of the world of historical being. This 'loneliest loneliness' is 'prior to and beyond every distinguishing of one to another, and of the individual from the community' (Heidegger, 1984: II: 24–5). There is here 'no trace of individuation as isolation', rather the loneliest loneliness ex-sists outside the world of everyday existence or being. It is nevertheless the place which we must 'grasp' in an act of '*authentic appropriation* [*Vereigentlichung*]' in order for the self to come into its own as that *Dasein* that grounds any relation to another (Heidegger, 1984: II: 24–5). In *Being and Time*, *Vereigentlichung* refers to the necessity that *Dasein* be founded on an appropriation of its own in-existence, its 'existential projection' of its own being-for-death (Heidegger, 2010: 252–3). The in-existence of our own singular death (including in the sense that we can only experience death in the image of another) is the very basis of our own existence, the death that we must appropriate as ours.

It is from this place of in-existence disclosed in the anecdotes concerning the deaths of Claretta Petacci, say, or Pier Paolo Pasolini, that obsessively evokes an outside-space and outside-time of history that, as I shall argue, Walker will subsequently re-evaluate his own practice, transforming it in its later form such that it becomes what it is, what it is in 'The Sun Ain't Gonna Shine Anymore'.

The x-humanism of existentialism

Scott Walker's association with existentialism has been regularly noted in interviews and biographical accounts over the years. That a pop star might express interest in philosophy and associated literature, art and film is conventionally treated with suspicion and contempt by British journalists and commentators for reasons that are historical, cultural and, it seems, immovable. British pop and rock journalism lives on a myth of sacred ignorance that it shares with conservatives who dismiss the culture as frivolous. Popular culture either does not deserve critical inquiry or it does not require it. At the time of *Portrait* (1966), the Walker Brother's album where Scott's interest was first noted, existentialism was still semi-respectable as a backdrop to a 'mod' chic interested in continental styles and fashions, black roll-neck sweaters, dark glasses, Gauloises cigarettes and so on. Nevertheless, even as Walker Brothers' drummer Gary Leeds acknowledged that 'Scott was increasingly portrayed as the intellectual one', Walker's biographer Paul Woods also notes that the libidinal 'fun-loving' Gary was quick to disassociate himself from such an image. 'John and I found all that a bit – dare I say it – boring?' (Gary Leeds in Woods, 2013: 49). For Scott, however, Woods acknowledges that existentialism became fundamental as 'an attitude for living', an 'ethos' that Engel has 'maintained … through all his fluctuating fortunes' (2013: ix).

If the career of Scott Walker has had its ups and downs, in the academic world the reputation of existentialist philosophy collapsed and has never recovered. By 1966 in France, this collapse had already happened. Its death was announced most spectacularly by Michel Foucault in his best-selling book *The Order of Things*, published that year. Sartre famously wrote in 1946 that 'Existentialism is a Humanism' (Sartre, 2007), only for Foucault to declare twenty years later that 'Man', the object of this humanism, had been erased like a face drawn in the sand at the edge of the sea. In an interview promoting his book, 'Foucault Responds to Sartre', Foucault gives the date of 1955 – when Sartre himself 'renounced philosophical speculation' in order to invest all his time into political activity – as the moment of existentialism's eclipse. Ironically, this was the year when it was gaining popular attention in Britain among the beatniks. 'Man disappears in philosophy ... as subject of freedom and existence', announced Foucault, since 'he' has been dissolved by 'structures', 'correlations', logical systems that form 'unconscious laws and determinations' (Foucault, 1989: 40). In his own philosophical career, Foucault moved on considerably in his last work from this high point of 'structuralism' to concentrate on the theme of care of the self in the practices and arts of existence. Here, Foucault's contention concerning the *bios philosophicus* that 'the true life takes shape and is given form only in a person's own life' (Foucault, 2011: 237) is not so far from either existentialism or Scott Walker's *bios poeticum*.

Nevertheless, the eclipse of existentialism (and indeed structuralism) not just in France but elsewhere in the Anglophone world needs to be acknowledged. Laws and determinations still reign supreme even if they are not the same as those identified by Claude Levi-Strauss's anthropology or Louis Althusser's scientific Marxism. These days the intellectual life of the Anglo-Americans is dominated by science, particularly the science of cybernetics. Again in 1966, in an interview with *Der Spiegel* magazine, Martin Heidegger conceded that 'the role philosophy has played up to now has been taken over by the sciences', claiming that cybernetics represented the completion of Western metaphysics (Heidegger, 1976). Sartre reiterated this view in his own response to the scientific turn in French philosophy which he connected to its Americanization. The ideological implications of the structuralist movement were evident in its embrace by the United States where 'a technocratic civilization no longer holds a place for philosophy unless the latter turns itself into technology' (Sartre, 1966: 94). In this context, philosophical concern with the self has followed technological innovation in two directions: one related to the image of the self that is manifested in various media, particularly digital media where it multiplies in the shape of various transitory images ('selfies'), avatars, icons, numbers, passwords and biometric data, while correlatively the other is concerned with its scientific image where the self disappears. Philosophers of neuroscience confidently proclaim that 'there is no such thing as a self', all its feelings, attributes and desires being merely the 'folk psychological' delusions of automata afflicted by the errors and misperceptions inscribed in natural languages (see Churchland and Churchland, 1998; and Metzinger, 2003).

Structuralism went to the United States in 1966 and quickly became 'post-structuralism', ultimately to become embroiled in 'culture wars' battling over the meaning of 'political correctness' in the constructivist politics of identity, particularly gender and race. Ironically, the existentialist thought at the basis of Simone de Beauvoir's feminism, the anti-colonialism of Franz Fanon, the struggle for civil rights of Ralph Ellison and Richard Wright, all of which was predicated upon a core of 'endless self-creation' (Fanon), has largely been forgotten. Essence, in the sense of the ontological, discursive, relational determinations of cultural identity, entirely over-codes existence. In the social sciences, the 'philosophical' response to both these developments is to form ethical committees which, in the absence of any idea of universality or the security of tradition, must calculate the benefits of the subject's normalization, which is to say assess its relative advantages and disadvantages in relation to statistical analyses. Ultimately, the subject has been erased by a tide of data. The cybernetic exchange and distribution of online identities provides the perfect condition for ethical committees to be replaced by algorithms, especially those second and third generation algorithms that can correct the historical 'biases' that condition their predecessors towards the goal of absolute transparency. It is an era when, it is claimed, computers can, on the basis of activities on social media, predict the thought, speech and actions of their users, can 'know' them better than they know themselves and can make better, more informed decisions regarding their everyday lives, their interests, their amorous partners and political choices. At such a time, users have clearly been brought to the point of an existential crisis, whether or not such users are described as 'human'.

'There is no human nature', wrote Sartre in *Existentialism is a Humanism* (1946/2007). 'Man' is not definable 'because to begin with he is nothing' (13). This view is of course not incompatible with the standard social science model in which the subject is a cultural construction, but there is still Sartre's contention that the subject is not simply a blank slate to be passively written upon but the source of an active 'will'. He or she is a 'nothing' that nevertheless 'wills': 'wills to be after that leap towards existence'. There is then also the question of desire that projects the 'nothing' of existence into the world of 'essence' or being. Though less certain, Sartre's subject in this world is nevertheless Cartesian; self-present, its 'for-itself' has no body other than an ego-image that it misrecognizes as itself. It is a semblance that indeed has an ontological dimension, but not an 'ontic' one in the traditional philosophical opposition. In fact, as I shall argue with regard to Sartre's fiction, a body is involuntarily produced in an event of song, a body that 'hardens' and enables him to enter '*in* the music', even as it enters him (Sartre, 2000: 38). Sartre's subject, however, is not an entity. Since it has no determined or determining physical manifestations, it can desire to be anything, but again that desire is conditioned by cultural images and objects. The data subject of modern algorithmic software is exactly the same except that its desire can be more precisely calibrated, calculated and predicted. The 'nothing' can be added-to indefinitely. This is ultimately the same situation we find when we move from the social science model to the science model proper in which the brain's neuronal activation vectors are conditioned by the evolution of electrochemical processes. Such vectors constitute a calculable coherence of forces dependent upon a numerical constant necessary for any neuroscientist to calculate how the brain is able to work.

It is for this reason that any re-engagement with existentialism, following Scott Walker, needs to reconceive the subject in an ontic rather than ontological dimension, as something in possession of a body. But this body is neither biological nor informational, since these bodies belong to the dimension of ontology. Rather, it is necessary to conceive of this body entirely as an effect of song, that is to say of a particular conjunction of speech and music that produces the body as a field of sensations. The body comes out of the voice, and song proceeds via the bodies that emit and receive it, affecting those bodies through the phenomena of resonance and echo, dissonance and repetition. What Sartre calls the 'will' is here less conscious will than a drive that is produced through the somatic events of sound and song. This somatic conjunction of speech and music is not therefore the Sartrean 'nothing' of the subject that is equivalent to the nothing that lies at the basis of enumeration. Only the destiny of the absolutely singular *one* that is 'honed' almost to nothing can be said to be unique and un-calculable. It is through the careful process of 'honing down', that is also a process of interpretation, which leads precisely to the un-interpretable, singular sound that provides the basis for meaning.

It is sound, then, a sonic event, that provides the contingent basis for the continual unfolding of the song of the one-all-alone. What is of concern here is not a subject, although it may be mistaken for one, nor is it a brain. What is of concern is a song that is continually being written even as it is sung in relation to a sound that is singular and thus outside-sense. It nevertheless becomes the basis for the sensation of a body produced in and by song that resonates with a mood and a tonality that is utterly distinct. In Walker's song, existentialism is not a humanism but an x-humanism, or an ex-humanism in which, on the basis of an indefinable sonic, non-human 'x', we exit from humanism, particularly the metaphysical form of humanism that seeks its completion in technology and scientific reason. In what follows throughout this book, the elaboration of the existentialist x-humanism of Scott Walker will also involve an 'exhumation' of three vectors in the work that constitute, traverse and exceed the human: animality, divinity and the Greek alternative to *techne*, the ancient notion of *epimeleia*.

'Archangel' (1966)

(Scott Engel)

One of the first Walker Brothers' songs to be credited solely to Scott Engel, 'Archangel' was the 'B' side to the single 'Deadlier than the Male', also written by Engel and his fellow 'brother', John Maus. Retrospectively, the 'B' side has much more significance in the context of Walker's oeuvre than the theme tune to a long-forgotten film of the same name, for two reasons. First, because 'Archangel' is one of the earliest examples of Walker's characteristic juxtaposition of mundane, quotidian life with extraordinary, swelling orchestral sounds and arrangements. Second, because of its ambitious engagement with existentialist ideas and concepts, here echoing one of the most famous passages from Sartre's *Being and Nothingness* (2003 [1943]) and Søren Kierkegaard's *Fear and Trembling* (2012 [1843]). No doubt one of the attractions of Jean-Paul Sartre for Engel was his philosophical use of everyday examples and ordinary scenes of contemporary Parisian life. 'This woman I see coming toward me, this man who is passing by in the street, this beggar whom I hear calling before my window, all are for me *objects*' writes Sartre at the beginning of his section on '*le regard*' from *Being and Nothingness*

(2003: 276). Like Sartre, Engel's persona in 'Archangel' is situated at the window of his rented apartment idly watching everyday scenes, children playing, young couples in the street below. He waits and watches all day for his lover to return, even to the fall of dusk as shadows slowly spread across the roof tops. This simple story is heralded and accompanied, however, by the huge, ominous sound of a church pipe organ – actually the organ of the Empire, Leicester Square. The use of the organ supports the idea of an 'Archangel', but the image of the angel floats apparently as a saving power above the organ's deep and oppressive resonance. The latter summons the anxiety-inducing presence of God and the looming imminence of death. The sun may not shine anymore, but the 'Archangel' – the protagonist's lover – appears as the moon rises at dusk to save him from the sepulchre that is his lonely apartment. Yet sonically, the song sustains the sense that there is something quite ominous and anxiety-inducing about this apparent deliverance. Speaking to Robert Sandall on BBC Radio 3 in 1995, Walker commented on his use of the organ on 'Archangel' and elsewhere. 'I've always used the organ at different periods of my career … the organ represents something to me always: organised religion; it's actually most of the times the enemy to me. It's this big looming gigantic thing.'

The church pipe organ is almost as old as established religion in Britain. The first pipe organ of Winchester Cathedral, for example, was built by Bishop Alphege in the tenth century. The monk Wulfstan wrote of its size and intimidating sound:

> Twice six bellows are ranged in a row and fourteen lie below. These are worked by 70 strong men covered in perspiration, each inciting his companions to drive the wind up with all his strength that the full-bosomed box may speak with its 400 men. Two brethren of concordant spirit sit at the instrument. … Like thunder the iron tones batter the ear. Everyone stops with his hands to his gaping ears; the music is heard throughout the town, and the flying fame there is gone out over the whole country. (Stanley Webb, 1988: 369)

The function of this sound is to tie the country together in the awe of God. The sound is full and painfully affecting. It batters the body such that everyone clasps their hands to their ears. It consists of 400 separate pipes that are here characterized by Wulfstan as 'men', each with its own distinct tone. As such, the organ provides the instrument and metaphor of their union in a thunderous sound, expressing the very breath of God's word and name. Often hidden, yet looming above and behind the congregation, the pipes shake and reverberate through their bodies, penetrating their souls.

In relation to this oppressive sound, 'Archangel' seems to be concerned with two versions of the *angst* or anxiety that is the existentialist basis for freedom – uncertainty and indecision being the necessary condition of choice. Sartre's unseen gaze and the demand of Kierkegaard's Old Testament God, who for no apparent reason commands Abraham to sacrifice his son Isaac, provides the basis for the anxiety that causes the subjective division inherent to self-consciousness. Self-consciousness and the desire for freedom can only be established in relation to the question of the Other's desire and the proximity of death. Both in *Being and Nothingness* and in 'Archangel', the sound of footsteps summons the 'look' of the Other. Sartre begins his famous passage with the example of a person looking out of a window, lost in the pure contemplation of the world. The example illustrates the 'nihilating' action of consciousness as a 'pure nothingness' that simply regards a world of objects rather than the existence of others. The existence of others is dismissed, just as Engel's character dismisses the young couples outside his window in the song. What establishes the potential for a relation to others for Sartre, however, is the experience of being looked-at. The experience of being looked-at is not the same as looking someone else in the eye. That would just be 'to apprehend a look-as-object in the world' (281). Rather than meeting another's gaze, the look is produced through sound. In the position of a voyeur, Sartre writes, 'all of a sudden I hear footsteps in the corridor. Someone is looking at me! What does this mean? It means that I am suddenly affected in my being' (284). Affected by the sound, Sartre becomes aware of his body, and can now see himself through the agency of an Other, the imaginary source of the sound, who he supposes looks at him. A field of otherness is opened that is not simply a world of objects but also the obscure source of affects: anxiety, shame, fear and desire. In this way, Sartre is brought to himself as a self-perceiving 'ego', an ego that is really an image. Sartre writes:

> I am that Ego; I do not reject it as a strange image [*l'image étrange*], but it is present to me as a self which I *am* without *knowing* it; for I discover it in shame and, in other instances, in pride. It is shame or pride which reveals to me the Other's look and myself at the end of that look. (284–5)

Coincidentally, no doubt, one of the strange features of the French word *étrange* is that it can be heard as an ellipsis of *être-ange*, 'being-angel' or 'angel-being'. The English word 'strangely' contains the celestial predicate 'angely'. The German word for 'angel' is of course 'engel', the strange name of the singer who became a Walker. The Walker Brothers' 'Archangel' by Scott Engel begins precisely at this Sartrean moment of heard footsteps walking down a hall, but as a repetition. Sitting in a shadowy silence, the song's protagonist longs to hear the approaching footsteps of his lover returning home at dusk, without the blessing of which the night threatens to entomb him. Here in Engel's song, the memory of footsteps clacking down a darkened corridor does not, as with Sartre, support the consciousness of the annihilating subject but threatens its dissolution in the darkest night – and thus the world of objectivity of which it is the correlate. What is disclosed therein in this early song is a more spiritual dimension in which sound patrols the boundary of a solitary existence defined by the ineffable in-existent reality of death. In his principled atheism, Sartre of course rejects any mystical or ineffable dimension to the experience of the look that grounds the relation to the Other, seeking it only in 'everyday reality' (277). But in this song, Engel takes the everyday reality of a love song and turns it into something strangely biblical in which the song's protagonist confronts his fate beneath the thunderous sounds of a church organ, as if he were both Abraham and his son Isaac. Just in time to save him from this doom comes the Archangel like the angel of the Lord in Gen. 22.11 who stays Abraham's knife, so that he might substitute the ram that is discovered behind him 'caught in a thicket by his horns'. In the Jewish tradition, the ram's horn becomes the source of the *shofar* that is blown three times at the end of the festive ritual that follows the Jewish New Year and the Day of Atonement. This sound produces the voice of Yahweh through an instrument shaped from the horn of the totem animal. In the Western Christian tradition, as can be heard in 'Archangel', this sound is mechanized and amplified a hundred-fold in the church pipe organ.

In Kierkegaard's reading of the tale of Abraham and Isaac, God's incomprehensible demand is matched by the enigma of Abraham's faith. Taciturn and solitary, Abraham chooses an act of murder that, from Kierkegaard's perspective at least and that of his time, goes against all morality. From motives that are represented as hidden and personal, Abraham sets himself up to undertake the task alone in a state of infinite resignation that allows him to transgress the morality of his time and achieve the transcendent summit of morality represented by God. Abraham at that moment becomes – in anguish – the equivalent of God, something that the Bible confirms in the New Testament when, according to the Christians, God will himself confront Abraham's dilemma and allow the son to be executed instead of the lamb.

Scott Engel's 'Archangel' playfully oscillates between the sacred and the profane, Kierkegaard and Sartre, with the angel of the Lord doubled as the protagonist's lover. He is a voyeur, roused by the echo of footsteps that summon the memory of the woman he imagines watching him. The song obliquely executes its own transgressive, sovereign reversal as the organ rises in its proud turgidity, only to fall in the lachrymose *tristesse* of solitary shame, awaiting the return of the angel who heralds its resurrection.

Sartre's body-event

Greg Hainge's excellent book *Noise Matters* (2013) posits an ontology of noise which lights hopefully on Sartre's seminal novel *Nausea* (2000) because of the etymological link between 'noise' and Sartre's title in the Latin root of *nausea*. For Hainge, following this etymological lead, 'noise makes the world pitch, roll, heave' just like the nausea that in Sartre's novel provides, Hainge suggests, his protagonist Roquentin's 'insights into the mobile and expressive nature of existence' (Hainge, 2013: 68). And indeed, Hainge does find that some of Sartre's nauseous descriptions of phenomena in the novel disclose the essence of an 'expressive ontology' that signals 'the necessary movement that subsists in all being' (2013: 68). This is Hainge's ontology, however, rather than Sartre's. Hainge's ontology of noise is essentially a vitalism, an expressive materialism that takes inspiration from the thought of Benedict Spinoza and Gilles Deleuze. As the promising title of Sartre's book suggests, Hainge's ontology of noise ought to find common cause with Sartre's own naturalist literary style that also seems to represent a kind of vitalism where presence similarly palpitates and oozes, sweats and groans to the point where 'nausea … spreads out at the bottom of the slimy puddle' (Sartre, 2000: 37).

But looking more attentively, in an exemplary close reading, Hainge discovers that when Sartre actually describes instances of *noise*, the nausea stops; things stabilize. Hainge registers his bafflement, as his disappointment turns to disapproval at Sartre's failure to 'follow through'

(68). 'Somewhat strangely, explicit instances of noise in the novel actually recontain and ground existence again, noise, when figured as noise, thus being elided as a means to reinstate an established and seemingly necessary order in the world' (68). For Hainge, instances of noise seem to disclose if not underscore an inherent conservatism in Sartre, cementing order in the world and in himself. Working through a series of examples, Hainge shows that while the field of vision frequently provokes disorientation in Sartre's protagonist, his auditory sense, 'noise in particular, even more strangely – seem to serve as a means to orient himself, as a fixed point of localization' (Hainge, 2013: 73). Footsteps are again mentioned twice, as well as speech, 'the slight hum of words', the chatter of the clients at the Café Mably.

Ultimately, it is the moment of 'vinyl noise' in the novel that confirms for Hainge the way that the 'full potential and operations of noise are ... co-opted by a coherent aesthetic project that attenuates or eradicates entirely the ontological qualities' of noise (70). One would think, given the previous examples of how sound provides points of orientation for Roquentin, that noise would also provide the basis of Sartre's aesthetic project, but Hainge argues that, on the contrary, noise is 'attenuated' and ultimately 'elided' completely (75). I am not so sure. Perhaps noise is not understood by Sartre in the way Hainge would like, as the essence of a relational ontology, but it does have an integral role in his aesthetic.

Sartre's protagonist has a passion for jazz, in particular for the song 'Some of These Days' which is described twice playing on a gramophone in the café Rendez-vous des Cheminots. In the first description, Roquentin makes a clear distinction between the sung melody that he prefers and its accompaniment, about which he is more equivocal, but no less attentive. The piping notes of the jazz affect his body, giving him 'a host of little jolts' that evidently mix pleasure with pain, excitement with dolefulness:

> They know no rest, an unchanging order gives them time to recover, to exist for themselves. They run, they hurry, they strike me with a sharp blow in passing and are obliterated. ... I must accept their death; I must even *will* it; I know few harsher or stronger impressions. (Sartre, 2000: 37)

The music is constituted in an 'order' that gives it an ontological consistency even as its sharp tones and pitches jolt, strike and die, offering Roquentin a pleasurable melancholy moment in which he is able to contemplate – and even 'will' – the fact of his own mortality. It is the voice of the singer, however (Sophie Tucker one presumes, though Sartre refers to a 'Negress'), that takes the song completely 'outside' of his feeling of nausea and 'this time in which the world is slumped' (37).

> How strange it is, how moving that this hardness should be so fragile.
> The last chord has died away. In the brief silence that follows, I feel strongly that this is it, that *something has happened*.
> Silence.
>
>> Some of these days
>> You'll miss me honey!
>
> What has just happened is that the Nausea has disappeared. When the voice sounded in the silence, I felt my body harden and the nausea vanished. All of a sudden: it was almost painful to become so hard, so bright. … The music filled the room … crushing our wretched time against the walls. I am *in* the music. (Sartre, 2000: 38)

This is a remarkable description of a body-event caused by sound, in this case the recorded voice of a singer on a record, that occurs in the space between Roquentin's normal, slightly queasy sense of himself and his body. Again, the word 'strange' appears to describe the fragile hardness of the voice that transfers its quality to his body. It is an intense but not especially pleasurable experience; it is 'almost painful'. The hardness comes from outside yet it is internal to him, even as he experiences an immersion into the music that envelops him as it fills the room, not only crushing space, but also 'crushing our wretched time', thus moving outside the dimension of being, as Roquentin will reiterate when he hears the song again.

When the record is replayed later in the novel, it has been scratched. This is of course the part that interests Hainge, and again to his disappointment the noise of this scratch is not celebrated by Sartre's character as evidence of 'the mediated and thus contingent nature of the tune he loves … he is able completely to elide this noise' (Hainge, 2013: 75). Since Roquentin does indeed notice and mention the scratch, he clearly doesn't completely elide it. On the contrary, it becomes the condition of his particular emotional response. The record is scratched precisely 'at that spot' of the chorus, the spot that produced the body-event

> and there is something that wrings the heart: it is that the melody is absolutely untouched by this little stuttering on the needle of the record. It is so far away – so far behind. ... Behind these sounds that decompose from day to day, peels away and slips towards death, the melody stays the same, young and firm, like a pitiless witness. (249)

It is understandable that Hainge is alert to the gap evident here between the sound of the melodic voice and 'the rest of existence' because he regards all of sound – indeed all phenomena – to occupy the same ontological dimension defined by noise. Everything is noisy and therefore the same. Indeed, as the double meaning of the title of Hainge's book suggests, *Noise Matters* because noise is material like everything else and it 'matters' because it provides the 'relationality' that produces effects of meaning, purpose or significance: a sense of something 'mattering'. On the one hand, noise is pure immanence: 'Noise is immersive because there is nothing outside of it and because it is in everything' (32); on the other hand, noise is matter's 'transcendent principle', the 'essence' of its 'relational ontology' (83). This is not as contradictory as it sounds because the 'essence' of this 'relationality' is the noise that separates two distinct elements. 'In essence, then, for it is indeed a question of essence, noise ... constitute[s] the nature or essence of the relation that is inimical to all expression when everything is conceived of as an expression' (Hainge, 2013: 14). The essence of relationality then, for Hainge, is actually non-relationality. Inspired by Spinoza and Deleuze, Hainge's ontology is likewise an ontology of the One, but that One is the noise that is inimical to its expression. The function of the non-relational One noise, therefore, can presumably only represent solitude. This is its function, it seems to me, in Sartre's text where noise is isolated from the usual 'nauseous' dimension of being as if it were the echo of some event or encounter outside of sense and signification, before even the apprehension of time and space. The scratch on the record isolates Roquentin as it isolates the vocal melody of the song, which rises above it such that it can no longer be said to exist: '*It* does not exist; it is even irritating in its non-existence', says Roquentin (248).

The noise of the scratch triggers the memory of the body-event, the moment earlier in the novel when Roquentin's body 'hardens' at the voice of Sophie Tucker and his heart is wrenched. Noise does indeed then signal the inimical, non-relational gap between Roquentin's being and his body, and between Roquentin and the song to which he relates as an Other characterized as the One-missing from existence: 'You're going to miss me honey'. The singer is dead, and yet the melody remains 'a pitiless witness' of the fact – as Sartre's use of language makes abundantly clear – that the one cannot link with the Other, particularly the sexual Other.

This fact introduces an indelible crack into any ontology. In *Nausea*, it produces three fissures between three different dimensions of existence, being and ex-sistence that can be correlated to the different dimensions of sound involved in music and song: noise, a principle of organization, and a 'voice' that may or may not be human. In the novel, Sartre differentiates the voice of melody from the rest of the music. 'There's no melody [to the jazz that's playing], only notes, a host of little jolts … an unchanging order gives birth to them and destroys them' (36–7). In *Nausea*, there is a movement between two points, between noise and the voice, but in reverse such that voice leaves behind music and returns to the condition of pure sound, or rather sound stripped of all signification, honed down to a 'fragile hardness', something like a needle, perhaps, a stylus. The contingency of the scratch literally 'hits the spot' where the voice earlier in the novel has produced the event, piercing his body 'hard', 'bright', 'painful', the memory of which now 'wrenches the heart'. The scratch sets the melody off on a path of ex-sistence even as it pins it to the reality of the body-event which, as Roquentin insists, is entirely outside the reality of social being and everyday existence. It is this body that will subsequently speak in the desire to write 'another kind of book', 'but not a history book: history talks about what has existed – an existent can never justify the existence of another existent' (252). The body speaks 'behind the printed words, behind the pages, something which didn't exist, which was above existence' (252). *Nausea* is the book that results, of course, its words and pages erasing the sound that they nevertheless repeat, symptomatically, in the form of the strangely inert noises identified by Hainge that pin the protagonist to some indefinite source outside existence.

'The Cockfighter' (1995)

(N. S. Engel)

Trevor Griffiths's drama *Comedians* (1980) is set among a night school class for budding comics taught by music hall veteran Eddie Walters. In the concluding scene, Walters is explaining to Gethin Price, his star pupil, the political rationale behind his teaching that is based on his disgust at the clichéd use of racial stereotypes popular at the time. Each racist joke is a mini holocaust. Walters has just seen Price take him quite brutally at his word in a chilling performance of icy, implacable class hatred. He wasn't funny, but that isn't the problem for Walters. In Price's righteous anger, Walters believes he is missing something – the truth. Walters begins to tell him about his visit to a German concentration camp, 'the punishment block', he says, 'was a world like any other; it was the logic of our world extended'. Price cuts him off. He's bored with people invoking the Nazis. He's concerned with now, with his life and the British ruling class. 'But', continues Walters, 'there was something else about it. It wasn't only repulsive, I got an erection – in that place! Something loved it too. We've got to dig deeper than hate. Hate's no help' (Griffiths, 1980: 45–6).

One of the most common instances of a body-event for young boys is an involuntary erection. For most, it is initially a disturbing experience, even frightening. Depending upon the situation, and the presence of a witness, a friend or family member perhaps, it can produce an unsettling sensation of shame and obscure desire. It signals that desire and intention, sexual feeling and appropriate objects will be continually at variance. The shock and embarrassment experienced by Griffiths's old comedian acknowledges that 'something else' is speaking voicelessly through the body from a site that lies 'deeper' than the normal assurance of moral certainties.

Scott Walker's song 'The Cockfighter' from the album *Tilt* (1995) is a track that attempts 'to dig deeper than hate', although masochistic, self-hatred is the threshold that it broaches. In his interviews promoting this album, Walker talked in some length about the song's *mise-en-scène* and the relation between the lyrics of the song and its particular sound. At the end of Sartre's novel *Nausea*, the protagonist hoped to reproduce the 'metallic transparency' of the melody of 'Some of these Days' in writing that would aspire to be as 'beautiful and hard as steel', so that it would make people 'ashamed of their existence' (Sartre, 2000: 37). Walker delivers this promise emphatically in 'The Cockfighter'. Its beauty is mixed with pain, however, and the shame (or guilt) externalized and internalized, is subject to severe sonic punishment that ultimately seeks to crack open the cycle of law and transgression, sin and retribution. The lyrics, Walker suggested, 'made it appropriate to have this metallic sound' produced by the use of extremely loud percussion instruments that crash terrifyingly into the song after moments of relative quiet or silence. In his interview with Robert Sandall for BBC Radio 3 in 1995, Walker attested to how painful it was to hear the harsh percussion beaters being played for the recording: 'When you hear them live, it's like having tin foil on your teeth' (Radio 3).

The song begins quietly with scratching and scraping noises, a slightly gothic, atmospheric wind sounding ominously in the background above which a reed instrument, something like an oboe, sounds a warning refrain. A man's voice murmurs and whimpers in his sleep, midway between speech and animal noises, murmuring, it seems in fear, about a scene of torture in which God lurks indiscernibly in the background. The warning reed becomes more insistent as the voice starts howling with the wind. There's the faint sound of a celeste, then the voice itself becomes percussive, rhythmic, clicking and clacking. At that point, with a shuddering jolt the industrial percussion crashes in, iron beating upon iron, pounding an ominous rhythm behind a shattering metallic shaker that hisses sharply back and forth, as if smashing to pieces a million steel fragments. 'I tried to imagine a man having a nightmare and the song begins like this' (Walker in Kijak, 2006, Bonus interviews). The man is a character, but also, Walker says, 'it's an extension of myself'. 'It's about an internal struggle, an attack and defence struggle within one man.' This internal struggle seems to bear on the man's relation to his sexual desire. Commenting to Sandall about the title of the song, Walker is explicit. '"The Cockfighter": choosing this image, raises the question: is it gross? Does it mean something as crude as cock fighter – geddit? – because it's an erotic song as well, I try to bring in erotic elements' (Sandall, 1995).

The eroticism, however, continually moves into an animality in which man and cock become indiscernible, fingers growing feathers exposing nerve endings to the outside. *Tilt* is teeming with animals: the buffalo of the title track, fighting cocks, of course, horses, butterflies, a halo of locusts. The animals plot a locus of animality that denotes savagery, eroticism and, as the latter also indicates, the sacred, evident throughout the album in frequent references to biblical and other religious figures: Angel Gabriel, Christ's swaddling hair, Mary Magdalene, saints, and the rosary of the closing track. There is also a reference to Jacob who broke his hip wrestling the Angel. Genesis relates that when the Angel saw that he was not prevailing against Jacob, 'he touched his hip, and Jacob's hip was put out of joint as he wrestled with him' (Gen. 32: 22–32). The story tells of Jacob's renaming as Israel, appropriate for Walker's song given the later references to Adolf Eichmann's trial in Jerusalem. The image of the Angel of the Lord (Elohim) is superimposed on to the cock at the place renamed Peniel, or 'Facing God', as animality conjoins with the sacred in an erotic struggle.

Animality, here, does not denote a degeneration back to a pre-human, pre-cultural animal substrate. As Georges Bataille insists, humanity represents an uprooting from 'nature', and 'that being who returns' to animality in acts of eroticism or savagery 'is still uprooted'. He or she remains 'an uprooted being who suddenly goes back toward that from which he is uprooted' in a process that ceaselessly continues the process of uprooting on a path of ex-sistence outside the dignity of human being (Bataille, 1991: 90). The uprooting springs from a centre of non-knowledge that is also the basis of mysticism. In a response to a question concerning his frequent allusions to animals, Walker commented, 'they're such a primal force. They're beings with us but we don't really know them. They're so unique so they keep coming in my mind' (Weidel, 2006). We do not experience the sensations of animals, any more than we know the ecstasies of God into which mystics seek to plunge.

Beneath the title of the song in the lyric booklet is a large black rectangle drawn by the white lines used for the text. It is perhaps there to signify the night of the nightmare, the unsayable that Walker has frequently said is the object of the song, the darkness of the unknown, the silence through which all speech has to pass, or pass over. For Bataille, eroticism is profoundly silent, figured as an open, divine mouth stripped of speech and song that moans, screams, laughs, rattles and sobs in a negation of the animal desire that it nevertheless seeks to regain in order to communicate from the mute site of enunciation overwritten by words and music. Without possibility of mediation, eroticism is also profoundly solitary, according to Bataille, because 'the final sense of eroticism' is death. Citing Sade with approval, Bataille contends finally that 'there is no better way to know death than to associate it with some licentious image' (Bataille, 1986: 11, emphasis in original).

'IT'S A BEAUTIFUL NIGHT' states the opening line, the lyric printed in capitals as the process of uprooting goes 'FROM HERE TO THOSE STARS'. The fighting cockerel is also an angel that mediates between the man and the cosmos. The dream-nightmare then takes a sudden historical loop as the lyric starts to feature dialogue from the public trial for adultery of Queen Caroline in 1820. In interviews, Walker explained this development as he sums up the song, and its method, in the following way:

> It starts with a nightmare, a man having a nightmare. And there are a lot of erotic images as well and banal sounds in the background. Finally, at the end of it as it transpires, the idea was to try and talk about the holocaust – this was a time when everyone was talking about the holocaust, it seems appropriate now. So, I wanted to talk about something that really can't be talked about, without a knee-jerk reaction, without riffing 'dirty Nazi, dirty Nazi'. I came across this thought. I wanted to attack the ludicrousness of the law. I also wanted to play with time, so I picked two trials that were in the public consciousness in a big way in their time, one was this big trial of Queen Caroline in 1820. The other's the Eichmann trial now in our time. So by using questions from one trial and answers from the other I managed to suggest this without really talking about it, to say 'this can't be talked about, this is unsayable, [but] here's a way we can find through this [method]', and then what comes through at the end of it all though they are both public things, because of using them in this way, they turn uniquely into the private again, into the internal where things really start, this kind of horror starts, so that's what I was getting at. (Kijak, 2006)

There would appear to be something of a contradiction in Walker's insistence on the unsayable with regard to the holocaust, particularly given that he is talking in the context of the 50th anniversary of the liberation of the camps. As he says, not only is everyone talking about and commemorating the catastrophe but he also agrees that it is appropriate to do so. Since it is clearly not a question of the sensitivity of the Jewish people, what precisely is unsayable? The two trials are deployed, Walker suggests, to attack the ludicrousness of the law. Why is the law ludicrous or 'absurd', as Walker suggests in another interview? Following this lead, it is possible to suggest that the song questions the problem of law with reference to two classic texts.

First, the designation of law's 'absurdity' of course recalls Camus and his novel *The Outsider*, another text centred around a trial. At the climax of the novel, Camus's hero Meursault verbally wrestles with the priest who has been sent to comfort him on the eve of his execution for murder. While he is guilty of killing 'the Arab', Meursault believes it was his perceived lack of empathy that condemned him to be 'executed for not crying at his mother's funeral' (Camus, 2012: 110). As the fatal dawn approaches, Meursault stands before a 'symbolic night bursting with stars', suggesting that memory of this scene kicks off the nightmare of Walker's own protagonist in 'The Cockfighter'. Gazing at the stars, Meursault opens himself 'for the first time to the indifference of the world' that provides the armature of his freedom, hoping that his execution will be attended by 'many, many spectators' greeting him with 'cries of hatred' (111). Far from representing a principle of rationality, the absurdity of the law not only fails to arrest violence but also precipitates it. The law's inherent violence is evident in every trial, especially a trial for murder where justice broaches an incommensurability – death – that it cannot adequately measure and, in Meursault's case, enacts.

Second, there is a chicken-and-egg problem with the origin of law. There is only crime from the perspective of the law that is brought into being to account for it. Culturally, then, the origin of the law always in some way has to account for the passage of a fall from innocence into sin or guilt. Given the song's territory of the dreamscape, we could invoke the Jewish father of psychoanalysis, Sigmund Freud. Freud's version of the mythical origin of the law is recounted in 'Totem and taboo' (1913), where law originates in the murder of the 'father' of the primal horde as an effect of the prohibition that results from the subsequent remorse of the parricides. The 'remorse' is an effect of the disappointed realization that none of the brotherhood can enjoy all the women for himself. The law, therefore, correlates the prohibition of parricide with the crime of incest, murder and sexual transgression. The result of this repression is that at the origin of law lies the fantasy of an exceptional, unlimited sexual satisfaction for which the 'father' has to pay with his life. This fantasy is subsequently displaced and commemorated, for Freud, throughout very many different cultures, by the sacrifice of the totem animal. The rooster, master of his brood of hens, is one such totem animal.

Accordingly, both trials in 'The Cockfighter' are tainted by the paradox of law's crime, just as they conjoin the question of murder with sexual transgression, the one 'answering' for the other in the mixing of question-and-reply at the end of the song, brought together in the dream-logic of the nightmare as the song turns 'uniquely … internal'. They both involve the unjust conflation of judge, prosecutor and plaintiff. In 1820, King George IV, known since his days as Regent to be debauched and adulterous, hypocritically prosecutes his wife for the adultery she has committed, even as judgement sits in the name of his Crown. In 1961, following its criminal act of kidnapping Eichmann from Argentina, the State of Israel itself (rather than an International Court for War Crimes) prosecutes and sits in judgement on the former German bureaucrat for the crimes he has committed against the Jewish People. Both were public show trials memorable for their theatricality, aiming at something beyond the stated terms of the trial. 'For the case was built on what the Jews had suffered', wrote Hannah Arendt, 'not on what Eichmann had done' (Arendt, 2006: 6).

This is the nub of law's ludicrousness, for Walker, that recalls Meursault's complaint about the jury in his own trial. The latter is condemned for his failure to register suffering in the form of grief at his mother's death and remorse for the murder. The register of suffering is the essential supplement of law's failure to account for the incommensurability of crime.

The problem with Eichmann, as Arendt goes on memorably to note, is that his banality failed to provide a sufficient objective correlative to the crime. On what scale of justice could this nondescript bureaucrat, isolated in the glass booth for his own protection, account for the immeasurable, unfathomable suffering of the victims of the holocaust? What monstrous lust could these deaths begin to satisfy? What possible punishment could provide a satisfying balance? How many eyes, how many teeth? Certainly, it would be possible to count them, but would the extraction of 12 million German eyes provide an adequate measure for the suffering and the grief and for the loss of the millions who would never be born?

The truth to which Walker's dream-work seems to be leading is the impasse represented by Eichmann, his inscrutable stupidity suggesting that there is something impenetrable about it that prevents identification, empathy, even hatred. This impenetrable wall repels us back into the interior prison of our own darkest fantasies that can themselves only take familiar shapes, the exterior 'turns into the private again, the internal'. Walker mentions the banality of the sounds in the background to his song, presumably not just the Gothic atmospherics, but precisely the big percussive, industrial noises no doubt engaged to represent the Nazi industrialization of death that the Gothicism haunts. The more the percussion attempts to smash through the limit of identification, the more it is defeated by the signifier that metonymically links industrial noise with industrial death. It is a cliché, to be placed next to what are now the clichés concerning the banality of evil and the impossibility of poetry after Auschwitz. The industrial noise that begins and ends the song, then, is also the wall of discourse forming the rectangle of silence drawn in the liner notes that is traversed by sacred animality. The structure of the song stretches the square into a strip of ribbon that it twists over, joining the beginning to the end in the process forming a Moebius band. Just as law and violence are not opposites but exist on the same plane, so too, at a certain point in the song, the cockfighter section becomes the trial section which, following the reference to 'Garcia' and the last cigarette, becomes the more frenzied middle cockfighter section which leads on to another trial section and so on. Indeed, most of the songs on *Tilt* have an A:B: A:B or A:B: B:A structure. As the song recovers from the frenzy of the central cockfight section, it drifts into another other-worldly moment projected out on a cosmic rim where 'calcium planets' grow in the darkness that is again the inner darkness of a 'flapping body'. The phrase 'clickety-click' is repeated twice before the song, swelling to the organ of the Methodist Central Hall, returns to the questions of Eichmann's prosecutors concerning his role and responsibility for the transportation of Jews to the gas chambers and the replies of defensive witnesses to Queen Caroline's arraignment in 1820. There is a pause as Queen Caroline is reported opening her tent to take the air and, like Meursault, look up into the starry night before dawn, returning us to the opening line of the song as the industrial noise crashes in again.

On a number of occasions, Walker has said that the goal of his art is to 'catch this terrifying moment as much as possible, the impact of this feeling as much as possible' (Sandall, 1995). The registering of such a moment can only come from the listener who registers the sonic terror as it oscillates between the two poles of attraction and repulsion. For myself, the most terrifying sound in the song comes in the middle cockfighting section with thundering bass metal and shrieking horns announcing the entry of the fighting cocks in which the word CRACK cracks sickeningly.

An onomatopoeia, 'crack' is an iconic sign whose meaning can be conveyed purely through its sound, without reference to another signifier, bursting through the network of differences: it is a signifier-all-alone that can crack open an abyss in the fabric of being. The cocks' ribbons are cracking and being cracked. As has been already noted, the song has the structure of a ribbon attached to itself at either end. Further, while the word refers to the ribbons sometimes worn by fighting cocks, operating as a metonymy for the birds themselves, they can also refer to the feminine ribbons worn in a woman's hair, just as 'crack' can be a word for female genitalia; in 'rosary' these ribbons are associated with snare wires, suggesting the idea of being torn to ribbons. A hairline crack suggests that something is about to break open, like the cracking of eggs, or of heads, a breastbone, something being broken – like the law. Freud's band of brothers crack open the head of the primal father in order to explore the cracks of his wives. And if not the dawn of civilization, then the end envisaged by King Lear on the blasted heath when he calls on the storm to 'crack nature's moulds, all germens spill at once / That makes ingrateful man' (Shakespeare, KL 3.2: 8–9). This would be the sound not just of the breaking of human law, but the cracking open of the moulds or laws of nature, its fundamental elements smashed into the smallest fragments: the very basis of regularity and consistency given over to an utterly lawless state of contingency and disorder. Significantly, it is the section of the song that Walker would use again over images of bombing raids and firestorms in the Second World War in his soundtrack to Leos Corax's film *Pola X* (1999). On the soundtrack album the track is given the Shakespearean title 'Time is Out of Joint'.

Perhaps, if the Freudian contention that a dream is the encoding of a wish is allowed, it can be suggested that the nightmare of the cockfighter concerns the problem of guilt, even self-hatred. The song's sonic violence betrays an almost hysterical identification with its subject matter that illustrates how empathy with the victims of violence, even pity, can constitute a masochistic projection of violence on to the other that cannot be reached. At the beginning and the end of the song, where the percussion beats loudest and most insistently in its attempt to crack open the circularity of the dream, there is the ghost of Meursault. He looks up at the bursting stars and 'the tender indifference of the world' with which he identifies his own fate. The wish takes the form of another identification, but a paradoxical one identifying only with a 'tender' indifference, a silence that provides the sovereign separation lacking in the infinite supplementation of law by human guilt.

ONE-MISSING

'Narcissus in Metamorphosis'

The title to Keith Altham's sleeve notes to *Scott 3* (1969), a stream-of-consciousness evocation of the songs' lyrical content and context, summons Ovid's well-known myth of the young man captured by his own image, although in an unsettling way. Altham's Narcissus is found 'tearing at his well-known image behind which he hides his unknown face'. This introduction to Altham's impressions of *Scott 3* implies that 'Narcissus in Metamorphosis' is a description of Walker himself, or perhaps of the creative process of song writing. These are works in which Scott Engel, the composer, explores the disjunctions between identity and image, self and persona, private and public, in works that will be sung by an alter ego, Scott Walker, defined by publicity images in a voice amplified, recorded, produced, disembodied, inscribed in wax, broadcast, played over and over, promiscuously, across the airwaves, in the imaginary intimacy of unknown bedrooms.

In Ovid's myth, the metamorphosis of Narcissus concerns the latter's transformation into the flower of the same name, but this is not the limit of the implication of Altham's idea. Narcissus's metamorphosis here is not the atrophying effect of his immobility, his fixation before his own image in the lake turning him into a flower, but of a creative movement that takes place in the disjunction between the 'well-known image' and the 'unknown face'. This creative movement is also destructive; it is a 'tearing' at an image that obscures and alienates the face precisely to the degree to which it becomes more familiar. The opening three songs of *Scott 3* prominently feature various windows and photographs as screens of delusional reflection, dreams and memory, all involving the misalignment of fantasy and reality. In 'Rosemary', disturbingly, the photograph 'speaks', even 'screams' at her to wake up from oneiric delusions initially fomented by the 'stain glass whispers' of her travelling salesman. Abandoned by her 'sad young man', 'Big Louise's' 'windows are broken' as the 'haunted house' of the aging transvestite's body fails to provide the requisite support for a desirable feminine identification. Narcissism, and its various failures, provides the structure for a commentary on songs in which even the self cannot make a satisfactory couple with its own image. The mirror or window is the 'empty space' of auto-amorous reflection in which 'we repeat our dreams to someone new' ('It's Raining Today'), the repetition acknowledging that this someone is always essentially the same, and also always missing, the enigma of ourselves.

It was Freud, of course, who placed Narcissus at the centre of his reflections on modern subjectivity, not as an aberration or perversion but, on the contrary, as an essential means of 'self-preservation, a measure of which may justifiably be attributed to every living creature' (Freud, 2001a: 75). Auto-affection is the necessary basis of any sense of one's future or historical being, or indeed affection for those objects and others who one might recognize, nurture, support, one's care for others happily providing a favourable reflection of one's own self-image. But as a template for the relation to others, it is curious. There is no 'other' in the myth – or at least not for Narcissus, who ignores the pleas of echo. The 'other' does not exist but is an effect of the one-missing. The other is misperceived in the image of the one who is all alone, unaware of its sonic partner in the sound that repeats.

The essentially solitary character of narcissism sustains the asymmetry and disharmony supposed to be resolved in the love of the couple, or the family or group. Indeed, in Freud's political text *Group Psychology and the Ego*, narcissism provides the ironic basis of the love for a Great Leader, precisely because of the extraordinary discordance that lies at the basis of love. Freud refers to 'Bernard Shaw's malicious aphorism to the effect that being in love means greatly exaggerating the difference between one woman and another' (2001b: 139). Ernesto Laclau cites Freud's reference in his own reflections on the affective politics of populism, noting that 'pure harmony would be impossible without affect' (Laclau, 2007: 119). Needless to say, love's exaggeration can take on monstrous proportions when it is projected on to the egotism of a populist or despotic leader, examples of which feature prominently in Walker's later work.

Shaw's satirical (if not 'malicious') aphorism implies that from the enlightened perspective of rational utility, all women are indeed of equal value, exemplifying for Freud the difference, fundamental to obsessive neurosis particularly, between love and sensuality, in which the presence of one results in the disappearance of the other. (The obsessive characteristically is unable to desire the person he loves, or love the person he desires.) Scott Walker's solo albums consist partly in a realist (or social realist) recapitulation of melancholic, even sentimental songs of loss involved in the scission between love and sensuality, from both male and female perspectives. Almost all the early songs are about lost love. Indeed the 'tears' of loss become the Walker Brother's special object of artistic fascination, in composition and selection, like Cézanne's apples or Hockney's swimming pools – to mention just some of the more lachrymose compositions, 'There Goes My baby' (1965), 'The Girl I Lost in the Rain' (1965), 'Young Man Cried' (1966) and 'Saturday's Child', about a party girl left weeping and abandoned. 'Where's the Girl' (1966) features a guy discarded like the nylon stocking he's left to cry over; in addition, there is Walker's intense vocal treatment of Hal David's 'Another Tear Falls' (1966), along with its 'B' side, John Maus's 'Saddest Night in the World' (1966); 'Archangel's' gloom concerns 'the tears of time all day' (1966), and 'Orpheus' (1967) where Mrs Blears's desertion before dawn by the song's lothario means she'll 'wake with eyes full of rain'.

The frequent metaphor of tears and rain, of course, extends the trope further in the solo albums such that the miserable English weather ('It's Raining Today', 1969) becomes the objective correlative for both amorous and existential misery. Indeed, these songs, featuring the *tristesse* of love's sexual conquest and the tears of love's disappearance, do indeed take a darker turn in Walker's solo records, a turn broaching boredom and shame that is nevertheless heralded by some of Engel's best compositions for the Walker Brothers, 'Orpheus' and 'Genevieve' from the album *Images* (1967).

'Orpheus' (1967)

(Scott Engel)

The use of Classical myth to give structure and meaning to an otherwise chaotic and absurd urban existence is a common literary device in twentieth-century modernist literature, evident most notably in James Joyce's *Ulysses* (1922). Engel's enigmatic reference to Orpheus in his composition for the Walker Brothers is testament to his literary ambition – if not quite as yet an achievement. The narrative seems to relate the sexual misadventures of a young man enjoying the favours of married women. Williams likens the tale to that of Lewis Gilbert's *Alfie* (1966), starring Michael Caine, that played in British cinemas the year before. The narration certainly betrays a similar laconic and ironic world-weariness. Pleasure and ennui are intermingled as first 'Mrs Blears' and then 'Mrs Brown' sleep contentedly while the singer lies awake contemplating his imminent departure, watching the smoke of his cigarette mark time as it drifts away on the ceiling. Bad conscience is everywhere as the gigolo contemplates his cheap theft of affection and shiny tributes; sins that are not expiated by his weekly gifts of pleasure that compensate briefly for a life without love.

Musically, the song's four main sections alternate in a style that will become familiar later in *Tilt* (1995) and *The Drift* (2006). A solitary trumpet heralds the cockiness of the voice that is then slightly undercut by more melancholy brass harmonics, suggesting the north of England evoked in contemporary social realist movie soundtracks. A significant pause announces the post-coital sections of the song in which the sonorous plucking of a stringed instrument – Orpheus's lyre, perhaps – is agitated by the high-pitched almost discordant insistence of orchestral strings that almost always signals existential disquiet in Walker from 'It's Raining Today' to the single-note drones of the post-*Tilt* work. These two sections are repeated, with the brass joining the strings in the fourth section only for the register to change again in the final, more dramatic climax. The strings bow short, sharp, high notes in a technique reminiscent of the shower scene in Hitchcock's *Psycho* (1960), as Walker intones somewhat morosely at the forgettable nature of this latest encounter before the music stops and the voice, treated with heavy reverb, sings a cappella into the void, mocking the madness of transgression.

The title of the song, of course, invites the listener to consider the narration in light of the Orpheus myth, something that most commentators attempt even as they ultimately concede bafflement. Stephen Kijak uses the song at the opening of his documentary *30th Century Man*, confessing that the song has little to do with the myth: 'If you listen to the lyrics it's definitely about something quite different', he says before adding ambiguously, 'Or is it, you know what I mean?' (quoted in Woods, 2013: 101). Rather than the song, Kijak was more interested in applying the myth to Walker himself which 'seemed to make perfect sense when you lined the various versions of the myth up. It fits kind of perfectly into that' (2013: 102).

The origins of the name Orpheus seem to predate Ancient Greek; it is suggested that the root *orbh* 'to put asunder, separate' derives from the proto-Indo-European language that has been inferred by etymologists from a number of common roots since there is no written record. Related, it is further suggested, are the Greek words ὄρφνη *orphne*, 'darkness' (Cobb, 1992: 240) and ὀρφανός *orphanos* (240) meaning 'fatherless, orphan', from which comes English 'orphan' by way of Latin. Noel Cobb's *Archetypal Imagination* (1992) also quotes Fulgentius, a mythographer of the late fifth to early sixth century AD, who, from the conjunction 'Oraia-phonos' gives the meaning 'best voice', perhaps interpreting retrospectively from knowledge of the Greek Orphic myth (240). If these etymological traces are correct then we see in the name Orpheus a conjunction in which song can be seen to emerge from a 'separation' in which a solitary 'one' – an orphan – is located in darkness, perhaps its own pool of darkness, without a father and without a name, like the 'Boy Child' of *Scott 4* (1969). 'Orpheus' is therefore the name of that namelessness. Just a sound, perhaps, the basis more for a yearning moan than speech, a tone giving shape to an indefinable sorrow. If there really is a connection to 'Oraia-phonos', then this sound is also perfect, 'the best voice', even if it contains within itself the loss from which it derives.

Nevertheless, the well-known myth of Orpheus is drawn from a variety of sources from Ancient Greece but, like Narcissus, is given fullest expression in Ovid's *Metamorphoses*. Orpheus is the archetype of the seductive musician, singer and poet, and as such has inspired countless iterations in music, art and literature: preceding the Walker Brothers' song, Jean Cocteau's Orphic trilogy of movies including *Orpheus* (1950) and *Testament of Orpheus* (1960), Pierre Schaeffer's opera *Orphée* (1953), Tennessee Williams's play *Orpheus Descending*, particularly its film adaptation *The Fugitive Kind* (1959) with Marlon Brando, and an influential essay by Maurice Blanchot from 1955, 'The Gaze of Orpheus' from his collection *The Space of Literature* (1982). Since he sings and plays the lyre (perfected from the teaching of Hermes), Orpheus combines both the Pythagorean and the Pindarian myths of musical origin, just as he conjoins both Dionysian and Apollonian traditions. His music and song were reputed to be so powerful and seductive he could charm nature and the gods. With regard to the latter, he is best known for descending into the Underworld to seek out his deceased wife Eurydice, managing to persuade Pluto and the Fates to release her from death on condition that he not look back on her while he leads her into the light of day. Variations on the myth such as told by Phaedrus in Plato's *Symposium* suggest that the gods failed to give up Eurydice at all and attempted to pass off a semblance (1985: 44). Whether it was this realization or simply impatience, anxiety or a change of mind, when Orpheus looks back she disappears returning into the night of death. Schaeffer suggests that it is only her loss that sustains his desire (2012: 96), and he is more interested in the semblance of himself: 'Orpheus bent down, picked up a mask – a replica of his own face – held it at arm's length, and began to sing a duet with himself' (Schaeffer, 2012: 100). It is an image very reminiscent of Altham's impression of Walker in *Scott 3*.

Subsequently foregoing women, yet continuing to exert a fatal attraction, Orpheus is murdered by a group of disappointed Ciconian women, followers of Dionysus, who tear him to pieces in a Bacchanalian frenzy. Notwithstanding the Walker Brothers' frequent encounters, during their boy band heyday, with frenzied young women – on one occasion Walker recalls in Kijak's documentary that they genuinely feared for their lives as their car was tipped over by screaming fans – it is probably the semi-legendary reputation of Walker's voice along with his prolonged disappearance into obscurity that Kijak has in mind when he compared Walker with Orpheus. And Walker disappears not just out of sight, but out of hearing. For Tracey Thorn, Walker consigned 'the most gorgeous, luxuriant, enviable voices of all time' to silence so that he could produce work that, for her, is 'hard to listen to *in the extreme*' (Thorn, 2015: 193). Walker had to silence that voice, she avers, in order 'to explore the depths'. His 'beautiful voice', Thorn acknowledges, actually 'confined him' from those depths from which he would produce art that is un-pleasurable if not unlistenable (Thorn, 2015, 193–4).

Walker's later work does indeed pursue Orpheus's '*Acheronta movebo*', foregoing heaven in order to raise hell. But Walker attempts to raise hell to the level of art, to put song in alignment with it: a hell beyond simple sensuous pleasure, towards sensuous unpleasure that ultimately aspires to the spiritual, though often in the darkest of ways. Perhaps this is what Engel's fictional persona is contemplating as he lies awake in someone else's marital bed, blowing his cigarette smoke at the ceiling. 'Orpheus' is not the name of the persona in the song, but the answer to the predicament, the question it poses. He's going 'round the bend'. Should he run from this madness, plunge into it, or do something with it, turn it into art?

Essentially this is Maurice Blanchot's reading of the Orpheus myth:

> The Greek myth says: one cannot create a work unless the enormous experience of the depths – an experience which the Greeks recognized as necessary to the work, an experience in which the work is put to the test by that enormousness – is not pursued for its own sake. The depth does not surrender itself face to face; it only reveals itself by concealing itself in the work. (Blanchot, 1981: 99)

Blanchot argues that the glory and power of the art of the Orphic artist is 'sacrificed' in order to 'look into the night to see what the night is concealing' (100). For the world in the light of day, this impulse is condemned as 'an unjustifiable act of madness', and it leads to his own 'death' or disappearance. The meaning of Orpheus's gaze, for Blanchot, is the impulse of desire that inspires it – a meaning that is multiple and indefinable – which condemns both Orpheus and Eurydice, who disappears a second time. All that is left is the song whose destiny is 'shattered' by the original impulse of desire that is uncontainable yet immanent to the work, disclosing a moment of freedom within the necessity of generic constraints. 'I am a formalist', stated Walker in 1968, 'I believe that an artist must work within walls, within boundaries. Greater originality emerges from this rather than from sporadic leaps' (cited in Woods: vii). In the Walker Brothers' 'Orpheus' the reflective gaze up at the ceiling, watching time and its burdens drift away, is the gaze through which the 'Alfie' persona disappears and becomes Orpheus in a Blanchot-esque writerly revelation of existential freedom: 'Orpheus's gaze is the extreme moment of freedom, the moment in which he frees himself of himself and – what is more important – frees the work of his concern, frees the sacred contained in the work' (Blanchot, 1981: 104).

Kierkegaard, Jacques Brel and the sensual erotic

'Orpheus' was one of the last songs Engel wrote for the Walker Brothers before he undertook his transformational solo work that would require another detour into the depths of the demi-monde of *Chanson Française* – a frequent metaphor for Hades in treatments of the Orpheus myth from

Offenbach to Schaeffer and Cocteau. Specifically, it would involve an encounter with Jacques Brel whose work is the culmination of a certain type of *Chanson Française* that owes its origins to the *Chanson Réaliste* moment of Aristide Bruant during the *Belle Époque*. Young intellectuals would gravitate towards the area around Montmartre sipping absinthe in *Le Chat Noir* with artists, workers and prostitutes. The themes of *Chanson Française* are more concerned with sex, sexuality, darker forms of enjoyment, abjection or suffering than love and romance. While Brel may not have been the first to emphasize these darker lyrical concerns, his artistic success was such that his example came to define the genre in a way that was new in the 1960s. After Brel, *chanson* favoured the grain of vocal performance rather than the kind of smooth, luxuriant voice associated with the Walker Brothers, just as they privilege words over music. According to Charles Aznavour, a master of the craft, 'the real difference' between French and Anglo-American popular song is that '*Chanson Française* is a good lyric, and if possible good music. *Chanson Anglais-Americaine* is good music and if possible good lyric' (Scott, 2015). Brel's example was critical for Scott Walker in two ways that persisted throughout his career, well beyond the moment of his 1960s cover versions. First, he would decisively favour words over music, indeed to a large degree stripping music down to sonic and *musique concrète* effects that enhance or counter-pose the power of the lyrics. Second, from the 1990s on he would increasingly seek to stretch and strain his baritone voice to the point where, as Tracey Thorn bemoans, aesthetic pleasure gives way to an, at times, almost unlistenable discordance in his attempt to achieve an emotional affect. This is not yet the case in the Philips solo records. Here, Walker is not simply concerned to combine music and lyrics in an Orphic conjunction, but to enhance his lyrics through ambitious orchestral arrangements. In the process his voice rises to the challenge of the orchestra in a way that is unmatched in popular music.

Nevertheless, in Kijak's documentary, Walker underscores the fact that it was the encounter with Brel that 'changed me, changed everything for me' (see also Woods, 110). The anecdote he tells concerning this encounter is prophetic of how Walker's versions of Brel's songs and their milieu would turn out. Walker recalls that 'it's a strange story':

> We went to the opening evening of the London Playboy Club – why I don't know. I was there with Gary just drinking, we did a lot of drinking in those days. It opened on Park Lane and everyone was invited. So we

got involved with the girls, we took up with the bunnies. I met this German girl who was a Playboy bunny, and we went home back to her place, and she was a really big drinker – I think it was Pernod, she was really into Pernod I seem to remember, and Jacques Brel. (see also Woods, 2013: 110)

To Walker's delight, the 'German girl' translated some of her favourite songs of Brel. 'This is fantastic!' exclaimed Walker, commenting also on the 'fantastic coincidence' that a week later Walker came across a demo of Mort Shuman translations recorded by Eric Blau while visiting former Rolling Stones manager Andrew Loog Oldham, who was happy to let him take them. It may be the plastic palace of the London Playboy Club rather than *Le Chat Noir*, Playboy bunnies rather than prostitutes, and Pernod rather than absinthe, but the half-world of swinging London provides the suitable backdrop for Walker's re-workings of Brel. Walker included nine Brel songs across the first three of the *Scott* albums, mostly from Shuman's translations. Critical reception has been mixed, particularly retrospectively where the contrast between the image of the young pop idol and the anguished lyrics of the *Chanson Réaliste* seems ever more marked. Gavin Friday in Kijak's documentary suggests that Brel's songs are known in the UK mainly as a result of Walker's covers. 'Brel was Flemish, he sort of dribbled when he sang, he was sweaty. Whereas Scott Walker took his songs and sang them like a Greek God' (2006). On the other hand, Woods quotes members of Jacques Brel tribute act Dead Belgian to represent the counter view that regards Walker's versions as camp and saccharine. Walker is considered too 'cool' a performer. He's 'cool, theatrical and laid-back. Brel was fucking sweat and blood and anger!' (2013: 116–7). Walker's performances of 'Mathilde' and 'Jackie' on Dusty Springfield's TV vehicle *Dusty* and *The Frankie Howerd Show* do indeed depict him making slightly camp hand gestures, his puppet-like 'slender frame and spindly legs' struggling to keep up with Wally Stott's breathless arrangements which – on 'Jackie' – have been likened to the *Thunderbirds* theme (Woods: 114, 117).

The stark contrast between the Scott Walker and Brel personas, then, along with some of the lyrical changes effected by the translation and the distinctive Stott arrangements significantly alter the tenor and meanings of the songs, such that some of them work interestingly in dialogue. Walker's reworkings are not just cover versions, but ironic commentaries on Brel's 'existential attitude' (Woods, 2013: 111), interpretations that come from an entirely different perspective, enclosed within the pop star's gilded trappings of *mauvaise foi*. This is perhaps most evident in the complex involution of 'Jackie' where Scott Walker, clearly the living embodiment of Brel's fantasy figure, has to convey the narrator's regret or nostalgia that he is no longer, or will never be, the very thing he actually is now: a crooner for the ladies who is beautiful, handsome but a total bastard at the same time. Brel's song is itself an ironic take and reworking of the theme of the charm of the amoral lothario, the 'Don Juan' who is every young man's fantasy, particularly Søren Kierkegaard, who raises the theme in the hands of Mozart, to the quintessence of music's demonic power.

'Jackie' (1967)

(Brel / Jouannes / Shuman)

'Where is the young man' asks Kierkegaard in the founding existentialist text *Either / Or*, 'for whom there have not been moments when he would have given half his fortune to be a Don Juan, or perhaps all of it; when he would have given half his lifetime to be a Don Juan for a year, or perhaps the whole of it' (Kierkegaard, 2004: 109). These sentiments are echoed perfectly by Brel in the chorus to 'Chanson de Jacky' in a way that also manages in characteristically brutal fashion to capture the ambivalent character of Mozart's *Don Giovanni*: '*Être une heure, rien qu'une heure durant / Beau, beau, beau et con à la fois.*' [To be for an hour, just an hour, beautiful, handsome, handsome and a cunt at the same time.]

Uncertainly poised, then, between nostalgia for the lost fantasies of youth and regret about the failure of adult potential, Brel's song summons an aged Don Juan anticipating his death and afterlife in which angels, saints and the devil sing his own song to him about when he was called Jacky, a refrain that immediately gives way to the chorus in which he longs to be again, for just an hour, the handsome devil he once was or perhaps never quite became.

For Kierkegaard, Mozart's opera *Don Giovanni* is a work of immortal greatness because it unifies form and theme, idea and sensuality in the immediacy of music. This immediacy is perfectly encapsulated in the main character in a combination that is, moreover, demonic. Kierkegaard argues that the modern idea or spirit of sensuality is both essentially

Christian and negative. Sensuality is brought into existence as an idea by the Christians in order for it to be negated and banished from the world of the spirit. It is thus a spiritual notion. While something like the Christian idea of sensuality existed with the Ancient Greeks, Kierkegaard argues, it was not defined spiritually but under the category of harmony, a modifying element to the idea. Unlike the Christians, the Greeks did not, for Kierkegaard, have a spiritual notion of the 'sensual erotic' that must be cast out. But before the Christians can cast it out, however, it must be posited or expressed in all its immediacy and loss, and that can only be in music. 'This is where the significance of music is revealed in all its full validity, and in a stricter sense it also reveals itself as a Christian art, or rather as the art that Christianity posits by shutting it out. … In other words, music is the demonic' (Kierkegaard, 2004: 75). The musical genius of Mozart, furthermore, manages to concentrate the concept of the sensual erotic in a single individual, in the figure of Don Giovanni. 'In the erotic sensual genius', Kierkegaard concludes, 'music has its absolute object' – it is beautiful and evil all at the same time (75).

Scott Walker will eventually grasp this musical and lyrical sound object in all its devastating ambivalence in work that is chilling in its violent beauty. His version of 'Jackie', however, following Mort Shuman's lyrical adaptation, wrings the bathos out of a debased Giovanni jaded by self-disgusted nostalgia for the lost immediacy of the sensual erotic. This is Don Giovanni in tight trousers, serenading respectable ladies out on the town, wiggling his pert Spanish butt. It is one future for Scott Walker himself, cabaret singer of easy listening classics. The demonic identity of music and its signature character updated to the swinging sixties – a pop idol with a series of hit records, surrounded by a harem of young women – now drunkenly performs a spectacle of dubious virility for grandmothers decked out in their finest tat and tinsel. The cruise ships and chicken-in-the-basket circuit awaits, an indefinite hell in which a grotesquely aged parody of his former self sings his chart hits forever. Rather than the longing for demonic beauty, the chorus culminates in a cynical image of youth and innocence – to be once again, just for a little hour, 'cute, cute, in a stupid ass way'. 'Is he still cute?' smirks Lulu in *30th Century Man*, reminiscing about a teenage crush on the Walker Brother in the 1960s. In its own quite complex way, as a prospective, retrospective self-description, Walker's version is bleaker than Brel's. When singing 'Jackie', Jacques Brel tribute act Dead Belgian cannot bring themselves to sing the final line of the chorus of Walker's version. 'We couldn't stomach that', they say (Woods, 2013: 115), perhaps recognizing its uncomfortable pertinence to tribute acts generally.

'If You Go Away' (1969)

(Brel / McKuen)

The final track from *Scott 3* (1969) engages in a similar dialogue with Brel's *'Ne me quitte pas'*, wherein changes in the delivery, arrangement and lyrics produce a different meaning from the original. The change is signalled in the title of the translation – not by Mort Shuman this time but American poet and singer Rod McKuen. The conditional statement, 'If You Go Away' has a very different meaning to the non-conditional 'Do Not leave Me'. In the latter, the song concerns an intense demand for presence that broaches the perverse, while the former seems to construct a fantasy of absence that would allow the speaker to continue to desire.

In Brel's performance there is an almost morbid desperation in which the reward for the lover's company threatens to smother her and in which the promise of 'gold and light' cannot shake off the initial, horrible idea of being buried alive. While *'ne me quitte pas'* makes a demand, it does not seem to be a demand for love, more the requirement of presence as an absolute condition, so that the singer may enjoy his servitude, his suffering and abjection. As the song builds to its emotional climax, the demand becomes mute in a manner that suggests perversion. He is no longer interested in engaging the lover in speech – he does not care if his love is returned – on the contrary, he is happy to hide and lurk nearby, watching from the shadows, watching her sing and laugh and enjoy, enjoying her enjoyment, watching indeed from the shadows like a dog, like the shadow of her dog.

The conjunction of 'hand' and 'dog' at the shadowy climax of the song leads us into an area of the sensual erotic also broached in 1969 by the Stooges' 'I Wanna be Your Dog'. It was clearly not an area that Rod McKuen wanted to go in his translation, where these words are cut, and mention of the shadow is there only to evoke being 'by your side'. In order for a dog to cast a shadow he needs to stand in the sun of course and, strangely, Walker returns to this image in one of his last songs, 'Sundog' (2018), that also gives the title of his collection of selected lyrics. Although this dog couldn't, it is suggested, 'take the heat' and so 'took my side' at midnight, demonstrating such prodigious fidelity that he is said to require 'a hundred bags and a shovel' (Walker, 2018: 191–5).

The romanticism of 'If You Go Away' is enhanced by Walker's performance which is steeped in both narcissism and that ambivalence in love that confounds the principle of non-contradiction. The insistence on the conditional 'if' sets up the song as a pleasurable fantasy scenario in which he can play the abandoned lover. And Walker's voice seems not to fear, but to savour the prospect of her departure in his repeated refrain 'if you go away, if you go away ....' The suggestion here is that it is precisely this scenario that is desired so that he can continue to desire, and love being in love. Significantly, the equivalent section offering the reward for staying lists a set of feats that are dubious, alliteratively trite and impossible, such as sailing on the sun or riding on the rain. And, moreover, he only seems to be asking her to stay one more day, so that he may quickly return to contemplate her leaving again. It is Scott Walker, after all, so one suspects he'd rather be on his own.

Simone de Beauvoir and the woman who doesn't exist

Of all the French existentialist philosophers who achieved something like popular recognition in the Anglophone world, by far the most socially significant has been Simone de Beauvoir. Beauvoir's feminist classic from 1949, *The Second Sex* (2009) remains an essential reference for contemporary debates concerning sex and gender – particularly in relation to the category of 'woman'. Not only does it remain in print, but also in the form of a new translation from 2009 that has restored important passages cut from the original translation by H.M. Parshley. Notwithstanding these restorations, there is in this text one famous sentence that is endlessly cited as the foundation of the 'constructivist' understanding of gender that will be developed most powerfully and radically in the 1990s by Judith Butler and her followers.

In the famous sentence, on page 330 of the new translation, Beauvoir states that 'one is not born, but rather becomes, woman' (2009: 330). This is sometimes taken to be a positive statement, but it is not. On the contrary, Beauvoir quotes Kierkegaard approvingly, who exclaims, 'What a curse to be a woman! And yet, the very worse curse when one is a woman is, in fact, not to understand that it is one' (Kierkegaard in de Beauvoir, 2009: 327). Beauvoir sets out in her book to correct that lack of understanding, and itemizes the many ways in which to become a woman is a disaster. For too long, she asserts, the character of this misfortune has been disguised, and the starting point of her book is to acknowledge this misfortune and the situation by which it is conditioned. The misfortune pre-eminently concerns society. The identity of woman is not primarily defined by biology, or by a certain psychic structure, or by economic relations; rather, it is by 'civilization' as a whole. Since that civilization has been overwhelmingly shaped by men, the category of woman has no identity that can be posited for-itself; on the contrary, it is a negative foil to set off the positivity of men. 'Humanity is male, and man defines woman, not in herself, but in relation to himself; she is not considered an autonomous being. ... He is the Subject; he is the Absolute. She is the Other' (26).

This situation was already changing in 1949. In America, Beauvoir observes, women 'are inclined to think that woman as such no longer exists' (24). This view is sometimes taken as evidence of the effects of the increasing numbers of women introduced into the American workplace in the early years of the twentieth century, particularly as steno-typists. As Friedrich Kittler argues, 'if the great word emancipation has any historical meaning, it is only in the area of word processing, which continues to employ more women world-wide than any other field' (Kittler, 1997: 64). The result of the increasing presence in the workplace of female bodies, Katherine Biers further suggests, contributed to the de-idealization of 'woman', even as it consigned women to a mechanized and sexualized world of office work (Biers, 2015). Formally, the Americans rejected the ideal of woman (what de Beauvoir characterizes as 'the eternal feminine') in favour of the plural designation 'women' whose identity became effectively subsumed under the unisexual form of universal worker. Except, there remained the problem of the sexualization of the workplace associated with residual elements of femininity – and masculinity – that provide the basis for an apparently ineradicable excess that rendered the workplace a new site for sexual transgressions from extra marital affairs to sexual harassment. This problem remains and is currently the focus of much concern in the wake of the publicity given to the Harvey Weinstein case, and the assumption of its general applicability. The solution is to de-sexualize the workplace which, in practice, usually means eradicating signifiers of femininity in favour of the template of a unisexual dress code predicated upon a traditional blue or white-collar male template.

In this section, I want to suggest that Beauvoir's challenge to the situation of women and the category of 'woman' informs some of Scott Walker's most important songs from the 1960s – as it does the work of other artists and film-makers of course. I also want to suggest that Walker's songs also anticipate Butler's critique and development of Beauvoir's logic. In her own classic *Gender Trouble* (1990), Butler challenges the idea that not just the category of 'woman', but also 'women' generally should be the subject of feminism. The meaning of 'women' is always already inscribed within the 'binary frame' exemplified by the heterosexual couple, whose coupling, Butler claims, society renders 'compulsory'. Her goal in this very influential book is to break 'the frame in which power operates' and consign the couple to history (Butler, 1990: viii). In 'Clara', Walker looks at the death of this couple with a degree of pathos, even as he exposes the fascist grotesquery through which the power of the state became manifested in the 1930s.

In common, perhaps, with the new wave of French and Italian films of the 1950s and 1960s, Walker's compositions in the eponymous solo albums chart the disintegration of the traditional heterosexual couple in the wake of youthful, restless desire for sexual freedom in movies such as Fellini's *Nights of Calabria* (1957), Antonioni's *La Notte* (1961), Godard's *A bout de souffle* (1960), Truffaut's *Jules et Jim* (1962) and so on. Such stories frequently end unhappily, if dramatically, with characters being gunned down by the police or forced into prostitution, the latter, for Beauvoir, a familiar trope for the fantasy of running away from the oppression of family life (de Beauvoir, 2009: 425).

In his use of swelling yet melancholic classical arrangements that reference twentieth-century composers like Sibelius and Delius, Walker gives a tragic cinematic treatment to scenes of transitory existence and social detachment, romantic betrayal, abandonment, social destitution, loss and loneliness. The combination was – and to an extent remains – virtually unique in popular music. The characteristic figure in these songs is the young woman, the street corner girl, or neglected wife, or women like Rosemary stuck in the maternal home, spending endless evenings staring at the images of time's passing in the sagging faces of her mother's friends over tea, pining for her lost love, the effect of a transitory affair. Rosemary wants to restart her life but can only watch her dreams disappear with the wind. Again, these women constitute, one might suggest, the demographic or target audience for the sad and lonely love songs of the young unspeakably handsome crooner. While in Walker's more narcissistic songs, he and his various personae function as agent, object and even spectator of the scene of – usually – amorous rejection, here Walker's songs inhabit the position of the solitary woman. Not only are there elements of the torch song tradition in the lyrical content of these tracks, Walker's performance also occasionally registers the homosexual or transsexual aspects of this tradition. This quality has attracted the admiration and imitation of artists such as Marc Almond among others.

In an interesting piece on Walker's crooning, Ian Penman notes that, in spite of his characteristic baritone, Walker's voice is oddly un-masculine; the voice 'doesn't seem sexually human' (in Young, 2006: 94). This is quite in keeping with the young Walker's angelic looks which at the time were more feminine than ruggedly masculine. Furthermore, Penman contends that, from this period at least, his 'best songs are sung from a woman's point of view' (Penman in Young, 2006: 94, 108). The de-sexualization that accompanies the apparent feminization is significant here since it is consistent with the twentieth-century history of crooners generally and the production of in-humanly proximate, machined voices, addressed particularly to 'housewives and working girls' (see Hoffman and Pitts, 2002: 14–16). Pioneer 'plugger-cum-performers', for example, were Whispering Jack Smith and Art Gillham, the 'Whispering Pianist'; the former, 'was famous for his sound: a deep-dish voice of clear and quiet authority with an amiable unctuousness that could sell a song or soap without leaving a trace of oil … [it was] hard to tell where the song ended and the sales pitch began' (14-15). These singer-salesmen through the means of the microphone and the wireless, successfully began the reorientation of the social bond away from the framework of the couple towards the media object: the song, the record, the radio show or TV special, and the media-scape generally. The media became the locus of a new kind of life, satisfactions directed towards commodities. Significantly, Rosemary's lost love is, precisely, a travelling salesman: Mr Jim, notable for his 'stained glass whispers'.

Big Louise (1969)

(Engel)

Described as an 'historic moment' (Woods, 2013: 144), 'Big Louise' is one of the most acclaimed tracks in Walker's oeuvre, complete with an extraordinary orchestral arrangement. It opens with a shimmering gong, building in waves of strings and a brass lament framing the opening lines that describe Walker's solitary protagonist humming quietly to her self while looking up to the heavens from the stairway outside her apartment. Another song of the one-all-alone, the arrangement lifts the figure of Louise in a manner that evokes an almost tragic heroism. This is captured in Walker's beautiful if quotidian image of her location, memorably used by Julian Cope in his 1980s compilation *Fire Escape in the Sky: The Godlike Genius of Scott Walker* (1981). As listeners we follow both the music and the lyric to look up to Louise taking the air outside her attic rooms; we look up and follow her direction towards the sky, a familiar metaphor in Walker for the space of freedom. The sky is a space of nothingness, of course, but, as Simone de Beauvoir maintains, nothingness is precisely freedom's prerequisite. Writing in *The Second Sex* about how a girl can take flight from the cursed situation defined by the negative definition of her sex, and the sort of fate represented by 'Rosemary', Beauvoir writes:

> This situation that the girl flees by a thousand inauthentic paths is also one that she sometimes assumes authentically. Her shortcomings make her irritating: but her unique virtues sometimes make her astonishing. Both have the same origin. From her rejection of the world, from her unsettled waiting, and from her nothingness, she can create a springboard for herself and emerge then in her solitude and in her freedom. (429)

Just as a springboard sends us upwards but only to fall down, so a fire escape descends, albeit outside the building. Appropriately, 'Big Louise' is, we discover from Keith Altham's sleeve notes, a 'he', or rather is outside-sex, exterior to the heterosexuality of the traditional binary couple. It is not clear whether Altham understands Louise to be a transsexual or simply a man in drag, but there is nothing in Engel's lyric to suggest anything other than a full-time commitment to a female identity. Exemplifying Beauvoir's famous statement in a remarkable way, Louise was not born a woman, but she has chosen to become one. The choice is significant – even perverse – given the cursed nature of the chosen sex, according to de Beauvoir after Kierkegaard. But therein lies the radical quality of the choice. Only through first adopting the negative position of woman, it seems, can one break free of the binary frame of the traditional heterosexual couple, assuming that is Louise's desire. It is, in any case, the effect of such a choice, as Judith Butler argues. No matter how authentically Louise has assumed the path of the woman, the choice discloses the 'constructed' or 'performative' character of gender, and its 'fundamentally phantasmatic status' (Butler, 1990: 146). In the song, Louise very successfully 'performs' the frustrated, unhappy state of the lonely, aging and abandoned woman. She could be Rosemary's sister. Her man has gone away, and she is equally concerned about the passing of time, developing bags under her eyes similar to those of Rosemary's mother's friends with whom she has to spend her evenings. Indeed, this emphasis on Rosemary's situation is the main emotional force of the song to the point that the aspect of transgender seems almost incidental.

Nevertheless, it necessarily poses Butler's question to Beauvoir, thirty years before. Interestingly, in so far as the adjective of the title 'Big Louise' indicates the awkwardness or 'unnaturalness' of the transition, the song also illustrates Butler's point about how drag 'allegorizes heterosexual melancholy'. For Butler, 'reciting a sexual position', as we are all required to do, 'always involves becoming haunted by what's excluded' (1990: 137). This is evoked in the song, of course, when Louise is described as a haunted house with broken windows. The image nicely evokes the discordance not only between gender and the body, but also the undead character of desire that refuses to accept the ravages of time and decorum. The image further condenses these ravages on to the hostility of those who don't just whisper all day behind net curtains, but sometimes throw stones.

The melancholy of 'Big Louise' marks Walker's song out from slightly later treatments of the theme, such as the Kinks' comic 'Lola' (1970), and Lou Reed's sensationalist 'Walk on the Wild Side' (1972). Socially, however, these songs were not as significant as the 'gender-bending' trajectory of popular culture generally in the early 1970s, spear-headed by David Bowie and supported by a dubious collection of 'spear-carrying', bricklayers-in-make-up glam rock bands like Slade and the Sweet. The 'pretty things' of the early 70s emphasized the de-naturalization of sex, re-configuring the signs of gender that flickered across an aesthetic-economic media-scape predicated upon the empty space of the unisexual universal worker. For Simone de Beauvoir, it was under the sign of the worker and universal brotherhood *promised* by the Soviet Union that the curse of femininity could be overcome:

A world where men and women would be equal is easy to imagine because it is exactly the one the Soviet revolution *promised*: women raised and educated exactly like men would work under the same conditions and for the same salaries. ... Within the given world, to carry off this supreme victory, men and women must, among other things and beyond their natural differentiations, unequivocally affirm their brotherhood. (2009: 856, 862–3)

In the capitalist West, we are still a long way from equal conditions and salaries. Women still exist in the workplace, even if the official ideology is that we are essentially neither men nor women but individuals who constitute our own capital, producers of our own mode of consumption and satisfaction. We are our own 'brands', choosing who we are through the services we offer and what we buy. In the West, the desire for sexual freedom being articulated in the 1960s was met, or rather re-defined by the market which facilitated the demands of the newly salaried 'baby boom' generation, empowered by their demographic dominance. The neoliberal response to the generation of 1968 was ultimately to emphasize the creative work of consumption through which the televisual spectacle of transgression turned into fashions for the repetition of the new. Nevertheless, the pop memory of that spectacle has been profound, judging by the reaction to the death of David Bowie in 2016. Most of the tributes and reflection pieces on Bowie's untimely death in January of that year concerned his social as much as musical legacy. Particular focus was given to the way his various personae, in the early 1970s especially, reflected and even enabled the transformation of traditional attitudes to gender, long before Judith Butler. 'The problem with writing about Bowie', commented Philip Hoare for *The New Statesman*, 'is that we are all writing about ourselves ... [he] pulled me into an entirely new world of art and otherness'; Bowie was 'a queer messiah in a man-dress' (Hoare, 2016). These changes were not just restricted to the liberalization of laws concerning homosexuality. 'Straight boys wore nail varnish, satin jackets, platform boots. The fluidity of gender that we are only now addressing seriously was exposed by Bowie. As Tilda Swinton said at the opening of the V&A exhibition "David Bowie Is" (2013), "we are all his freaks" (in Hoare, 2016). As this reference to the Victoria and Albert Museum suggests, while gender difference and identity were certainly a matter of political positioning, they quickly became more about style than sexuality, a form of cultural self-expression. Inevitably, in an era that ushered in neoliberalism, such self-expression was also a form of self-promotion and self-marketing, transgression riding the 'cutting edge' of the new, to use the discourse of advertising. Bowie was in the avant-garde here too, John Gray commenting on the 'streetwise shrewdness' that saw him, in 1997, issuing $55million worth of 'Bowie Bonds' just before the bottom fell out of the music business (Gray, 2016). But when gender becomes fluid in this way, purely a question of image and style, a shifting play of identities that are unconstrained either by biology or social convention and in which the order of reproduction is itself being transformed by twenty-first century advances in bioengineering, it makes less and less sense to speak of gender at all.

This raises a problem about how to define the couple. As we have seen, the Walker Brothers', and Scott's solo work specialized in songs of love's loss, and the tribulations of romance between essentially narcissistic partners. Mirrors of misfortune, portraits of solitude and images of abandonment are everywhere. But in a few mysterious songs, there are hints at a different conception of the couple; the mirrors of narcissism become darkened and begin to crack. For example, 'Boy Child' from *Scott 4* responds to love's fantasy by returning to 'If You Go Away', citing its last lines as its own, but with a twist. Unlike 'you', the addressee of the song, the boy child is no longer a shadow, but rather the embodiment of freedom in the enigmatic figure of the one who lies at the heart of the singular couple.

THE SINGULAR COUPLE

'Boy Child' (1969)

(Engel)

With 'Boy Child' Scott Walker comes out of the shadow of the Walker Brothers and of Jacques Brel – there are no Brel songs on *Scott 4* – even as he seems to embrace obscurity, anticipating the stripped down, allusive lyrical style of the more mature work. If there is still an element of interpretation, here of his own interpretations of Brel and others, this is only to invite further interpretations – as the quotation from Camus on the back of the album sleeve suggests – but with the acknowledgement that they cannot but fail. We are advised by Camus that it is not meaning as such, or some kind of statement, that we should attempt to discover in following the (retro) trajectory of the artist's work. Instead, it is in one or two significant images.

Who or what is 'Boy Child'? Two specific references, one Christian one Classical, are given in the song. The opening lines suggest St Christopher, the boy child riding on his back being therefore an image of Christ. In a later reference the boy child is 'Love', who is called upon to catch fragments of affection swirling through the winds of night. Ironically, Cupid is traditionally depicted as blind, but he was also originally nameless – like Engel's boy child. According to Hesiod, Love is born along with the Earth from Chaos and thus is an orphan like Orpheus. In the courtly love tradition, Cupid is represented as blind because the arrows he fires are random, the love-struck smitten unawares. Engel's lyric concerning the cost of giving the boy child back his sight thus may concern a wish to restore some order or rationality to love such that he may be seen to provide narrative consistency to the fragments. If he does, it is only because he is called to do so, blindly, which is precisely the situation of any listening to the song. Is this the burden that we bear on our back: to try and make sense of things, to ask the basic questions of childhood concerning the enigma of our existence, the question of our parents' love and desire, or God's demands or the gods' enjoyment. Is it only through asking these existential yet unanswerable questions that, paradoxically, we will not lose our way since they are fundamental points of orientation?

Love is the main tenet of Christianity, although in a very different register to the Classical tradition. We are commanded by Christ to 'love thy neighbour as thyself' (Mk 21.31). The problem with this formulation is that it requires, as Kierkegaard notes, love to be considered purely as an idea that is evacuated of all sensuous content. Further, since it is universalized beyond any specific neighbour, it becomes attenuated to the point of meaninglessness. It is not possible to meaningfully love everyone, which is why it has to be predicated upon the relation to oneself. As such, for Freud this sole Christian commandment has the structure of the superego. Christ issues a command but does not ask if it is possible for people to actually obey it. The superego is that punishing sense of moral authority and bad conscience that rides on your back nagging you about your shortcomings, the fundamental guilt of your existence. 'It is impossible', Freud complains, Christ's commandment 'admonishes us that the harder it is to obey the precept, the more meritorious it is to do so ... [such] ethics has nothing to offer here except the narcissistic satisfaction of being able to think oneself better than others' (Freud, 1989: 109). But perhaps the biggest problem with the narcissistic basis of loving one's neighbour as oneself is that it is not always easy to love oneself. As the superego never ceases to remind us, deep down we are not good, we are fundamentally bad, and this primordial guilt leads us to suspect that we do indeed nurse unspeakable fantasies that we would prefer not to approach. One may as well utter the command: 'Torture thy neighbour as thy torture thyself!' The next lines of 'Boy Child' immediately imply this shadowy aspect to narcissism with their reference to cracked and darkened mirrors.

Sonically, the song also cracks with beautiful but brittle sounds, the sharp, high-pitched notes of hammered dulcimer strings. Their staccato melody, tapping out the cracks in the mirror perhaps, clacks above the lush, swirling string arrangement that suggests a depth of field extending through different cosmic or spiritual dimensions, lyrically evoked later, that are still somehow lacking in affect. Walker's voice follows the melody clacked out by the dulcimer until voice and instrument come together in the final lines of the opening section that refer to the closing lines of 'If You Go Away'. They signal that this is a revision of the idea of love contained therein. Up to this point, there has been little indication about the identity of the 'you' that is the object of the lyrical address whose wayward direction, life and trajectory is described, and who is continually enjoined to do this and seek that. The address to this 'you' initially implies the listener of the song, but the information that 'he' is not the shadowy 'us', indicates that the 'you' is the alter ego of the singer, or at least the singer of 'If You Go Away'.

Only the lover's point of view is presented, in different ways, in 'Ne me quitte pas' and 'If You Go Away'. In the latter, the beloved's absence is the condition of either demand or desire. With 'Boy Child', however, there are two 'voices', that of the singer and the hammered dulcimer, just as there are two main protagonists in the song. The singer and the 'you' he hammers with the question and direction of existence. The singer offers advice on the choice of love object, a choice that broaches the importance of love's economy. We're advised to seek someone who'll give rather than take, who'll offer the promise of happiness and sexual fulfilment. Yet the night where she rests, in post-coital contemplation perhaps, empties even as her song begins. That this is another song of loss is confirmed by the evocation, in a complex image, of eyes that are swollen with tears that are figured as the town's flickering windows for lonely travellers that are hidden from sight. This loneliness is exacerbated by the echoing laughter of inaccessible enjoyment deep within the city. We've lost our way again, hidden in the shadows of the city's shadows.

The song ends with the enigmatic lines repeated from earlier concerning the freedom of the one. This would seem to reaffirm the sovereignty of the existential wanderer, except for the previous line that suggests an amorous couple cleaving together. In the line there is a double emphasis on the act of holding as one as if anticipating imminent separation. It is not simply the narcissistic couple, however, that has provided the context for the singer's monologue about the 'you', the image of his alter ego in the darkened mirror. There is also the boy child, of course, the 'he' that is referred to throughout who occupies neither of these positions. He is rather the 'one', or the metaphor for the 'one', that one must remain in order to stay free. This freedom does not require the renunciation of love, quite the contrary. The love of the one, personified by the boy child, remains as the sole point of orientation for a heart to keep holding to the promise of renewal that is the basis of freedom in which the promise of a new life is within reach. On the one hand, the blind and nameless boy child is the metaphor for the one-missing, but on the other he is the nameless name for the distinctive quality that defines the singular couple. The one of or from which someone might be or become, the one on the basis of which one might be loved, the one from which the ways, qualities and dimensions of love might begin to be counted but never quantified.

Walker's song suggests that the enigmatic boy child is the symbol for this indefinable quality that is hidden, and about which neither lover nor beloved knows anything. This would be consistent with lyrics to other of Walker's songs, notably his lyrical contribution to Tony Hatch and Jackie Trent's 'Joanna' (1968) which he released as a single in 1968, and his own composition 'Copenhagen' from *Scott 3*. Here, the album's cover highlights, under a miniature of Walker's Danish future wife Mette Teglbjaerg, the lyrics 'you're the end, gone and made me a child again'. The ungraspable quality of 'our love' – like two snowdrops, according to 'Copenhagen', melting in an extended hand – is nevertheless retained in the memory of the form in which one's heart first opened, encrypted and endlessly circulating like an old song reverberating in a fairground carousel. (The Walker Brothers were playing in the Carousel Club in Copenhagen when Scott first met Mette in June 1966.)

If the relative lyrical obscurity of 'Boy Child' sets a precedent for the style of the later works, *Scott 4* also set a precedent for that work's relative unpopularity. Unlike *Scott 3* (1969) which, released earlier in the same year, managed to reach number 3 in the British music charts, Scott's fourth eponymous album failed to chart. As the Mercury Records CD release from 1980 notes, *Scott 4* 'was credited as being by Noel Scott Engel [and] was deleted soon after release'. Walker released one more album, *Til the Band Comes In* (1970) which again 'sold next to no copies' (Woods, 2013: 105) before lapsing into song-writing silence. Throughout most of the 1970s, Walker went on to record albums of cover versions of easy listening standards and movie themes such as *The Moviegoer* (1972), *Any Day Now* (1973), *Stretch* (1973) and *We Had it All* (1974). Lewis Williams insists that these albums are much maligned yet have fine examples of Walker's vocal abilities and interpretative skills. Notwithstanding this view, they do not really contribute to the theme that concerns this chapter and this book that is focussed, for the most part, on Walker's own compositions.

Scott Walker began writing again in the late 1970s in the context of the Walker Brothers' reunion album *No Regrets* (1975), another covers album whose title track became a chart hit. However, it was ultimately not enough to secure the Walker Brothers' comeback, not least because their record company, GTO, found itself going out of business. The Walkers were given a further opportunity to produce a final album that, given GTO's disinterest, had no commercial or company prerequisites: they could write what they liked. This gave Scott Walker the chance not only to rekindle his song-writing ambitions, but also introduce into the form of the pop song elements beyond his previous rock and orchestral repertoire, such as electronic and experimental music. While these are areas normally outside the usual expectations of popular music, they were increasing in popularity after 'Krautrock' and post-punk. Indeed, in the mainstream, Brian Eno and David Bowie were advancing a similar sound from Berlin, out of the Hansa Studios.

For the resulting album, *Nite Flights* (1978), each member of the group contributed their own compositions led by Scott, under their own names of Engel, Maus and Leeds. The stand-out track of Engel's four songs, 'The Electrician', is a stunning and chilling example of the love song of the one-all-alone that returns to realism – if not in the mode characteristic of *Chanson Réaliste* – in combination with a deeper descent into the Orphic underworld and music's *Acheronta movebo*. Here, however, what is at stake is not Orpheus's power to make music reach beyond the realm of society to tame nature or speak to the gods. On the contrary, at issue is Kierkegaard's conception of music as the antisocial vehicle of the sensual erotic, 'the triumph of sensual nature over spirit' (Dolar, 2002: 57) that is evoked beautifully, but with the most brutal and sinister literalism.

'The Electrician' (1978)

(S. Engel)

Remarkably, 'The Electrician' is a love song. It seems to be a dialogue between a couple, one of whom has the power to make the other yield, like Don Giovanni who prefers to take his lovers one by one. In the Walker Brothers' song, this power is evoked in an extraordinary way by both music and the subtle use of industrial sounds to convey the utility and effectiveness of instruments of torture that are deployed for erotic purposes by the 'Electrician' of the title, a state interrogator. In a 1984 radio interview with Alan Bangs for the German programme *Night Flight*, Walker said that the context for the song 'is how the Americans sent in these people who train torturers in South America. I imagine these lovers in a conversation. If you listen to the words of 'The Electrician' it really explains itself' (Bangs, 1984).

The song's 'intro' is characteristically cinematic, almost Hitchcockian: a high frequency drone of sustained strings immediately establishes a sense of tension and high anxiety that is intensified by the sound of wire being scraped on metal, sharp enough to put your teeth on edge. Beneath this piercing drone there is the sinister intonation, low in the mix, of a Gregorian chant that is introduced by an ominous bass guitar note, left to resonate for four bars before sounding again, heralding the arrival, as the sound of scraping metal gets louder and more insistent, of Walker's double-tracked baritone at its most intimate, seductive, rich and enveloping:

Baby it's slow
When lights go low …

The seduction implied by these slowly whispered lines is rendered sadistically ironic by the soundtrack, the grinding drones, the bass note that punctuates each short line, and the screech of metal that heightens the anxiety during the long pause in the line that eventually concludes that there's no help, no. For Lewis Williams, the song is horrific because lyrically it connects breaking the spirit of his victim with 'defiling' the holy spirit itself (2006: 147). This is truly demonic work, then, though who is speaking here, and enjoying the spectacle of hips twisting in the darkness, is uncertain.

'The Electrician' is often credited as the track that signals the profound change in Walker's oeuvre. It is seen as the hinge or fulcrum upon which the generic lightness of *chanson* and pop balladry lurches into something disturbing and unique. There had always been darkness in Walker's songs, but from now on the sun would truly no longer shine in his work. Darkness would become its primary theme. The notion of such a turning point is not unknown in accounts of the work of writers, artists and philosophers. A frequent reference for Walker, along with Camus, Sartre and Franz Kafka, is Samuel Beckett whose biography is marked by a similar caesura in that it touches on the formative role of darkness. Deirdre Bair quotes a letter from Beckett to Ludovic Janvier around the time of the Second World War in which he announces that he will no longer attempt to fight off the darkness that had been consuming his life. 'He stated that the "dark that he had struggled to keep under" was ultimately to become the source of his creative inspiration' (Bair, 1980: 298). For Beckett this darkness concerned the pessimism and depression that he was now determined to accept and 'make work for me'. For Walker, in contrast, it concerns deep fascination for the intimate solitude of a degradation that plunges someone beyond all hope of redemption, sunk into a place where there is indeed no help.

However, there is also a consistency of theme from the solo works of the 1960s in so far as romance and erotic seduction involves a crisis of narcissism, as identity fractures in the darkness of a cracked mirror. In the 'lover's conversation' articulated in 'The Electrician', it is never easy to tell who is speaking. The indeterminacy of the duologue is immediately apparent in the song when, after the repetition of the first verse begins to provoke a listener into wondering who, precisely, is beyond help, a drum roll straight out of an 1980s American power ballad changes the register from the first to the third person as the act and object of torture is briefly described before collapsing again into a series of agonized or ecstatic demands. The positions of torturer and tortured alternate and are ultimately rendered indistinct in the parallel rhymes of the repeated lines that conjoin the demand to kill and thrill the one or the other.

If this is a sadomasochistic psychodrama, it nevertheless bears a number of specific lyrical and musical references that locate the narrative historically and politically. The use of Spanish guitar and references to Mambos or 'Manbos' – voodoo priestesses – establish cultural coordinates that are musically underscored and nuanced as the brief clatter of a castanet announces the middle eight and its incorporation of Latin American melodies. This section provides a brief respite to the droning sonic menace and hint at a world, a time and place outside the claustrophobia of the torture chamber. We know broadly where we are: in an Office of Public Safety (OPS) or CIA interrogation room somewhere in Central or South America in the late 1960s or early 1970s. William Blum's authoritative history *Killing Hope: US Military and CIA Interventions since WWII* (2003) details the post-war activities of the CIA and the OPS in Vietnam, Cambodia, Haiti, Guatemala, Brazil, Uruguay and Chile. In his research for the song, Walker has evidently consulted accounts of these activities that were reported increasingly often, particularly after the CIA-supported coup against President Allende of Chile. The line that describes jerking a handle is highly specific, referring as it does to a technology of electric torture first deployed by the French and then the United States in Vietnam. This hand-cranked device is called a magneto or dynamo. Darius Rejali describes the device in an essay on 'Electricity: The Global History of a Torture Technology' (1994). He quotes a US Marine who learned the technique from the French: 'Take a field telephone, the TP 3–12, and put the connecting wire to it, then take the other end of the wire and attach it to a person's testicles and crank it – this causes a high-voltage shock, there is no amperage behind it, just voltage, but it is extremely painful' (1994). Rejali suggests that by 'the late 1960s, virtually all police forces that used electric torture in interrogation were either former French colonies or had received extensive American training. The devices and methods remained the same until the 1980s' (1994). This would fit Haiti where the CIA were involved in covert operations to support the notorious regime of Jean 'Papa Doc' Duvalier, but the general Latin American milieu suggested by the Spanish elements of Walker's song and the strong suggestion of sexual excess also evokes a different technique and scene of electric torture.

The torture device of choice for most Latin American regimes in the 1960s and 1970s was the *parilla*, the name taken from the word for a Spanish barbeque or grill, because of the way the victim would be spread-eagled and strapped naked to a metal bed or steel frame. Wires and electrodes would be used to torment the most sensitive parts of the body, particularly the breasts, nipples and genitals. Sheila Cassidy, a doctor who was tortured by this method in Chile during the Pinochet regime, offers an account of her experience in her memoir *Audacity To Believe* (1977); and in an interview for *The Times* on 1 January 1976 that Walker is likely to have seen, she describes 'electric shock torture in a prison "sex house"'.

But if there is a real model for the 'Electrician' himself, it is likely to be Dan Mitrione, who was the head of the OPS mission in Montevideo, having previously worked under the auspices of the CIA in Brazil in the 1960s. In the mid to late 1960s the CIA-backed Uruguayan government were concerned with an oppositional group known as the Tupamaros and sought increasingly violent means to suppress them. Mitrione's leading role and enthusiasm for pursuing all means to these ends eventually so alarmed the Uruguayan Senate that it undertook an investigation that concluded that torture in Uruguay had become a 'normal, frequent and habitual occurrence' (Blum, 2003: 201). Mitrione's story is told in Blum's *Killing Hope* and includes some revealing quotes and anecdotes. For example, Mitrione considered electric torture an art form in which he was master at delivering 'the precise pain, in the precise place, in the precise amount, for the desired effect' (201). He liked to boast about his prowess and demonstrate to witnesses his skill and his power over life and death, explaining to Manuel Hevia that 'a premature death means a failure by the technician ... it's important to know in advance if we can permit ourselves the luxury of the subject's death' (Blum, 2003: 203). In his home in Montevideo Mitrione built a soundproofed cellar to enable him to hone his technique and demonstrate his knowledge of the most vulnerable and sensitive parts of the human anatomy and nervous system. In the process he afforded himself the licence of killing five beggars in the perfection of his art (202).

Unfortunately for Mitrione, Hevia proved to be a Cuban double-agent who presumably advised his opponents of his whereabouts because in July 1970 he was kidnapped by the Tupamaros. Shortly thereafter he was found shot dead in the back of a car. Back in the United States in his home town of Richmond, Indiana, Mitrione was honoured in a funeral attended by Secretary of State William Rogers and President Nixon's son-in-law David Eisenhower. Blum notes that the occasion was also marked by the presence of American light entertainment and popular song when 'Frank Sinatra and Jerry Lewis came to town to stage a benefit show for the Mitrione family' (203).

After the brief glimpse of light and hope offered by the Spanish guitar part, 'The Electrician' returns to the confined horror of the torturer's low-lit cellar, returns to the stretched and bloody strings, the drones, the bass, the rumbling chant, and the metal that evokes the frame of the *parilla*. Walker's voice repeats the opening verse, reiterates the subject's utter helplessness and abandonment. The song's fade-out lasts more than 30 seconds as the high-pitched note is sustained above a bass sound effect that pulses and gasps, signalling perhaps the perpetual exhaustion and anxiety produced by the presence of torture.

'The Electrician' provides, for the twentieth century, a starker metaphor for the demonic nature of music in conjunction with the sensual erotic than Kierkegaard's description of Mozart's *Don Giovanni*. In his own commentary on this text, Mladan Dolar underscores how for Kierkegaard music is the quintessence of demonic sensuality, such that it results in the destruction of the spirit and the annihilation of the subject. Indeed, Don Giovanni is the embodiment of music precisely as 'the pure principle of non-identity' (Dolar, 2002: 53) and therefore the affirmation of existence without being. He retains the voice, the music and its 'subtle connection' to sensuality at the point where its demonic nature places it at the 'antipodes of ethics and religion'. Kierkegaard's position, like Walker's we should add, is paradoxical. This is not the celebration of the darkness, but a condemnation of it in the form of American torture and its sadistic sensual excess. But, at the same time, to paraphrase Kierkegaard and his Christian concern with ethics and religion, 'whoever cannot give himself to the fascination of [evil] should remain silent with respect to ethics and religion' (Dolar, 2002: 57–8).

While *Nite Flights* failed commercially, it alerted Brian Eno and David Bowie to the re-vitalization of Walker's writing career. Eno noticed that Walker's tracks resembled, in ambience and tenor, some of the work he and Bowie had been doing on the 'Berlin' albums, *Low* (1977) and *Lodger* (1978). This acknowledgement from within the more avant-garde parts of the industry, along with recognition from a younger generation newly informed by Julian Cope's compilation album, provided the context for a solo record deal with Virgin records. When *Climate of Hunter* (1984) eventually appeared, it was evident that the new sound and bleak lyrical concerns announced by *Nite Flights* had been further pursued.

At the same time, there are echoes of the past. 'Sleepwalkers Woman', for example, the final track on side two, invokes the myth of Orpheus but is sung from the perspective of Eurydice. The song returns to the

Orphic myth and re-works the sounds and imagery of the solo works of the 1960s, particularly 'Boy Child'. Here I want to conclude this section with a brief assessment of 'Sleepwalkers Woman' and its companion song on *Climate*, 'Blanket Roll Blues'.

'Sleepwalkers Woman' (1984)

(Scott Walker)

Climate of Hunter (1984) is significant for a number of reasons, not least because it marks the beginning of Walker's long collaboration with producer Peter Walsh and arranger Brian Gascoigne. Lyrically, *Climate* continues themes introduced in Engel's songs for *Nite Flights* (1978), but also begins the process where lyrics are painstakingly pared down to the point where they become fragmented and elliptical. As 'Boy Child' announced in 1969, the role of love is to catch 'fragments' which from 'Sleepwalkers Woman' are more likely to be characterized in a darker vein as 'splinters' and 'fracture'. There remains an Orphic register on *Climate* that gives lyrical consistency in the general suggestion of various kinds of underworlds comprised of hunters and the hunted. The line 'this is how you disappear' opens the first track of side one, and the songs descend into a many-shaded Hades of obscurity and the unknown, whether this be the pre-historic world of 'Cro-Magnon herders' in the opening track 'Rawhide', the night of prowlers and junkies in 'Dealer', the sleepless yet shadowy night world of crime and murder of 'Track 3', the force-fed hostages, electrocuted and jettisoned in the rain in 'Track 5', the half-lit, low-ceilinged prisons that house more scenes of torture in 'Track 6', leading perhaps to possible escape in 'Track 7' in the gathering gloom of deserted, unburied corpses. Above all this is the restless nocturnal domain of insomnia, bad dreams and somnambulism. Indeed, across the record there is the lyrical flow and consistency of a two-act concept album, as each track on side one of the vinyl disc parallels its partner on side two.

The songs that end sides one and two both reference Orpheus via two versions of the myth: a ballet and a movie. The final song on the album is Walker's cover version of 'Blanket Roll Blues', the Tennessee Williams tune sung by Marlon Brando at the heart of *The Fugitive Kind* (1960) directed by Sidney Lumet, the film adaptation of Williams's play *Orpheus Descending* (1958). Both the play and movie are set in the Deep South, another 'underworld' of violent racism and social injustice, hatred, sexual frustration and vengeance. Brando plays Valentine Xavier, the Orphic figure as a wandering rural drifter-minstrel, strumming his guitar in a snakeskin jacket. But as with Walker's 'Boy Child', his name suggests the Christian promise that love is a saviour. Indeed, Xavier is called 'boy' frequently in the movie, especially by the redneck racist police, in a way that codes him in the movie as black – just as the saxophone motif colours Brando's character Stanley Kowalski in Elia Kazan's version of Williams's *A Streetcar Named Desire* (1951). In *The Fugitive Kind*, Orpheus's Eurydice is 'Lady' Torrance played by Italian actress Anna Magnani whose situation as a middle-aged woman trapped in a loveless marriage with a sadistic elderly and invalid husband recalls some of Walker's women in the Philips albums of the 1960s – and, indeed, the Walker Brothers' song 'Orpheus'. Brando's character attracts the attention not just of Lady, but a number of other 'Bacchae' like the alcoholic, libidinally charged Carol Cutrere and unhappily married Vee Talbot, who could be decaying, Southern Belle versions of Mrs Brown and Mrs Blear.

Lyrically, it is not immediately obvious that 'Sleepwalkers Woman' concerns Orpheus. Retrospectively, the album's track-matching hints at this, as does some of the imagery that recalls elements of Williams's script. Xavier is an 'exile' from New Orleans who does emerge from the 'jails of another' – not just the courthouse jail of the opening scene but the cage supervised by Vee Talbot in the following scene in which he seeks refuge from the rain. The most recent occupant of this cage having escaped, the police now noisily pursue him with hound dogs. His death by gunshots is heard by Talbot and Xavier, heralding the even more gruesome fate of Brando's character at the hands of the police at end of the movie. But before he dies, in a movie in which everyone seems to be sleepwalking in drunkenness, insomnia and tireless malice, Xavier does bring two female characters briefly back to life. First, Carole Cutrere (Joanne Woodward) who takes him to the 'bone orchard' in the cemetery scene, and while Brando comments about the how he could splinter the fragile bones of her wrists, echoes the cry of the dead to 'live, live, live'. Ultimately, he brings vivacity and new life to 'Lady' (Magnani), albeit briefly and tragically – she discloses that she has become pregnant by Xavier before she dies.

It is not so much lyrically as musically, however, that the Orphic dimension is most audibly announced in 'Sleepwalker's Woman'. Unique to *Climate*, 'Sleepwalkers Woman' returns to the stunning orchestrations of the Philips albums, but this time with a different tempo and reference. In interviews, Walker acknowledged his interest in German *Lieder*, and indeed 'Sleepwalkers' has a similar *adagietto* pace and vocal melody to Mahler's *Kindertotenlieder* ('Songs on the Death of Children'). However, the opening of Walker's song directly cites the opening and apotheosis of Stravinsky's ballet *Orpheus* in which the plucked melody of a solo harp descends step by step down a Phrygian scale over sustained bowed notes. 'Sleepwalkers Woman' repeats this arrangement, although the melody of the harp does not simply descend but seems to hover, poised at the threshold of Hades, an ambiguity registered lyrically in the repeated phrase: 'For the first time unwoken I am returned.' This opening also recalls 'Boy Child', even as the vocal melody's resemblance to *Kindertotenlieder* suggests that this song may concern the aftermath and mourning for the death of the boy child, love's enigmatic *agalma*. Following the release of Julian Cope's compilation album *Fire Escape in the Sky* (1981), the songs from the Philips albums were certainly in Walker's mind while he was composing parts of *Climate of Hunter* (1984). 'I was sent Cope's compilation', he told the *NME*, 'and I put it on and listened to this young guy singing [and] thought, hey that's not bad. But one play was enough' (Woods, 2013: 229). Those days might be gone, but at the same time they were just asleep in the grooves of the record, returning here unwoken, yet haunting the present. The 'boy' Xavier dies at the end of *The Fugitive Kind*, along with his unborn child.

'Sleepwalkers Woman' has the same complex, seemingly triangular mode of address as 'Boy Child', involving more than one speaker, more than one 'I', who addresses a 'he', a 'you' and a 'she', suggesting different voices, even if in Hell there are no voices, only belated and redundant confessions. The most complex image in the song concerns the idea of the 'he' whose refuge has been exposed only to be hidden away again, his secret enfolded by 'her' in his damaged hand. This action of the hand recalls the scene immediately following Brando's singing of 'Blanket Roll Blues' in *The Fugitive Kind*. It is a scene where he fondly anticipates crossing the dark river without a single soul for company that paradoxically begins his seduction of 'Lady'. Back in her Mississippi store, up close, Brando puts his hand in Anna Magnani's hand and asks her 'what do you feel?' 'Your hand', she replies. 'That's right', he goes on

and you can feel the size of my knuckles and the heat of my palm ... that's how well we know each other. All we know is just the skin surface of each other. … Nobody ever gets to know anybody. We are all, all of us sentenced to solitary confinement inside our own lovely skins for as long as we live on this earth. (Lumet, 1960)

Though no optimist, Lady does not agree with this melancholic assessment and indeed an affair begins, hand in hand, palm in palm. It is an image that not only recalls 'Boy Child', but also looks ahead to 'A Lover Loves' from *The Drift* (2006). Their love begins in flames of passion, but ends in an inferno when her jealous, dying husband sets fire to her building, shoots her and her unborn child while the Sheriff and his deputies send Brando into the flames with their water cannon.

What is left, and what replaces them? asks the Sleepwalkers Woman. The apparently missing apostrophe of Walker's title recalls James Joyce's *Finnegans Wake* wherein death and its ritual celebration is supposed to prefigure an awakening – perhaps even the political awakening of the Irish ('Finnegans'). Here, similarly, while the possessive apostrophe is heard in speech, it is absent in writing, suggesting the idea of multiple sleepwalkers, from the one to the many. The conjunction of sleeping and wakefulness, then, is implied in the literary allusion. Sleepwalking is an effect of the 'zombie brain', the ability of a non-conscious person to function effectively in the dream of habitual reality. Joyce's *Finnegans Wake* famously delivers its readers from the dream of meaning through its excess of multi-lingual puns and equivocations that destroy the realist novel through pushing sense into nonsense. While not remotely on the scale of Joyce, Walker's songs will from now on also seek to wake their listeners from the dream of meaning through a lyrical half-saying that requires the participation of *readers* as well as listeners. Moreover, such a participation will necessitate the isolation of a symptomatic object, anecdote or sound by which the song and its listener can become a singular couple.

In the movie, all that remains of Brando is his snakeskin jacket, taken as a souvenir by the lonely 'lewd delinquent', played by Joanne Woodward, as a symbol of her intended escape beyond the county line. A premonition of the counterculture to come, she is the only character in the movie to have explicitly raised the political context of this nightmarish depiction of Mississippi – her soubriquet being earned through the abuse, arrest and conviction she earned as a result of her solitary 'civil rights' march in protest at a lynching. Convicted of 'lewd delinquency', she adopts the name, description and lifestyle as a mode of rebellion.

In the next section we will turn, accordingly, to cinema and politics, though not to the politics of Tennesse Williams and Joanne Woodward who in *The Fugitive Kind* seek to re-form a social link by way of an object of fascination that holds the place of the one-missing. First, we will look at how Walker uses cinematic techniques in order to 'play with time' and disorient common modes of temporality and perception in order to communicate differently to the listener at an existential or disordered level rather than at the socially sanctioned level of ordered discourse. Then we look at how Walker's songs – and his soundtrack to Brady Corbet's film *The Childhood of a Leader* – engage with the political theme of disorder and of the One who would become an exception, thereby giving a universal definition to the being of the many.

ONE

Cinema and politics: The death of Pasolini

In numerous interviews Scott Walker expressed his distaste for overtly political songs. 'I don't like out-and-out protest songs. … I don't like some fellow strumming and preaching in my face' (Kijak, 2006). And yet, there is almost always a political dimension to his work, particularly the work from 1978 on, where the violence (often sexual) that is the surplus effect of political power becomes one of his major themes. But, even in the solo albums of the 1960s, Walker is as politically engaged as Bob Dylan or Neil Young. 'We Came Through' (*Scott 3*, 1969) references the deadly struggles of Che Guevara and Martin Luther King; the Dylanesque '30th Century Man' actually has Walker strumming like a protest singer about being caught between 'Dwarves and Giants' even as he references Charles de Gaulle. 'Two Ragged Soldiers' (*Scott 3*) and 'Hero of the War' (*Scott 4*, 1969) offer narrative vignettes illustrating the bitterness and futility of armed conflict. Supremely, 'The Old Man's Back Again' (*Scott 4*) is 'dedicated to the Neo-Stalinist regime' and is written in part in protest at the Soviet Union's regression, following the relative openness of the Khrushchev era, to Stalinist domination of its satellites in the Eastern bloc, evident in its invasion of Czechoslovakia by Warsaw Pact tanks in 1968. Notwithstanding the element of protest in this song, Walker seems to have taken at the time a very Sartrean view about the crushing of the 'Prague Spring'. He suggests that it might ultimately have been required in order to thwart counter-revolutionary forces, commenting that 'what was done to [the Czechs] was cruel but probably necessary to prevent the break-up of somethin' for which so many people have worked so hard and suffered so long' (Woods, 2013: 154).

Walker in the 1960s had, it seems, much more clearly defined political views than many of his 'freewheelin'' musical peers in the counter-cultural movement of the 1960s. In his apparent support for communism and the Soviet state, indeed, he may well have shared Pier Paolo Pasolini's disdain for the student unrest in 1968. Notoriously, Pasolini published a long poem about the Italian students' revolt, denouncing them as 'spoiled kids' more concerned with resistance as a form of style. He considered it a 'rock 'n' roll' revolt against paternalistic constraints on their pleasures rather than a genuine desire for socialist revolution. 'When yesterday in the Valle Giulla you came to blows / with the cops, / I sympathized with the cops! / Because the cops are sons of the poor!' (Schwartz, 2017: 486–7). While Pasolini would later acknowledge his 'provocation', and regret a little the way it was exploited by the bourgeois press, he did not apologize and maintained his political analysis. In 1973, he would write that 1968 represented only 'a form of self-criticism of the bourgeoisie (with the bourgeoisie using the young to destroy the myths that bothered it)' in order to clear the way for the emergence of the 'new consumers' (Schwartz, 2017: 489). Catastrophically, the self-criticism and self-correction of the bourgeoisie that facilitated the spread of 'neocapitalism' represented its triumph and the eradication of the workers and the peasants, and thus any kind of alternative perspective. 'In effect, through neocapitalism, the bourgeoisie is becoming the human condition. Whoever is born of this entropy cannot, by any means, metaphysically exit from it. It is all over' (491).

By 1975 Pasolini was dead and Walker's career in the doldrums, deep in the mire of his 'bad faith' years. The year marked the brief Walker Brothers reunion, the successful comeback album and single *No Regrets* (1975), followed by *Lines* (1976) which flopped. The contractually obligated third album, containing their own compositions, resulted in *Nite Flights* (1978) Engel's return to politically committed songwriting. The subject matter of the highlight track, 'The Electrician', in its chilling evocation of US government sanctioned use of torture, might seem consistent with a communist sympathizer. But on early copies of the vinyl edition of *Nite Flights*, Engel's song 'Fat Mama Kick' was dedicated to Bernard-Henry Levy, who had recently published *La barbarie à visage humain* (*Barbarism with a human face*) in 1977. Levy's accusation of barbarism referred specifically to that of communist states. Levy was one of a small group of *nouveaux philosophes* making their name at the time denouncing French philosophers of the previous generation, particularly

Sartre. They accused these philosophers of accepting with insouciance news about mass executions, forced starvations, and the labour camps of the gulag archipelago because ultimately they would be redeemed by the triumph of the working classes, as guaranteed by the iron laws of History. While left unnamed, criticism of the US government in 'The Electrician' can easily be inferred through the Latin American context and specific reference to the technique of torture. The political reference of 'Fat Mama Kick', however, is much more oblique. In this state in which searchlights and 'armed angels' police the city and patrol the borders, the 'sunfighters' – forces of enlightenment, perhaps – wage war 'on the night'. Even though its streets are patrolled by 'angels' – God's traditional police and bureaucracy – the state is described as Godless. Indeed, the gods are dead; the angels' 'master corpses peeled raw, betrayed'. Revolution and its continuation involve perpetual disruption, constant betrayal.

Hannah Arendt states in her magisterial account of *The Origins of Totalitarianism* (2017), that the violence of the Soviet state was strictly impersonal, the necessary effect of the sacrifices demanded by the law of history (Arendt, 2017: 611). State terror is not the result of the arbitrary power of one man but must be incorporated into its bureaucratic processes – indeed bureaucracy is itself a form of terror, introduced initially by Western states as a form of imperial domination (Arendt, 2017: 241). State terror is the expression of the 'suprahuman' force of history. The state 'far from wielding its power in the interest of one man, … is quite prepared to sacrifice everybody's vital interests' including, of course, the lives of the previous masters of the revolution (611), Stalin's former Bolshevik comrades.

For Arendt, it is the form of what Jean-François Lyotard, in *The Postmodern Condition* (first published in 1979), would later call the 'grand narrative', that defined the totalitarian structure of both Marxism and Nazism insofar as the latter sought to ground its idea of racial superiority in Darwinian evolution. In both, 'the movement of history and the movement of nature are one and the same' (Arendt, 2017: 608), in the sense that both were seen to drive the cause of progress. Further, both directly inter-implicate one another since, insofar as nature describes a linear movement, it becomes swept into history just as Marx's notion of the productive forces of labour-power is natural. 'The "natural" law of the survival of the fittest is just as much a historical law and could be used as such by racism as Marx's law of the survival of the most progressive class' (2017: 608–9).

It would be easy to suggest that the political register of Scott Walker's oeuvre after *Nite Flites* becomes increasingly ambiguous and oblique. But I want to argue that it actually becomes more profound in the sense that it is precisely history that comes under scrutiny and is placed into a radical disjunction with an existentialist conception of time; no longer the subject of history in the shape of the proletariat or the bourgeois individual, nor even its semblance in the multicultural, postmodern microhistories of Western academia, there is instead the time of the one-all-alone. This is evident in his songs' frequently oneiric and cinematic evocation of time, but also in his everyday mode of composition in which one day can drift into another while he occupies himself with 'hanging out. Doing a little travelling. Nothing constructive' (Young, 2006: 195). The discipline of linear clock time is of course a product of modernity and the productivity demands of industrial capitalism (see Thompson, 1967), including the music industry of the late twentieth century. After the 1960s and 1970s, Scott Walker was having none of it. Over ten years separates *Climate of Hunter* (1984) from *Tilt* (1995). Another ten years would pass before *The Drift* (2006). While the writer suffers the entropy experienced as the passing of human time, the muse inhabits a temporality all of its own. It could even be said to be outside time and space since its impossible domain is silence. 'I can't tell you where it comes from. It comes from silence, most of it. I sit around and I'm waiting. I'm waiting and waiting' (In Young, 2006: 195).

'Farmer in the City' (1995)

(N. S. Engel)

In the 1980s and 1990s in philosophy and culture, following Lyotard and others, it becomes the fashion to no longer think of history in a grand linear fashion, but rather think in terms of what Lyotard called *petit récits*. These little stories or narratives addressed the problem of legitimation in philosophy where truth can only be assessed as the effect of specific 'language games'. Like different cultures, different discourses and disciplines have different principles of veridiction ('difference' being the keyword of the time), irreconcilable conceptions of the world. For theoretical physics at the quantum level, for example, time does not exist: there is no cause and effect; there is an entropic process in which events occur (or do not) without reference to the laws and temporality of being. In a Walker-esque description, quantum physicist Carlo Rovelli compares such events to a kiss. 'A kiss is an "event" [but] it makes no sense to ask where the kiss will be tomorrow' (Rovelli, 2017: 87). For the discipline of history, where time is subsumed into narrative, some notion of cause and effect is essential. Culturally, writers, artists and film-makers produced fragmentary works marked by pastiche, parody and anachronic forms that sought to open up the problem of history: the impossibility of establishing definitive historical facts out of the chaos of an event. In the promotional CD to *Tilt* (1995), Walker highlights this aspect in the writing of the album's opening track, 'Farmer in the City' which is subtitled '(Remembering Pasolini)'. 'My interest was in writing a song about Pasolini ... who was murdered in a brutal way, but no one seems to know the bottom line on that, there are conflicting stories about it: where it happened, was it on this road, was it by a deserted football ground, what was it? So, I'm quite a fan of his films, but the whole thing fascinated me as an internal exercise, I felt, "Well, I'll play around with this idea"' (Promotional CD issued by record company Fontana, 1995). In the sound and in the lyrics, Engel's 'play' involves the interlacing of two different but closely related perspectives of a displaced 'farmer' and a 'citizen', perhaps also Pasolini and his long-term companion Ninetto Davoli. They are conjoined around the central idea of displacement, but also the (a-historical) repetition of an 'inexhaustible singularity' that provides the resources for the journey of a life (Pasolini, 1971 in Satrielli, 2014).

The brutal murder of Pier Paolo Pasolini in 1975 can be seen retrospectively as a symbolic endpoint to one form, characteristic of the 1960s, of the politically committed artist, intellectual hero and champion of the proletariat. The official version of events is that Pasolini was murdered by Pino Pelosi, a teenage boy he picked up in the back streets of Rome. Pasolini drove him to the beach at Ostia, a short distance from Rome, one of his favourite places for sexual encounters with boys like Pelosi. According to his court testimony, Pelosi rejected certain advances, there was a fight and, while Pasolini was on the ground, he ran him over whilst fleeing in the director's car. But Pasolini's body was run over more than once, and the extent of his injuries during the 'fight' strongly suggested that Pelosi could not have acted alone. They were consistent with Pasolini having been beaten by a group of men. Uncertainty remains about the perpetrator, or perpetrators, then, as does the reason for the crime, whether it was the result of sexual aggression, a mafia assassination condoned by the government, or aggravated homicide by an extortionist. Pasolini's friend Sergio Citti gave testimony where he spoke about several rolls of film from *Salò* being stolen, and that Pasolini was meeting the thieves.

In reports of the official version of events, Pasolini's erotic investment in the objects of his political and artistic concern were stressed – and indeed the element of compromise or exploitation this implied. Even in his sympathetic biography, Barth David Schwartz notes Pelosi's similarity to the street boys in Pasolini's novels – and to Ninetto Davoli. 'His poetry throughout the 1950s and his films up to 1968 were grounded in the love of the *borgatta*, the slum world no one else wanted to know about. The erotic link he had to the slums was a utopian vision of the *popolo* and an ideological commitment to the left' (Schwartz, 2017: 32). Compounding this view was the fact that Pasolini had recently completed *Salò*, his take on Sade's *120 Journées de Sodome* set in Mussolini's last redoubt on the shores of Lake Garda in 1944, the very short-lived 'Italian Social Republic', also known as the 'Republic of Salò'. Here, Sade is superimposed upon Italian fascism but with actors who are recognizably modern, the libertines tormenting and sexually exploiting mostly passive and compliant contemporary Italian youths. The purpose of *Salò*'s anachronistic conjunction of eighteenth-century France, 1940s Italy and the present seemed to be to convey the idea that 'neocapitalism' represented the continuation of fascism by other means in its depiction of 'the young as "victims" of a consumer culture that turned willing boys into monstrous hustlers' (Schwartz, 2017: 32). Was Pasolini's own monstrous death the result of a similar encounter?

In response to the question 'sex, is it political?', posed by a French interviewer interested in the meaning of the film, Pasolini concurred replying with the statement 'everything is political' (a scene reproduced in Abel Ferrara's *Pasolini* (2014)). But it seems that statement could also be reversed or mirrored in the idea that everything is also sexual; or at least everything can be sexualized. There is no word in the dictionary that cannot, given a certain nuance, be given a sexual meaning, as the actress said to the bishop. Everything can be sexualized because there is no 'natural' sexual relation. Sex has to take a detour through language, negotiation, commerce, politics, every element thus being potentially affected by innuendo. Similarly, everything is political because there is no definitive political arrangement or system that could produce a perfect order of civil society or total equalization of economic goods. Since every interaction is unequal to a greater or lesser extent, every relation can be regarded as exploitative in some way, however minor. Sex and the political circulate in a chiasmus that revolves around points of incommensurability.

This is something that Pasolini acknowledges frequently in his poetry, examples of which pre-empt and anticipate the conditions of his death. In 'Lines from the Testament' (1969) for example, Pasolini writes that his love of the boys from the *borgatta* provide the pretext for his joy before death precisely because they exacerbate the very gap or isolation necessary to desire, and the experience of life. Sex constituted only 'moments of loneliness; / the warmer, more alive the gentle body / that anoints you with semen and then leaves, / the colder and deadlier the desert around you; / this is what fills you with joy like a miraculous wind' [from 'Lines from the Testament' in Sartrelli, 2014: 387, 389].

It is another of Pasolini's poems '*Uno dei tanti epiloghi*' (1971), however, translated as 'One or Many Epilogues' by Norman Macafee, that also pre-empts the drive that became the culminating journey of Pasolini's life, and provides the point of reference to Engel's 'Farmer in the City'. At the mid-point of the song, as the farmer's perspective switches to that of the citizen, Walker hails Pasolini's lover Davoli, recalling him to the dream to which they so often referred. As Pasolini writes in his poem, the 'dream makes a part of reality'. The dream partakes of reality and frequently disturbs or reorganizes the linear sense of historical time. Dreams are unconscious constructions that, as Freud suggested, have no history in the sense that they are an effect and product of a repression caused by the event of symbolization. This event, that is repeated in a singular way with every subject of language, is constitutive of civilization itself and is therefore the pre-condition of the unconscious discourse that interprets the truth of its desire in the dreamwork. Walker's dream-songs are like dreams in that they deploy memories and representations of historical and contemporary events, but only to confound the fantasy of their chronological significance. The desire for chronological significance is annulled in real fictions that bear on the first apprehensions of the body in sound. From *Tilt*, Walker's songs largely begin with an enigmatic sound object: a faint bell at the start of 'Farmer', the obscure scratching at the beginning of 'The Cockfighter', the metallic buzzing and clicking of locusts that opens 'Bouncer See Bouncer...' Sound opens another dreamlike or hallucinatory dimension that consists of content that does not signify in the same way as the historical material. Jacques-Alain Miller writes of how these two dimensions operate unconsciously in dreams and hallucinations, such that while 'meaning and the laws of language are deployed in history, on the other side of the coin we have the real cut off from speech – as Lacan says more precisely, a real that talks all alone' (Miller, 2018: 99). Miller cites Lacan's Seminar XXIII on James Joyce, where he speaks of 'a noise in which one can hear anything and everything' (2018: 99). Evidently, the real talks all alone in a dimension that is sonic.

Increasingly, Walker's songs from *Tilt* onwards will introduce hallucinatory sounds and images that resonate with the enigma of singular existence in its discordance with historical being.

'Farmer in the City' conveys its dream-like quality in a way that is appropriately cinematic, but in a different manner to the social realist vignettes of the *Scott* albums. Certainly, it has an orchestral score, arranged by Brian Gascoigne rather than Wally Stott, but this time there is a deliberate a-historical deployment of a pastiche baroque opening which evokes the iconography of many of Pasolini's films such as *Mamma Rama* (1962), *The Gospel According to Saint Matthew* (1964) and *The Canterbury Tales* (1972). Over the baroque theme, following the sound of the bell, a livestock auctioneer (if such it is supposed to be) calls out the number '21', in a way that is heavy with emotional significance though apparently detached from any context. It is unclear what he has to do with Davoli-Pasolini's journey of a life; he seems to occupy a different, a-historical dimension. He calls this figure out no less than thirty-six times, in three batches of twelve, the number never getting higher or lower, the commodity thereby seemingly poised forever at the point of (non)sale. Along with what Walker himself describes as the 'cliché baroque theme', he added 'Italianate bits in the orchestral sections' because the idea with the song is 'to play with time'. The song plays with time musically, then, but also cinematically. Walker 'remembers' Pasolini through evoking the style of his movies, and indeed some of his cinematic techniques, or at least in so far as they are sketched in his famous lecture 'The Cinema of Poetry' (Pasolini, 1976). In this lecture, Pasolini favours an idea of cinematic poetry over the cinema of 'narrative prose' – where the cinema of poetry has not been 'recuperated' by bourgeois culture in the shape of the internal revolution of capitalism (that also replenished itself in the 1960s by obliging the counterculture to objectify its sexual desires in the commodity form).

In the cinema of poetry, Pasolini contends, 'image-signs' replace words in a visual language whose prime objective is not communication in the sense suggested by speech. Rather than words representing movement and actions in a world of cause and effect, the cinema of poetry constructs 'a world of memory and dream' in which 'all dreams are a series of im-signs which have all the characteristics of the cinematic sequence: close-ups, long shots etc' (Pasolini, 1976: 1–2). 'Farmer in the City' is a song not a piece of cinema, but the lyrics evoke camera 'shots' that, moreover, adopt what Pasolini describes as the mode of 'free indirect subjectivity'. This is the technique where 'the author penetrates entirely into the spirit of the character' (4). While the idea is derived from the technique of the modern novelist, cinema, for the most part, uses visual and sonic techniques. Similarly, Engel eschews the means of literary prose or poetic narrative to achieve a similar effect through the poetic adoption of two aspects of a particular stylistic operation. In his essay, Pasolini describes the technique of free indirect subjectivity in relation to the cinema of Antonioni and Bertolucci. First, 'the close follow-up of two view-points, scarcely different from one another, upon the same object' (5). In the two – farmer / citizen and Pasolini / Davoli – sections of the verse, the long shot of the row of darkened farmhouses and the close-up of a horse's harness are repeated, but the second time there is a small difference, the latter is not this time 'wrinkling' but 'withering'. It is a subtle change, but it is part of a montage of images and statements that repeat with a significant difference. Second, Pasolini argues that it is important to have characters enter and leave the frame 'so that the world appears as ordered by the myth of a pure pictorial beauty, which the characters invade [but] while submitting to the rule of this beauty instead of profaning it' (5).

The two, if it is two, characters (three if we include the auctioneer), certainly enter and leave the lyrical frame, their speech and perception conveyed through the voice of Walker that is attuned to the simple, structural beauty of the song. Two sets of injunctions ('don't go …') relating to various choices are posed in either section. They are characteristically elusive, and indeed their form is taken from another song, 'Man from Reno' (1993) written a year or so before the release of *Tilt*. Co-written with Goran Bregovic from the former Republic of Yugoslavia (now Bosnia), the song features in the opening and closing credits of Philomene Esposito's film *Toxic Affair* (1993). Lyrically it seems to be about the 'Zodiac' serial killer (or others like him) who operated in Northern California in the early 1970s. These serial killers are friendless, but deadly figures of the fatal encounter. In the Walker-Bregovic song we are enjoined not to pursue the 'Man from Reno', as he or others also pass through various cities across the world. The song further attributes these men, poetically, with the strange and disturbing qualities of brain grass and eye gas.

Grafted into 'Farmer in the City', these lyrical formulations take on a different atmosphere even as they underscore the stylized, cinematic sense of horror. Indeed, the replacement of the place names in the first set of sanctions seems to refer to cinematic choices: the action movie represented by 'That Man from Rio' (1964), a James Bond spoof directed by Philippe de Brocha and starring Jean-Paul Belmondo; the reference to 'Vigo' perhaps an allusion to Jean Vigo, seminal French film-maker from the 1930s who pioneered poetic realism. 'Ostia' is obvious, although the person who actually described himself as 'the man from Ostia' was Benito Mussolini (it was the place where he first met Claretta Petacci after she pursued his Alfa Romeo along the same road that Pasolini drove with Pelosi in his own silver Alfa). The second series of injunctions refer to the choice of various shirts, and perhaps is a reference to Pasolini's dubious fashion sense, his habit of dressing like the objects of his sexual desire. 'He went around dressed like his boys: tight jeans and jean jacket cinched at the waist, polyester shirts far cheaper than he could afford, often with loud patterns' (Schwartz, 2017: 33). The final two injunctions grafted from 'The Man from Reno' now look to be poetic evocations of Pasolini's corpse, still in his tight jeans and polyester shirt but with a flattened nose and smeared eyes, his smashed head ground into Ostia's football pitch by the wheels of his own car, his brain now one with the grass.

Pasolini's idea of free indirect subjectivity concerns a style that can be brutal when it seeks to rediscover the power of cinema by 'rediscovering [its] technical means' 'in its original oneiric, barbaric, irregular, aggressive, visionary qualities' (1976: 6). This is a very apt description of the poetic technique that Engel employs in 'Farmer in the City' and throughout the production of *Tilt* (1995). But these sonic and lyrical qualities are always attuned to the voice and to a chiastic structure in which two main lyrical and musical strands intertwine each other, disclosing through repetition and difference the incommensurable gap around which they cannot close. Framed by the auctioneer (of sex's fatal commodification, perhaps), the lyrics of 'Farmer in the City's two monologues start first with the accusation of a mistake, that is in the next section followed by an assertion of certainty; the first ends with a question concerning

Ninetto Davoli's dream, and the section with Ninetto's desperate plea to accompany Paolo that he articulated in the dream, lines that direct us to Pasolini's poem. Davoli takes his place next to Pasolini in his car, the same place that will later be taken by Pelosi, on the journey of the end of a life. Pasolini's poem ends poignantly in a powerful declaration of his desire: 'I am insatiable for life / because one singular thing in the world can never be exhausted.'

Arendt and the totalitarianism of the isolated being

Pasolini's characterization of 'neocapitalism' anticipates the Anglo-American regimes of Thatcher and Reagan that implemented the ideas of American neoliberalism, the theory of human capital that led ultimately, after the collapse of the Soviet Union, to capitalism itself taking a quasi-totalitarian form. *Salò* (1975) anticipates or suggests this in a startling way through bringing together disparate elements that share a governing theme in which the enjoyment of transgression becomes an oppressive imperative. Sade's libertines are commanded to their monstrous crimes by Nature's law. All simple attachments and pleasures must be sacrificed in the name of this imperative which quickly moves beyond the field of pleasure into Sadean horror that results ultimately in the very opposite of enjoyment: boredom and apathy, the latter state being for Georges Bataille the ultimate truth of Sade's philosophy (Bataille, 1986: 170). In Pasolini's film, the four fascist bosses initially delight in their deviance which they justify with reference to avant-garde art and philosophy, quoting lines from Baudelaire and Nietzsche. They claim that 'the Fascists are the true anarchists', an idea that would find approval among the 'alt-right' libertarians of the twenty-first century. In interviews around the shooting and release of *Salò*, Pasolini drew attention to the allegorical nature of his film, of how, in his view, the counterculture compelled people to pursue commodified sex and its representations. Pasolini wrote in the *Corriere* on 25 March 1975 during shooting: 'Sex today is the satisfaction of a social obligation, not a pleasure taken against social duty. ... Sex in *Salò* is a representation, or a metaphor of this situation: that we are living in these years: sex as an obligation and ugliness' (CDS, 29 April 1975).

But does it really make sense to think of what Pasolini calls neocapitalism as a mutated form of totalitarianism? The main features of totalitarianism for Hannah Arendt are its attack on the social, legal and political traditions in a particular country, the deconstruction of classes into a mass of isolated individuals and the introduction of a de facto one-party system to which there is no alternative; these are also complemented by the militarization of the police in actions against an enemy within and 'a foreign policy openly directed towards world domination' (Arendt, 2017: 604). From 1979, through successive governments pursuing essentially the same economic policies irrespective of their traditional class allegiances, the United Kingdom and the United States saw the marketization of public institutions and services, the attempt to dissolve society through the reorientation of the social bond away from communities towards commodities, and a drive for world domination through the globalization of finance capital, governance by the World Bank and the IMF and, in the 1990s, the project for the American Century that led to the global policing actions of the US military, most notably in Eastern Europe, the Gulf, Africa, Afghanistan and elsewhere. Throughout the nineteenth and twentieth centuries capitalism was considered by some to have subversive effects on imperialist and authoritarian regimes insofar as its reduction of cultural and social institutions to the money-form threatened to turn the world upside down. Money's famous class, race and sexual blindness was even presumed to enable forms of social mobility for those who could make it. However, the total operationalization of the market as a mechanism of national and world governance changes matters – particularly when allied to new technologies that have rapidly exacerbated inequality.

Pre-eminently, for Arendt, 'what prepares men for totalitarian domination in the non-totalitarian world is the fact of loneliness [which] has become an everyday experience of the ever-growing masses of our century' (627). Loneliness has not diminished in the civilization defined by neocapitalism in the twenty-first century. Indeed, it has been intensified as an effect of capitalism's conjunction with ubiquitous networked computing that orients sociality via technological gadgets linked to automated systems. The 'mass' is now networked in a highly individuated – or rather uni-dividuated – manner in which dataflows increasingly inform the algorithms of predictive computing based in machine learning such that the control of data subjects becomes effectively locked-in. For Arendt, totalitarian domination as a form of government isolates individuals by destroying 'the public realm of life' (624). In the twentieth century this was done through the offices of state ownership of mainstream media, control of public institutions and discourse, state censorship and the secret police. In the twenty-first century, it is achieved through cybernetic command and control systems, and the dismantling of the distinction between public and private in which both state and commercial institutions operate ubiquitous surveillance over ever more intimate areas of personal life, thought and morality. Online, all intimate life is rendered transparent even as it becomes commodified and sold to data companies. In the digital lallation of social media 'the most intimate personal choices and requests central to your personal dignity will be sung' (Walker, 'Lullaby', *Soused*, 2014). What Pasolini called the social obligation of enjoyment is now technologically mediated, satisfaction oriented towards the 'i-object' (phone, tablet, screen) that is coded with innumerable applications that structure maximum usage in the form of pleasures structured by an addictive pattern of usage. Addiction and solitary forms of pleasure are pre-scripted by design to the point where pleasure becomes compulsive and therefore ultimately a non-pleasure, a beyond-of-pleasure that is ultimately destructive.

In her discussion of isolation, loneliness and solitude, Arendt is keen to distinguish between the isolation and loneliness that prepares totalitarianism, and the solitude that is actually essential to the freedom of genuine sociality. First, there is the contention that the basis for communication is the solitude in which one can reflect upon oneself in relation to oneself. In solitude one is nevertheless *with oneself*, even talking with oneself as an imaginary interlocutor. In her book *Reclaiming Conversation* (2015), Sherry Turkle discusses how the intervention of i-gadgets intercedes not only in conversations between members of social institutions, workers, families and couples but also in the internal dialogue that individuals hold with themselves. Turkle's research with students and young people shows that alone, people are almost always instantly bored with themselves, instinctively reaching for their gadgets, thereby intensifying their loneliness in the virtual space of automated communications (see particularly the chapter 'Solitude' in Turkle, 2015: 59–79).

Second, Arendt draws a classical distinction between the different modes of production that shape a society. 'Fabrication (*poiesis*, the making of things)', which she distinguishes from action (*praxis*) on the one hand and sheer labour on the other, 'is always performed in a certain isolation from common concerns, no matter whether the result is a piece of craftmanship or of art' (624). Sociality in the age of intelligent machines is driven first and foremost by consumption in which both elements of fabrication are largely automated – or performed in the general context of cybernetics according to the same logic and protocols. Indeed, desire and consumption are also automated in the shape of predictive computing based on pre-processed data that variously informs the media-scape. Walker has always been interested in how the media-scape conditions the scope of creativity, artistic work and its reception, being particularly scathing about so-called audience-driven entertainments in 'Hand Me Ups' from *The Drift* (2006). For Arendt, this is the threat that is most devastating for any notion of human freedom: 'When the most elementary form of human creativity, which is the capacity to add something of one's own in the common world, is destroyed, isolation becomes altogether unbearable' (624). Of course, creativity is not destroyed by the new empire of technology; it is simply transformed into digital utterances – those of many million YouTube vloggers, for example – generated by an online world whose commonality is solely measured by metrics linked to advertising, the default of which is the condition where everyone is an artist with an audience of one.

Arendt's opposition between the totalitarianism of isolated being and the creativity of solitude is a distinction that can be mapped on to the notion of the one-all-alone that signifies the singularity brought into existence through sonic contingency, and the one-all-alone that signifies the isolation of the social being whose sociality is oriented towards objects. In the twenty-first century these objects are not just social but the intimate means through which one's being is integrated into the totalizing system of techno-capitalism. Whereas the individual of classic liberalism was established in the discourse of rights and property in which subject and object remained distinct, the 'one' of neoliberalism is defined by number rather than name, and its being totally subsumed into data systems. Just one information system among others, there is no existential dimension for the techno-scientific understanding of being that is predicated on number, be it formula or statistic. As science tells us, information cannot be destroyed (in spite, it seems, of Stephen Hawking's provocation about the evaporation of black holes). This is why it is important to distinguish being, as it is understood discursively – particularly by scientific discourse – from existence. Addressing precisely this existential dimension, Arendt writes 'we have only to remind ourselves that one day we shall have to leave this common world which will go on as before and for whose continuity we are superfluous in order to realise loneliness, the experience of being abandoned by everything and everybody' (625). Even as the existential dimension is overwritten and erased by the world of being-digital in which the uni-dividual is pixelated in statistical patterns with all the other ones with whom it cannot establish a relation, not even with itself, solitary existence precisely ex-sists outside that world as lonely superfluity, excess and waste. The former not only cannot absorb the latter, it produces it and thus reproduces a form of totalitarian domination that bases itself 'on the experience of not belonging to the world at all, which is the most radical and desperate experiences of man' (Arendt, 2017: 624).

Walker's songs from the 1980s onward are littered with characters who find themselves for one reason or another in this situation of non-belonging. Not just farmers displaced in the city but characters, often through their own excess, rendered heterogeneous to the dominant system in which force is grounded in economic reason and the totalization and acceleration of the 'hedonistic calculus'. The predicament of the excess-of-the-excess provides the backdrop to the political dimension of Walker's later work. From *Climate of Hunter* (1984), his themes become more elemental and primordial in their conjunction of rapacious violence and those surpluses of neocapitalism identified by Pasolini in *Salò*. In so doing, his songs take wider geopolitical, historical and even pre-historical reach as they remain contemporary and perpetually mediated by the globalized world of telecommunications.

Tilt (1995), for example, engages directly with its contemporary moment at the height of American hubris about the 'end of history' (see Fukuyama, 1989 and 1992) and George Bush Sr.'s declaration of a new world order, just six years after the fall of the Berlin Wall and the collapse of the Soviet Empire. 'Farmer in the City' is not the only song on *Tilt* to look at the proclaimed death of communism in the image of the death of its intellectual heroes. While side one of *Tilt* examines the libidinal basis of fascism in 'The Cockfighter' and 'Bouncer See Bouncer ...', side two considers the tragic and pathetic remains of communism in the 1990s in the midst of a ferociously aggressive capitalism that became and remains continuous with war and crime.

The torment of the listener

Tilt begins a trilogy of albums, along with *The Drift* (2006) and *Bish Bosch* (2012), in which Walker and Peter Walsh hone a highly distinctive style with the same core of musicians: Ian Thomas on drums, John Giblin on bass, Brian Gascoigne and Mark Warman on piano, David Rhodes and Hugh Burns on guitar and Alasdair Malloy on percussion. The songs on these albums develop to the point where they start to torment and re-define what a song is – a song that doesn't know how to *be*. Everything starts from the lyrics, as Walker will re-iterate in every promotional interview when he is asked about the construction of his songs. They thus remain in the tradition of *Chanson Française*, German *Lieder* – and indeed of folk ballad and protest song. The difference, evident in 'Farmer in the City', the first track of the first album of this trilogy, is that the songs are now much more cinematic. They are cinematic but in this they pursue a trajectory in which words, music and sound are stripped and honed down over the course of the albums such that they never manage to crystallize a scene, story or statement that isn't ambiguous. But at the same time, these fragmentary and hallucinatory scenes are conveyed by an agonized voice extended in emotion often at the limit of its range. Thus, in these songs at stake for the listener is always desire, anguish and torment – in so far as the listener is interested in trying to hear the song and its disturbance of discourse, rather than simply regard 'the meaning of the song [as] whatever the listener gets from it' (Williams, 2006: 89). Simply making whatever one likes of the song is likely to leave the listener undisturbed in the narcissism of his or her own solitary pleasure, sense and meaning selected precisely to the degree to which it confirms the listener's understanding of being in the world, reaffirming listener-as-discourse. As we have seen, it is the self-enclosure of this narcissism that Walker's songs attempt to breach.

Scott Walker's work broaches the notion of the one-all-alone both at the level of being and existence, but with recourse to song rather than discourse or number. For the songwriter, song is the medium of the social bond between the singer and the listener. Of course, song finds its being in language, discourse and number. There is no song without words, rhythm and generic conventions. But the 'there is' of this statement is something of the one that sings (or is sung). This is the one whose existence is precisely founded upon in-existence, from the contingency of what Heidegger calls 'thrown-ness' (*Gerworfenheit*) (Heidegger, 2010: 133–7). One is thrown or called or sung into existence such that one does not know how to be as being. Consequently, such existence seeks support from what Heidegger calls *Ek-sistenz* (ex-sistence), from something that is not. Walker's songs, I want to suggest, provide a locus of ex-sistence between obscure ones-all-alone who do not know how to be in the world – for better or worse. Or perhaps both for better and worse. Ultimately, Walker's songs do not communicate anything at all. This is of course quite normal; poetry and song are not modes of communication like transport or freight haulage. Poets and songwriters cannot communicate meaning – thought and feeling – to a listener as if they were goods and people conveyed by road and rail. Language would have to be a means of telepathy for this to happen. Brought into being by language, everyone has a different relation to the discourses to which we listen even as they enable us to speak in return. Broaching a similar idea with regard to his poetry's attempt to communicate 'inner experience' Georges Bataille writes:

> The reader who acts on me is discourse – it is he who speaks in me, who maintains in me the discourse intended for him. And no doubt, discourse is project, but even more than that it is *other* … without whose present insistence I could do nothing, would have no inner experience. Not that in moments of violence – of misfortune – I don't forget him, as he himself forgets me – but I tolerate in me the action of project in that it is a link with this obscure *other* sharing my anguish, my torment, desiring my torment as much as I desire his. (Bataille, 1988: 60–1)

To rephrase: the listener who acts on the one-all-alone is song – song itself is the listener (a listener is an effect of the discourse through which we understand what is a song) who sings a song intended for the one who listens. Song is an effect of discourse, but even more so of the one who is an *other* also exposed to the anguish, torment and desire about which it sings and for which song provides a link in the form of a barrier between the one and the other. It is the present insistence of the *other's* anguish and torment that becomes the predominant theme in Walker's work from the 1980s reaching a defining point in 1995 with the album *Tilt*. With this and the later albums, the challenge is to confront one's lack of understanding, precisely in that which is *obscure* because therein is the trace of the *other*, who is another one-all-alone. But the location of obscurity requires the prior action of providing a structure or context for interpretation in which the obscure can be isolated, a context which, in liner notes or in interviews, Walker will always offer.

Following the baroque theme of the opening track that was used to evoke Pasolini, the choice of music on *Tilt* does not just create the mood of the song, but also its *mise-en-scène*: a situation, domain or dilemma. On *Tilt* and other songs of the 1990s there is an increasing use of electronic, industrial and 'found' or synthesized sounds deployed in the tradition of *musique concrète*. Essential to the successful expansion and exploration of Walker's sound-palette is Malloy's invention and expertise on percussion, and Walsh's ability to source unusual instruments and devise or improvise unusual sounds through ingenious means such as the braying donkey on 'Jolson and Jones' or the 'big box' constructed by Tim Painter used on 'Cue', both from *The Drift* (2006). These concrete sounds often do not always function as Pierre Schaeffer would approve. They are not simply one element of a system that retains the sense of musical abstraction in which the sound primarily functions in relation to other sounds in the piece, rather than the material object (instrument or some sort of device) that produces it. Sounds in Walker's songs function as elements of both Walker's cinematic realism and his cinema of poetry. The donkey in 'Jolson and Jones', for example, is meant to sound like a donkey – and indeed one being punched. Through following the lead of the lyrics, percussive sounds in Walker's songs are frequently indexical or deictic, or even iconic in the sense of imitating the sound of images in the text. Alternatively, sounds counter-pose sense, almost threatening to obliterate the words. Other times, sounds function precisely in order to indicate not necessarily an external reality but the reality of the sound-image, as in the cinema. The sound produced by the big box on 'Cue' functions in this way: it is not a pure sound object in Schaeffer's sense, but neither does it indicate the box that is its source. It is rather something like the 'death's door' of a medieval plague victim. The box produces a sound-image that makes sense in the context of the soundscape produced by the fragmentary narrative and its sonic arrangement.

By the time of *Bish Bosch* (2012), the close tie between lyric and sound occurs almost on a line-by-line basis both enhancing and undermining sense (see commentary on 'Corps de Blah' below). Throughout these albums, unsettling even nauseating blocks of sound and noise, usually neither in nor out of tune, lurch from one register to another, crushing sense. For Schaeffer, musical works whose sound objects operate with a double meaning (because they remind us of the source they came from even as they operate abstractly through being organized in the musical ensemble) 'are possible and interesting ... but they do more than choose an expressionist or surrealist aesthetic; they explore a particular type of art halfway between music and poetry' (Schaeffer, 2017: 7–9). This is an excellent description of Walker's songs from the 1990s onward, though one would need to add another hyphen connecting music-poetry to cinema.

The songs on *Tilt* are relatively straightforward, except that in their cinematic poetry they play with time. This is not the cinema of classic Hollywood. Different figures, situations, historical time periods are juxtaposed and even superimposed upon one another. On *Tilt* this method is used to approach very contemporary political concerns, for example in 'Bolivia 95' and 'Patriot (a Single)'.

'Bolivia 95' (1995)

(N. S. Engel)

Contemporary with *Tilt's* release date, the subtitle suggests that the concerns of the song are current. It is about the Bolivia of the 1980s and 1990s that is being riven, like many Central American states at the time, by political corruption, drug cartels and gangster capitalism. 'Opiate me', pleads the voice at the beginning of the song, its speaker voiced by Walker apparently begging a 'doctor' to supply him with cocaine or some combination of cocaine and opium. But Walker's promotional interview with Robert Sandell, on BBC Radio 3, informs the listeners that the doctor is Che Guevara. 'It's a man who is talking to the corpse of Che Guevara who was murdered in Bolivia. I was trying to summon up that kind of atmosphere. What would it be like on a night like that? What would it be like in this strange hut somewhere?' (Sandell, 1995). This is the drug withdrawal-affected fever dream of an addict, condensing dealer and doctor with the ghost of communism in the form of Guevara's bullet-ridden cadaver, decomposing in a dilapidated rural school hut deep in the heat of the Bolivian rain forest. That would seem to be the suggestion supplied by the scene and atmosphere set by the music. The song has another AB structure that opens with a Chinese Ba-Wu flute suggesting a smoky opium den, over the nervous tension of a heavily dampened yet jittery cimbalom. Percussive chains rattle, suggesting captivity, along with other percussive sounds that educe clicking insects in the night of the rainforest. In the B section of the song, repeated three times, an ominous beaten tom drum marks time as a slow, mournful refrain from an acoustic baritone guitar adds a melancholic yet consoling patina of regret. In the second iteration, the drum is a bass pedal, and in the third a snare, impatient for the end. The hallucinatory feel of the song is highlighted by the spirit that is addressed as a potential saviour or companion and who is given the name 'babaloo'. According to the Urban Dictionary, the name has an interesting provenance and is both a mambo Latin American term of endearment, something like 'baby love' (famously used by Desi Arnaz in an ejaculation of heightened affection for Lucille Ball in an episode of *I Love Lucy*) and an Orixa god of the Lukumi tradition known as Babaloo Aiye. Like Guevara and the promise of communist revolution, Babaloo Aiye is supposed to be the god of healing and protection from illness, pestilence, war and famine. Engel has a fondness for words that bring together contradictory meanings. 'Babaloo' connects American TV and a fetish god in ironic equivalence with the imaginary corpse of Che Guevara. The chorus that links the A and B sections consists of a chant, over the drumbeat and the slow guitar refrain, about 'lemon bloody cola' that similarly conjoins the deadly sweet sourness of the soft drink with the hard drug. It resolves in the preparation to sponge down the corpse of Che as if for a sacred burial or even Christ-like resurrection. Indeed, the speaker, utterly alone in his stupefied vigil, describes himself as a saint. But the dead body does not stir or respond to his adorations; the only reflective surface is the floor tiles, his solitude speckling darkness around his feet.

'Patriot (a Single)' (1995)

(N. S. Engel)

The title refers to the MIM-104 surface-to-air missile (SAM) introduced by the US Army in Operation Desert Storm, the operational name of the Gulf War of 1991. The name 'Patriot' derives from the 'backronym' used for the radar component that rendered it 'smart' and able to track and intercept its targets: 'Phased Array Tracking Radar to Intercept on Target'. The word also suggests, perhaps ironically, an ardent American nationalist – an irony accentuated further by the fact that the arms dealer featured in the song will sell his arms to anyone. He's referred to in the third person, whereas the speaker is more concerned about shopping for nylons in New York. These are described in loving detail, some having butterflies, some flecks, others clinging vine or specks. Another AB song, the A section places on the same plane commodity fetishism, violence, global capitalism and the 'liberal way of war' (see Dillon and Reid, 2009). Musically, its two sections are highly distinct. The first section begins after a pause of about 15 seconds with a bank of strings playing a single continuous note that, as always, brings ambient tension as the date of the Gulf War is uttered *in media res*. But this time the drone is set off with a gentle three-note bass melody rising and falling, accompanying the pleasures of hosiery consumption. The strings then rise in crescendo as the singer, now like a CIA interrogator, informs us about the good news and the bad news brought by neocapitalist evangelism: the good news is that resistance is futile, the bad news is that its endless production of goods actually offers nothing genuinely new at all – except death, as the song underscores by leading into the section about the arms dealer. Rapid bleats of massed trumpets low in the mix convey an effect like that of ranks of Patriot missiles firing off and raking across the sky. The song then pauses again before it changes register entirely and musically the song tilts towards Weimar Germany with Bertolt Brecht and Kurt Weil. The singer, now a quite different speaker, mournfully and apparently drunkenly bemoans the fate of the *Luzerner Zeitung* to a Weilian piccolo, bass and snare drum. The *Luzerner* was a Swiss newspaper whose oppositional stance on the Gulf War proved unpopular, it seems. In Engel's mordant humour, it never sold out, so consequently never sold out. Rather like *Scott 4*.

The *Luzerner* section fades as the block of strings slowly lurches in again building the tension before the assault missiles start hitting their Muslim targets. Missiles, commodities and body parts explode in tiny fragments recalling the detail on the nylons: 'See how it blows … it swirls and collects … twisting butterflies, swirling flecks' (Walker, 2018: 32).

'Face on Breast' (1995)

(N. S. Engel)

Two songs on *Tilt* seem to summon the torment of psychotic isolation, paranoia and hostility, both of which play on the ambivalence of maternal love. 'Face on Breast', the song that opens the second side of *Tilt*, is not a song full of amorous or maternal tenderness, although the question of pledging one's love is repeatedly posed. The phrase may well come from the song 'Pledging my Love' (1954) by Johnny Ace that was a posthumous hit for the rhythm and blues star after he accidentally shot himself in a bar. For a love song, Ace's record has a slow, even mournful tempo and was used in a macabre way by John Carpenter in his horror film *Christine* (1983) about a psychotic car. As the vehicle attempts to kill the heroine, the song blasts out of the car radio at top volume.

'Face on Breast' opens side two of *Tilt* and begins with a rapid bass drum rhythm like a heart racing with fear or excitement. Walker's voice is sharp and agonized, the notes strained and twisted in emotional pain and anticipation. An electric guitar duels with the voice, mimicking its high discordance.

The image next to the lyrics printed on *Tilt's* CD booklet makes clear that the song is not about a face resting upon a breast, but a face being drawn or painted or etched on to a breast. But by whom, upon whom is not clear. As with a number of Engel's strange and ambivalent love songs such as 'Sleepwalkers Woman' and even 'Boy Child', the pronouns are difficult to follow. Referred to in the song is a 'you' – presumably 'Swan' whose breast is exposed as the catches are released and her wings are strained behind her back. Then there is someone to whom the demand 'paint his eyes' is addressed. Whether this someone is real or imaginary is not evident. Then there is an 'it' who, it is claimed, won't lick the eyes on the breast. The speaker begins to be spoken by movie dialogue, mouthing Lauren Bacall's famous lines to Humphrey Bogart in *To Have and To Hold* (1944): 'You know how to whistle ... put your lips together and blow', but in a recriminatory rather than seductive way – 'that's what it said' – as if they explained the torture, or as if the torture is designed to produce the whistle. Scott Walker and Peter Walsh blow the ensuing whistles on the track, making piercing, high-pitched screams that repeat along with a simulated human scream as the song proceeds to its discordant conclusion. The song ends with the speaker repeating in an increasingly mordant and deranged way that this could be him 'only pledging his love', a gruesome play perhaps on the courtly idea of literally fulfilling the binding promise of love. Historically, courtly love sonnets are a form of prosopopoeia – the personification of inanimate objects from the Greek root *prósōpo*(n) meaning face. The poet's persona is inscribed, through the praise of the body and attributes of the beloved – a body in the most familiar trope decompartmentalized, described piece by piece in the form of the courtly blazon (her eyes are jet, her lips rubies, her breasts alabaster). The mutilation in which the poet seeks the indefinable object of his love from among the isolated body parts is a metaphor, but metaphors are problematic in some forms of psychosis and are often taken literally; the metaphor collapses.

No doubt it is his own face that he is inscribing on the breast of the woman in the pledging of his love, but, as the confusing pronouns and the cacophony of screams, whistles and distorted, wailing electric guitar notes suggest, at this point it is difficult to tell. Just as 'The Electrician' blurred the distinction between torturer and victim, here too identity is evidently coming apart, spilling across relations of affect. As Walker will later sing repeatedly in the song 'Phrasing' from *Bish Bosch* (2012), 'Pain is not alone. P-a-i-n is n-o-t alone'. At a certain point in Walker's songs the pain of the one and the pain of the one-as-other are one and the same thing, in a relation of affect that also spills over to the listener. The song is painful to listen to.

'Tilt' (1995)

(N. S. Engel)

The title track seems to concern a psychotic cowboy's hostility towards his hometown and the maternal home, but in this song the violent subject matter is ameliorated by the narrative form of the 'country song' and the mostly third person delivery. Its hero is a singular man – 'when they made him they broke the mould' – who is described with awe and trepidation. It seems that when he returns home he stampedes his herd through the town looking for his old jacket in the park, the only hope being that 'they' will somehow be able to turn or divert the buffalo away from town. In the 'B' section of the song leading to the brief and enigmatic chorus, the third person switches to the first-person perspective of the cowboy, convinced that the people of his town enjoy a good stampede. Whether this is simple delusion or sarcastic menace is not sure, but he seems more concerned with his lost jacket and the maker's name on the label than with the 'mother' whose cold vigil in the moonlight suggests that she might be the one who made him. It is on the label of the jacket that the answer to the question of the title 'Tilt' seems to be hidden.

Before I examine how Walker brings the cinematic sensibility of his songs into actual cinema, I want to consider a particular song on *The Drift* that returns to some of the political themes raised in *Tilt* in the wake of the first 'event' of the twenty-first century to represent a setback for globalization, the point where the edifice of American power started to implode.

'Jesse (September song)' (2006)

(Scott Walker)

Describing it as his '9/11 song', 'Jesse' was written about a month after the hijacked planes crashed into the Twin Towers of the World Trade Center. The subtitle refers to the American jazz standard written in the 1930s by Kurt Weill and Maxwell Anderson for the musical *Knickerbocker Holiday*. It belongs to a genre of songs whose protagonist reflects back on his or her life, sometimes using the metaphor of a single year. In the CD booklet Walker provides a note giving the information that 'Jesse' is the name of the twin brother of Elvis Presley who died stillborn, buried in an unmarked grave. It is to Jesse that the King of Rock 'n' Roll would turn 'in times of loneliness and despair'.

In interviews, Walker would again deny that his '9/11 song' was an 'out-and-out protest song ... there were a lot of songs and albums that came out after 9/11, I don't like some fellow strumming and preaching in my face', he reiterated again (Young, 2006). However, the familiar denial does itself acknowledge that this is indeed some kind of protest song, even if of a very unconventional kind. Protest songs conventionally involve a singer addressing a particular political situation from a defined perspective, from a position of political or outraged virtue. Billy Bragg, for example, would presumably be happy to acknowledge that he speaks from a socialist perspective. Other singers might take up the burden of representing one group or another. Walker's political songs, in contrast, project the speaker deep inside a particular situation to the point where any sense of political representation collapses. Throughout the songs on *Tilt*, it is never entirely clear what role the protagonist has, or what the relation between political antagonists is, even when specific roles – arms dealer, chief of police, Nazi bureaucrat, communist revolutionary – are mentioned. They could be phantoms, projections, characters in a dream, fantasy figures. 'Jesse' is similar in that it begins with the topical matter of '9/11' but 'finally zeroes back in to the existential moment – the self – for the very end of it' (Young, 2013: 251). Qualifying what he means by the 'self' in the same interview with Rob Young, Walker said 'not the ego self, but the other self' (251). The importance of the *other* (even if it is imaginary) is essential to the idea of any political project – or any project at all: writing songs, singing them. In Walker's songs, especially his (non) protest songs, the 'I' is always also this 'other'.

There are then (at least) two selves: ego and other. Later, in the interview in 2013 with Stuart Maconie, Walker would elaborate further that, 'I'm not quite sure what the self is that I'm meant to be. Or if there is this construction going on all the time. What is it? You know I don't have this strong identity' (Maconie, 2013). The idea of the self as a continuous construction is consistent with the current idea from neuroscience, popularized by philosophers of science such as Thomas Metzinger in *Being No One* (2003, MIT) and *The Ego Tunnel* (2009, Basic, NY). Walker's interest in questions posed by contemporary science including scientific scepticism concerning the self is a recurrent theme. At the time of *The Drift* (2006), however, there are evidently at least two selves in play. Perhaps they are twins. The notion of the identical twin immediately disturbs the idea of the unity or self-identity of the individual. In the twin the mirror image is realized in flesh. But which one is the authentic one, which one is the copy? Am I two? Identical twins are attributed with many of the same aspects of being, as if they were two beings in one (dress the same, think the same, same DNA and so on) even though the death of the other discloses the reality of their separate existence.

Certainly, it is the idea of twins that initially brings together Jesse Garon Presley who died on 8 January 1935, the same day that his twin brother Elvis was born. The latter died forty-two years later on 16 August 1977. The Twin Towers of the World Trade Center were hit on 11 September 2001 and collapsed soon after, one after the other. In 'Jesse' these two very different sets of twins are condensed or superimposed upon each other. In the song this impossible, dream-like condensation is done in a very ingenious way, musically and sonically. The opening of 'Jailhouse Rock' is taken apart, recomposed and slowed down, such that the opening two chords of Presley's famous hit from the 1950s are 'darkened' through being strummed on a baritone guitar supported by a bass over a familiar background of ominous strings playing a sustained note that builds in intensity as the planes approach the towers. Walker describes the idea in the following way: 'It starts with the basses sounding like planes coming while substituting the "Jailhouse Rock" drum riff with whispered "pows" for the planes hitting the towers. Like "Clara", it's really a big dream sequence' (Weidel, 2006). From whose dream-like perspective are these two sets of twins brought together? The dream is mentioned towards the end of the song when the speaker, who in his dream is on his hands and knees trying to smooth out the dents and gouges of the prairie, suddenly exclaims: 'ALIVE! I'm the only one left alive'. The exclamation is repeated five times. This is Walker's 'existential' moment, and not simply an exclamation of survivor's guilt (Williams, 2006: 176).

'Jesse' and the last man

The notion of the last man is a well-known existentialist thought experiment dating back to Mary Shelley's novel *The Last Man* (1826). This work develops the romantic vision of the individual as 'essentially isolated and therefore tragic', a theme shared by Percy Shelley, Lord Byron and William Wordsworth (Luke in Shelley, 1965: xvii). Shelley's novel is set in the final years of the twenty-first century where world civilization has become devastated by plague. This is a topic that features also in 'Cue' and 'Psoriatic', defining tracks on *The Drift*. In the context of this worldwide devastation, Shelley's novel features among other post-apocalyptic groups, Americans marauding Europe and violent, fanatical religious sects. Eventually, only one man remains, shipwrecked on the shores of Greece in the year 2100. Perhaps 'Jesse' is a 'September song' precisely in this sense, in that it marks the end of a culture, a civilization, even the end of 'Man' rather than a particular person like Anderson and Weill's character Peter Stuyvesant in *Knickerbocker Holiday*, the proto-fascist dictator of New Amsterdam.

Nietzsche uses the idea of the last man in a very different way, but one that gained currency in the 1990s following Fukuyama's quasi-Hegelian treatise on *The End of History*. Fukuyama notes Nietzsche's caveat about the 'last men' in *Thus Spake Zarathustra*, the pacific, comfortable and complacent citizens of the bourgeois state like those currently representing 'the American way of life' that are objects of the *Übermensch's* contempt (Fukuyama, 1995: 310). This contempt, amplified by then fashionable right-wing philosophers Leo Strauss and his acolyte Allan Bloom, was applied to the nihilism of contemporary American society, particularly its cultural relativism and popular culture (Bloom being particularly averse to popular music). According to this view, American democracy and the formal recognition represented by the state equalizes everyone and reduces every cultural value to the lowest common denominator defined by economic reason. The role of politics is simply to guarantee physical security and material plenty by economic means. Apart from necessary military actions directed at securing essential resources and global markets, there is no longer any need to sacrifice one's life for an idea or a greater value – in sharp contrast, perhaps, to the hijackers of the American planes that crashed into the towers. Quoting Hegelian interpreter Alexandre Kojève, Fukuyama contends that while 'Man remains alive' at the End of History, 'he' remains only as a biological animal, sunk in bovine satisfactions seeking contentment in consumer goods. As noted before, much of the political content in *Tilt* concerns American hubris of a kind represented by the Twin Towers, while the death of Elvis Presley provides a graphic image of the fate of one of these Nietzschean 'last men' at the dead end of all possible libidinal pursuits: pumped full of pain-killing drugs and junk food, impotent, unable even to defecate, slumped insensate on his bathroom floor beneath his commode, drooling on his rug (perhaps for a while attempting to smooth out its dents and gouges) (see Alden, 2014 and Williamson, 2014: 18).

The idea of the last man also interested existentialist fellow travellers Maurice Blanchot and Georges Bataille, although more in Mary Shelley's sense than Nietzsche's, but with elements of both. Blanchot published a book with this title concerning a character who resembles Bataille. He also bears a certain resemblance to the myth of Walker's reclusive modesty and detachment. The novella begins: 'I always thought of him: that he was the last man .... Certainly he talked very little, but his silence often went unnoticed. I believed that he had a kind of discretion, sometimes that he was a little scornful, sometimes that he withdrew too much into himself or outside of us' (Blanchot, 2007: 4). In a section of Bataille's work *Inner Experience*, composed in 1942, Bataille reports Blanchot suggesting to him that he might 'pursue his inner experience as if he were the *last man?*' For Bataille, the prospect is dizzying. The last man would suffer an 'anguish [that] would be the most insane imaginable!' This is precisely because it would represent the impossibility of any kind of reflection or communication. It would constitute an inescapable prison (or jailhouse): 'I would remain before infinite annihilation thrown back into myself or yet still: empty and indifferent' (Bataille, 1988: 61). The last man would be witness to the extinction of humanity and the archive of human civilization – except that the function of witness would thus lose all meaning. There would be no more reader, no more discourse, therefore no possibility of reflection, not even the self-reflection and internal dialogue mentioned by Arendt. There would be only the most unbearable isolation, 'enclosed in this self as in the depth of a tomb' (61), buried alive ... like Jesse Garon Presley in an unmarked grave.

It is the absence of any 'reflective quality' that in his interviews Walker insists he was trying to evoke in different ways by combining the Twin Towers with the role of Jesse for Elvis. The Twin Towers simply represented brute, non-reflecting American muscle and hubris, as unthinking as an erection. Although if an erection did have the ability to reflect on itself, it would no doubt immediately collapse in a detumescent state of pure anxiety. Jean Baudrillard suggests something of this when he advances the fanciful notion that the towers 'committed suicide' after being struck (Baudrillard, 2002: 4). For Walker, the towers 'had no reflective quality, of course Elvis's twin brother wouldn't either because he's not there, Elvis couldn't see him, he's not there. He spoke to him, but he couldn't see him, so there was no reflective quality' (Young, 2006). For Elvis the predicament of non-reflectivity is different; it concerns the stability of the mirror image of the self as other, the alter ego that provides support for the ego. This is something that the existence of a twin disturbs, yet as the autonomy of the uncanny sibling is increasingly established the twins may successfully develop separate identities. Jesse died stillborn, however. He has (or will have had) no image other than Elvis himself. Elvis is the one-all-alone as the (non)reflection of a non-existence. 'No dupe' because there is no other whose cause one might serve or rival; 'no chiming' because there is no sound or action to echo; no twin babies' harmonic burbling; no Presley Brothers to sing 'Bye-Bye Love' before the Everlys.

Instead there are the dual darkened chords and snare echo of 'Jailhouse Rock'. The 'chiming' here, however, is 'less harmony than the passage (or return) of harmony to dissonance (in its history and in each work)' (Bataille, 1988: 56): 'pow' 'pow'. The opening words of the song encapsulate this harmonic dissonance in the vivid detail of a cinematic close-up of nostrils filled with a substance resembling earth or soot. They could belong to an interred Jesse or a victim of 9/11 buried in rubble.

Soundtracks

Between *Tilt* (1995) and *The Drift*, Walker produced his first film score for Leos Carax's *Pola X* (1999), a movie loosely based on Herman Melville's novel *Pierre: or the Ambiguities* (1852), set in contemporary France. Walker's score deploys both his 1960s ear for sumptuous orchestral music and his 1990s flair for industrial noise. The former, in tracks like 'Light' and 'Meadow', convey in conventional cinematic style the pastoral yet *haut bourgeois* lifestyle of the main character's life in a French chateau in the first half of the film. The latter evokes the derelict demi-monde of the paramilitary cult into which the hero descends in the second half. The opening of the film, titled 'The Time is Out of Joint', features the 'strutters' section of 'The Cockfighter' in the midst of archive documentary footage of the Second World War firestorms and bombing raids. The themes of *Pola X* chime nicely with some of those of *Tilt* and later *The Drift*. As the reference to a line from *Hamlet* would suggest, the initial premise concerns the problem of 'setting right' paternal dereliction in the context of an out of joint temporal and spatial dereliction produced by the absence of the paternal principle, conditioned by the question of the mother's desire. This is underscored geopolitically by the opening montage of US and German bombers obliterating French graveyards, paternal names and ancestors being smashed to smithereens. Walker's score establishes a sonic continuity between this and the post-industrial, apocalyptic cult in the warehouse scenes. There is the accompanying theme of the twin (rival brothers) and the lost uncanny sibling. The latter becomes the focus of an unavowable sexual relation conveyed in a somewhat Jacobean manner through an incestuous sex scene filmed in pitch blackness that fails, as the film concludes, to resolve into anything other than insanity and solitude.

Walker has produced two soundtracks for Brady Corbet: *The Childhood of the Leader* (2016) and *Vox Lux* (2018). *Childhood* returns to the themes of fascism and totalitarianism that have fascinated him throughout his oeuvre. This soundtrack is more closely tied to the mood if not psychology of its subject, a precocious, manipulative and violent child. This time the theme is the exceptional 'one' who commands alone, in the default of paternal authority, through chaos.

The Childhood of the Leader (2016)

(Scott Walker)

Corbet's film looks in forensic detail at the transgressive impulse to fascism from the perspective of a small child called Prescott destined to become the leader of a totalitarian regime. Set in the immediate aftermath of the First World War, the boy's rebellion against the Church and family is set in the context of the formulation and signing of the Treaty of Versailles, an event which is commonly assumed to have set the social and political conditions for the rise of National Socialism in the 1930s. Walker's mostly orchestral score frames the film and provides atmosphere and tension at various points in a soundtrack which, for the most part, consists of the diegetic sounds of a chateau in France where the action of the film is set: the village, countryside, the occasional gramophone record of opera and light jazz, and dialogue. For his score Walker along with Peter Walsh engaged the services of a formidable orchestra conducted by Mark Warman consisting of twenty-seven violins, eight violas, ten cellos, five double basses, five trumpets, five French horns and six bass trombones. Combined, these instruments produce huge blocks and pulses of sound. While neither the movie nor soundtrack resemble Walker's songs, there are themes and sound elements in common. The interest in dictators and solitude, of course, but also in the arrangement of a soundscape that is stretched from very high to very low registers. Rather than the baritone guitars familiar from the songs, cellos and double basses frame the film with a fast, short-bowed agitated rhythm, a signature staccato melody of eight notes. In the overture, a further six notes complete the line before it is repeated again and is set off, over a montage of images of trench warfare and displaced refugees of the First World War, by high-pitched strings, octaves above the bass notes, adding a sense of tension, distress, even building panic. The film ends in chaos and confusion as vertiginous strings and lurching camerawork greet the emergence in the crowd of the mature Prescott in full military regalia. In the finale and over the credits, just the first eight notes of the movie's opening refrain repeat, leaving the cinema audience to imagine the sound of further tension, distress and panic leading to the start of the Second World War.

Generally, throughout the film the high-end and low-end notes contrast and connect Prescott the Boy – the future Leader – with the conflict promised in the shaping of the Treaty of Versailles, its consequences and fascist aftermath. The bass notes accompany scenes related to the adult world of politics while the higher notes suggest the inner world of Prescott. The high and low sounds cut across each other, connecting otherwise quite distinct family and geopolitical narratives. The score is often very loud and out of kilter with the narrative images. But in this way the disturbing music suggests turmoil and building conflict even though this tension is, on the surface, asynchronous with the relative quietude of domestic life or the scenes of bureaucratic work and discussion related to the treaty. Appropriately, the disjunctive use of the musical score follows ideas from the theory of film sound first introduced in the Soviet Union in the 1930s. In V. I. Pudovkin's 'Asynchronism as a Principle of Sound Film', for example, the Soviet film-maker and theorist writes: 'It would be entirely false to consider sound merely as a mechanical device enabling us to enhance the naturalness of the image' (Weis and Belton, 1985: 86). Sound augments the expressive quality of the film's content through contrast or 'interplay with the action', not through sound and image being tied 'to one another through naturalistic imitation' (86). 'Music', Pudovkin maintains, 'must in sound film *never be the accompaniment*. It must retain its own line' (89). As an example, Pudovkin cites his own film *The Deserter* (1933) about the communist re-education of a disillusioned young worker from a Western country who is sent by his trade union to Russia to re-find his enthusiasm for the approved methods of class struggle. Pudovkin states that the film music does not accompany the images of the vicissitudes of political struggle, attempting to elicit pathos with melody, or generate menacing sounds with the introduction of the police. Rather, Pudovkin instructed his composer Shaporin that, in contrast to the progress of the narrative images which 'curves like a sick man's temperature chart', 'the dominating emotional theme of [the music] should *throughout* be courage and the certainty of ultimate victory. From beginning to end the music must develop in a gradual growth of power' (90). Remarkably, Walker's score manages to produce music that develops a gradual sense of power *and* sickness, in contrast to images that are often banal, even sweet, though darkly lit throughout in a chiaroscuro that does indeed complement the music.

There are one or two sections of the score that are not purely orchestral and feature instruments that are not mentioned in the credits. These are also related to inner mental states, specifically to a mode of thought and feeling that resolves itself in a drive to control and manipulate. *The Childhood of the Leader* is partly based on a short story by Jean-Paul Sartre published in 1948 in the collection *Le Mur* (*The Wall*, 1975). While there are one or two moments where Sartre is echoed, it is really only the opening scene of his story that is used in the film. The war-and-devastation montage of the opening section of the film gives way to a shot of the chateau's candle-lit window in which the boy Prescott is discerned dressed in an angel's costume, rehearsing his part for the church nativity. Like Sartre's character Lucien, Prescott looks adorable in his costume, charming in his gauze wings, long robe, 'small bare arms and blond curls' (Sartre, 1975: 84). Prescott also shares Lucien's concern that he looks more like a girl than a boy. Sartre writes of Lucien's own confusion on the matter, as everyone looks at him and says 'my sweet little darling; maybe it's happened already and I *am* a little girl; he felt so soft inside that it made him a little sick and his voice came out of his mouth like a flute' (84). Nevertheless, Prescott shows no sign of wanting his long blond curls – the main signifier of femininity that he bears – cut off, even though the gender confusion produces resentment and aggression at significant points in the film. His hair affords him a degree of narcissistic pleasure, but, at the same time, there is a growing if unstated understanding that Prescott likes his hair to provoke misidentification precisely so he can enjoy acting up about it. Indeed, later in the film such a misidentification provokes Prescott to expose his burgeoning virility to the entire Versailles committee debating the contents of the treaty in the drawing room of the chateau – much to his father's fury.

Belying the angelic quality of Prescott's image and the innocence of the nativity rehearsal, Walker's score characteristically hints at something darker. The bass strings from the overture remain but have slowed and become more broodingly foreboding. Above the bass notes pipes a slightly discordant, high woodwind sound – not a flute exactly, but the sound of a piccolo, synthesized a little in order to enhance the discordance. The instrument is not counted among those in the orchestra, but it nevertheless appears at various points in the film where Prescott is silently planning his actions. Much later, at the end of the film, another piccolo (along with a military snare) provides the accompaniment to scenes at the party headquarters where members of the government are meeting to discuss security measures. The piccolo then seems to connect Prescott's childhood plotting to that of his state security and his secret police.

The Childhood of the Leader is organized into four sections or chapters. The first three name episodes in the child's life in the chateau that are organized around a particular 'tantrum'. The fourth section relates to the child's maturity as a young and charismatic fascist leader. Prescott's angelic appearance at the window dissolves to the first caption: 'The First Tantrum: A sign of things to come.' The tantrum relates to an act drawn not from Sartre's book but the biography of Benito Mussolini. Mussolini was by all accounts a violent child, stabbing another pupil at school and attacking his teacher. But it is the anecdote about the eight-year-old Benito throwing stones at parishioners leaving church that is reproduced in Corbet's film. This act is interesting not just because it provides an early sign of violent malevolence, but also because it is reminiscent of what André Breton defined as the primary 'surrealist act'. In the *Second Manifesto of Surrealism*, Breton writes that 'the simplest surrealist act consists of dashing into the street, pistols in hand, and firing blindly as fast as you can pull the trigger, into the crowd' (Breton, 1930: 125). Breton naturally never shot anyone and his provocation is clearly a fantasy directed at his frustration at the 'system of debasement and cretinization' represented by the herd-like passivity of the crowd (125). For Prescott and Mussolini, however surrealist the act, it is undoubtedly real. While they don't have access to pistols, throwing rocks at church-goers offers a satisfying means of taking a pure pleasure in violence and confusion. Prescott offers no explanation for his act despite all the attempts of his parents and others to elicit a reason, including the parish priest to whom he also refuses to apologize.

At this stage it seems Prescott's violence is not a symptom; his parents have not yet refused him anything. The film does not suggest at this point that his aggression is a form of 'Oedipal' rebellion against the paternal law of the Church and his family. Indeed, he rejects the priest's suggestion that he was 'angry with his mother' and his reason for refusing to apologize to Father Laydu is that the stones were not directed at him. The act of throwing stones does not, from his point of view, at this moment at least, place him in conflict with the Church, family or the village community, but locates him outside it. It is an expression of his existential solitude and an affirmation of his freedom.

But if solitude is at the core of his autistic enjoyment of violence, it soon becomes socialized. The most disturbing section of Walker's musical score concerns the dream that Prescott has following his mother's attempts to call him to account for his 'surrealist' act. In her questioning of his act, Prescott's mother situates his apparent desire to hurt someone in symbolic rivalry to her love. His response is to question who these people are to him or to her, asking: 'Do you love them more than me?' Assigned to the place of violence by his mother and told to say his prayers, Prescott's nightmare is evoked by Walker in a non-orchestral ambient section of synthesized, sinister growling bass sounds against an industrial rhythmic noise low in the mix reminiscent of some of the films of David Lynch, especially the quieter moments of *Eraserhead*. Stylistically, this part bears no relation to the rest of the orchestral score and therefore heightens for the audience Prescott's sense of disconnection, alienation, even otherworldliness; it is as if he exists in his 'own sound world', a sound world, of course, that bears a certain resemblance to Walker's own. Greeting his mother next morning, he states, as a matter of fact, 'I had a dream that you weren't there.' The dream is a premonition of the subsequent narrative in which he will manage to alienate, dismiss or lose everyone around him – mother, father, language teacher, maid – even as, in the solitude of his room, he manages to exert 'control over the house' – in the words of his distracted, exasperated and mostly absent father.

The second tantrum concerns a narrative sequence in which Prescott follows a post-Freudian trajectory of paternal provocation and refusal of the benefits of maternal goodness, and its displacements. In Sartre's original story, the teenage Lucien and his louche, sexually ambivalent mentor Berliac discuss psychoanalysis, the latter enthusiastically confirming his childhood desire for his mother, while Lucien shrugs in agreement with a nonchalant 'naturally' (Sartre, 1975: 103). The scene illustrates the post-Freudian problem with the psychoanalytic cure that arose in the 1930s when the Oedipal structure of repression became common knowledge. Indeed, the pre-pubescent Prescott's actions are such that it is as if he is himself using Freud as a textbook for the emotional manipulation and control of family members.

The second tantrum section of the film begins with Prescott being taught French by Ada, a young and attractive local woman engaged as a tutor by his mother. During the lesson the camera focusses, from Prescott's point of view, on a close-up of Ada's breast and nipple that can be seen prominently through the translucent material of her blouse. It is quite a long shot, sustained for the duration of the scene of her teaching him to read the fable of the mouse and the lion. The lesson ends with Ada promising to bring Prescott his lunch after the rigours of the lesson but does not return. Venturing out of his room, he discovers her with his father. She has forgotten his food. His father asks his son to give him a hug, but Prescott ignores him and walks away. There follows a short sequence of Prescott ascending and descending the stairwell when Walker's film score reintroduces the sinister high string and brief piccolo notes that indicate the boy's interior machinations.

Later at the dinner table, Prescott refuses his food and, still ignoring his father, asks his mother pointedly whether 'Ada was giving father French lessons today?' There begins a struggle over the food, with his parents attempting to force Prescott to eat by banishing him to sit with Edith the maid to finish his meal even if it takes all night. Taking pity on the boy, Edith eventually scrapes the food into the waste bin. Prescott obligingly confirms the breast-food connection by stroking her breast, forcing Edith to smack the hand away. The metonymic logic of the classic Freudian connection leads back, of course, to his question concerning maternal love and his mother's denial of his pleasure (in the form of the stone throwing). Ada's neglect of his lunch through the distraction of his father repeats and confounds the sense of rejection and exclusion which he embraces and which, from that point, becomes the guiding principle of his behaviour. He withdraws to his room, finding strength and even satisfaction in the injustice of his exclusion that sustains his determination to control and manipulate his environment. The exclusions rebound as first Edith, then Ada, are dismissed and his parents' marriage starts to disintegrate. The father's frustrations mount so much that he threatens to rape his wife before beating his son for his unrelenting disobedience following a further series of provocations.

The third tantrum conjoins and raises to a higher level the previous two. The Treaty of Versailles signed, Prescott's parents host a party at the chateau to celebrate. The party culminates in a sumptuous banquet prepared by his mother who asks her son at the table to lead a prayer blessing for the meal following his father's terse and awkward speech. Prescott's improvisation consists entirely in him shouting repeatedly, 'I don't believe in praying anymore', before slapping his mother violently in the face, fleeing as she falls to the ground. The sharp high string notes of Walker's score pipe in triumph as bass strings deep below them dissolve into a sinister growl. The following scene brings the New Era and the score turns fully industrial-military as the printing presses of the new fascist regime print out materials headed by Prescott's Lion regalia.

There is, of course, an irony in the situation of a sumptuous banquet celebrating the Treaty of Versailles that provides the context for Prescott's third tantrum. It is generally assumed that aspects of the treaty, notably the 'Guilt Clause' demanding crippling levels of reparations, led to the economic failure of the Weimar Republic. Unlike the Marshall Plan following the Second World War, in 1919 the Germans were excluded by the treaty from the banquet of American wealth and generosity. But Prescott's response to his parents' dinner party suggests the immense resources that can be found in the experience of being excluded, or excluding oneself from, the banquet of others so that one can seek in solitude the much greater if more negative satisfactions found in violence and horror.

Foucault and the bureaucratic personality

The Childhood of the Leader (2015) seems to confirm what is generally assumed about totalitarian regimes: that they demand the presence of a charismatic leader. The masses cannot be mobilized without the 'strong man' or the 'great leader'. Certainly, that is how they like to characterize themselves. 'Conducator', for example, with its roots in the Latin term for *ducere* (to lead) that provides the basis for cognate terms like 'duke', 'duce', 'doge' and *führer*, was the title that Romanian president Nicolae Ceausescu gave himself. But in his promotional commentaries on this and other songs concerning totalitarian leaders, Walker diverges from the generally held view. 'All dictators are fascinating clowns', he claims in the 2013 interview with Stuart Maconie, the fascination no doubt arising in this strange combination of the risible and the sinister. Prescott, the subject of Corbet's film, does not combine these two qualities in quite that way, but the childish cunning of his tantrums is clearly meant to offer a significant insight into his character.

Certainly, he is an outsider, and this is one of the important aspects that Hannah Arendt notes of the leader in her book *The Origins of Totalitarianism* (2017). Just like his supporters (as opposed to his bureaucrats), the leader is the product of a social machine that isolates people in a mass of solitary individuals. The masses, or the 'mob', as Arendt calls them, hate 'society from which it is excluded' (428–9), finding its focal point in a fascinating image of this exclusion. The main twentieth-century totalitarian leaders illustrate this model: Mussolini's buffoonery, Stalin's gauche provincialism, Hitler's frustrated bile and incontinent rage incongruously decked out in a Chaplinesque little-man persona. In his lectures on the 'Abnormal', focussing on frequently absurd character analyses of delinquents in psychiatric discourse, Michel Foucault pauses to consider the function of the 'grotesque' or 'ubu-esque' figures who manage to produce effects of power, even though such power should be disqualified through the intrinsic qualities of the discourse or individual. The function has a long history, and Foucault cites figures from Ancient Rome – Caligula, Nero, Elagabalus – suggesting that their role is not to provide an image of the limitation of power, but, on the contrary, of 'giving a striking form of expression to the unavoidability, the inevitability of power, which can function in its full rigour and at the extreme point of its rationality even when in the hands of someone who is effectively discredited' (Foucault, 2003: 13).[1]

The idea of the 'extreme point of rationality' also concerns art, of course, and Walker makes this connection in his talk with Maconie: not only are dictators fascinating clowns but they are also 'failed artists in a way. They are failed and frustrated artists. They are all very eccentric characters' (Maconie, 2013). Following Hannah Arendt, however, we need to modify the idea that the frustration of artistic failure might have produced more destructive forms of creation in the theatre of politics and war, although this is sometimes claimed. German film-maker Hans Syberberg, for example, once suggested that 'the Third Reich [was] a total artwork of the perverted West' (Syberberg, in Lacoue-Labarthe, 1990: 62). The problem for Arendt is not the art per se, or whether, following Adorno, Nazi art can be regarded as a failure and condemned for its 'kitsch'. The problem is the identification of the artwork with the 'personality' of the artist that derives from German Romanticism. The roots of the personality cult of totalitarian leaders lies in the German romantic intellectuals of the eighteenth and nineteenth centuries and their 'idolization of the "personality" of the individual'. What they prepared was not 'the development of any single opinion', but 'personality as an end in itself' which could mean the co-option of an ideology – any ideology – with which they could identify and customize and colour with the genius of personality. She writes that the attitude of these intellectuals was 'fairly well represented by Mussolini, one of the last heirs of this movement, when he described himself as at the same time "aristocrat and democrat, revolutionary and reactionary, proletarian and anti-proletarian, pacifist and anti-pacifist'" (Arendt, 2017: 218). Arendt writes that the ruthless individualism of romanticism never meant anything more serious than everybody is 'free to create for himself his own ideology'. 'What was new in Mussolini's experiment was the attempt to carry it out with all possible energy' (Arendt, 2017: 219–20). Syberberg makes much the same point about Hitler in *Die freudlose Gesellschaft* (1981), a book written following the release of his movie *Hitler, a film from Germany* (1977): 'It is precisely in this very identification – Hitler equals Germany – that we find the explanation [of his willingness to see the total destruction of Germany]: it was the horrific and total suicide of Hitler in the form of Germany' (see Lacoue-Labarthe, 1990: 63).[2]

'The Day the "Conducator" Died (An Xmas Song)' (2012)

(Scott Walker)

In 'The Day the "Conducator" Died (An Xmas Song)' from *Bish Bosch* (2012), Walker once again combines the catastrophic with the quotidian, totalitarianism with consumer culture in an 'Xmas Song' complete with sleigh bells. The song has for the most part a conventional verse-chorus structure. The verse reproduces a Lickert-style personality questionnaire; the chorus concerns the apparently chaotic situation of Nicolae Ceausescu and his wife Elena when they were executed following a brief show trial on 25 December 1989. Both parts are therefore linked to the problematic notion of personality, central to both totalitarianism and consumer culture. Walker comments: 'Nicolae Ceausescu had a cult of personality – that's why there's a personality test there. And of course, I'm sick of seeing personality on TV and everything else, its driving me crazy' (Cocker interview, 2013).

Walker's juxtaposition of a grotesque example of the cult of personality with the bureaucratic anonymity of the personality questionnaire re-sets Arendt's analysis of totalitarianism in a typically Foucauldian framework (think of the opening juxtaposition of sovereign and disciplinary power at the beginning of *Discipline and Punish*, 1983). It also broaches the three principles of organization – law, the norm and truth – that were the main objects of Foucault's research throughout his career. Further, 'The Day the "Conducator" Died' can also be seen, somewhat obliquely to be sure and ironically, to broach Foucault's final seminars at the College de France about the ethics of existence and the care of the self. Walker's song is the concluding track on *Bish Bosch*, an album that is very interested in the status and purpose of art. Foucault's framework can provide a means of elaborating Walker's interest because of the efficacy of this (no doubt co-incidental) juxtaposition. The two main elements of Walker's song illustrate the transition from the dictatorship of sovereign power characteristic of twentieth-century totalitarianism to what Foucault calls the 'dictatorship of the norm' characteristic of contemporary biopolitics and neoliberalism. There is also a third element to Walker's song that brings in the element of contingency and 'truth' which, for Foucault in his last work, is an effect of *parrhesia* or speaking-truth-to-power. In the song, however, this speech takes the form of direct action. This third element is celebrated in a decorously mournful fashion in the chorus of 'The Day that the "Conducator" Died'. It was apparently the case that none of the firing squad waited for the command to 'fire' before pulling the trigger on the Romanian dictator. This fact provides the line for the chorus, a line repeated in an insistent and emphatic manner eighteen times in three batches of six.

The result of a very hastily assembled court that Nicolae and Elena Ceausescu refused to recognize, the aspect of the execution that interests Walker in the song is its chaotic prematurity with the executioners contravening or failing to recognize, or heed, the authority of law – and indeed the law of spectacle. The shooting occurred too quickly for the film crew to capture, and thus had to be re-staged with their corpses. Needless to say, the execution of the Ceausescus nicely illustrates how law – the law of the new post-communist state – is founded in exceptional violence, that is to say the violence of the exception appropriately exemplified by the figure of the Conducator himself. As they were led off to die, Nicolae sang 'The Internationale'. His wife Elena, meanwhile, who had complained about the shame of being tied up, saying to the soldiers, 'I brought you up as a mother', now screamed 'Motherfuckers!' adding a nice Oedipal touch to the proceedings. Like the fate of Claretta and Benito, this is the death of another last couple. The romanticism of this idea was encouraged by Captain Ionel Boyeru, the chief executioner.

Boyeru was the paratrooper who claims to have single-handedly killed the couple, recalling that Ceausescu and his wife were 'still very much in love' [and] had asked to die together in defiance of a sentence that ordered separate executions. He granted their last wish. 'I shot them very fast', he recalled, 'I feel I helped them to die with dignity'. Not so much chaos, then, but compassion. The anti-sovereign sovereign act of the freelance executioner who, through his compassionate act, puts his own life at stake. Boyeru strongly suspected that he'd be shot himself by the machine gun situated behind him in a 'clearing up' exercise by the new authorities of those personally responsible for the death (Graham-Harrison, 2014).

Alongside this defining feature of the execution for Walker, the rest of the song, in bizarre contrast, concerns a speaker reading aloud a personality test questionnaire, the first enquiry of which poses the question of care:

I am nurturant, compassionate,
caring.

⚬ Not so much

⚬ Very much

(**WALKER**, 2018: 139)

The questionnaire proceeds to offer binary alternatives to queries concerning social activities, ideal partners, the chaos of life, decision-making, control of desire, relation to ethical obligations, even a question concerning the type of garden one considers oneself to be. Personality tests go back to the late eighteenth and nineteenth centuries when the notion of 'personality' began to emerge in the context of romanticism, on the one hand, and the origin of psychiatric discourses, on the other. Various temperaments, personality and racial types could be assessed by phrenology, the study of skull shapes, and the assessment and measurement of physiological features. Of particular interest were types of 'degeneracy'. The first personality questionnaires were pioneered in the United States in the first half of the twentieth century and were also concerned with psychological factors, aptitude and fitness, particularly for military service and work.

The questionnaire provides a mechanism for decompartmentalizing and recording along quasi-rational lines the intimate lives of individuals so that this life may be framed and thereby shaped, counted, assessed and evaluated as part of a sample, as one-among-many. The questionnaire embeds each one in an apparatus of writing which makes everyone directly comparable relative to a statistical norm. There is no outside, no exception, just a more or less. Excellent. Good. Fair. Fairly Fair. Poor. Not so much, O very much. In the song, Walker sings the 'tick boxes' (or ○s) as apostrophes, as if he were a romantic poet. It reminds us that this is poetry and song reduced to the mechanism of the questionnaire, the modern form of self-expression. An apostrophe both in punctuation and in poetry, marks the place of absence, the one-missing: an absent letter, an absent other or object whom or which one summons: 'O for a draught of vintage! ... O for a beaker full of the warm South' exclaims the thirsty John Keats in 'Ode to a Nightingale'. On the one hand, the call summons the empty boxes of the writing apparatus into which one places oneself in the form of a plus or a minus. One ticks a box or leaves it blank. On the other hand, the apostrophe calls to the reading machine that evaluates and assesses the sample. It is a modern form of confession in which speech is transformed not just into discourse but into mindless machine-readable data.

In his discussion of the grotesque leader as one of the essential processes of arbitrary sovereignty in *Abnormal*, Foucault's aim is to show how this 'stupidity' function passes to the practice of assiduous bureaucracy. 'Since the nineteenth century', Foucault writes, citing literary examples from Balzac, Dostoevsky and Kafka, 'an essential feature of big Western bureaucracies has been that the administrative machine, with its unavoidable effects of power, works by using the mediocre, useless, imbecilic, superficial, ridiculous, worn out, poor and powerless functionary' (Foucault, 2003: 12). In his final lectures, Foucault begins to construct a historical pantheon of 'dangerous individuals', recalcitrant 'degenerates' who are defined against regimes of power such as bureaucracy. As he returns to the study of antiquity, the dangerous individual takes on philosophical weight and even a certain comic grandeur in the figure of the Cynic. Diogenes the Cynic, famously refused to condemn incest and cannibalism, and masturbated in public, wishing that his hunger could be so easily satisfied. The Cynic is both rejected and rejects being, reverting to a position of poverty and bare existence, intimately exterior to society. From the position of existence rather than being, the Cynic, Foucault argues, makes of himself (through breaking laws, flouting customs, ignoring taboos) 'a blazon of essential truths, often taking direct action in his own right' (2003: 361). In these last lectures, Foucault's methodology changes again and he inverts the usual relation of priorities between subjectivity and power, truth and knowledge, the body and its pleasures. Foucault adopts the Cynics' practice of organizing his method not primarily around the study of 'treatises and texts', although of course he continued to do that, 'but rather around the study of exemplars, figures [mythic or real that] the Cynics admired and treated as standards' (360). Foucault's own exemplars included the Cynics themselves, but also contemporary examples including 'a series of intensely disquieting modern poets, painters and artists, from Baudelaire to Beckett' (Miller, 1993: 362). These figures exemplify the 'true life', Foucault maintains, which 'takes shape and is given form only in a person's own life. The true life could only be embodied' in a mode of existence that is 'radically other' to the determinations of social being. In his own modest way, Scott Walker has sought to be true to the cause of truth in the sense of remaining faithful to the enigmatic cause of his art of song. It is precisely with regard to the enigma of this cause that the locus of truth is pursued in a way that takes him away from all preconceived notions of what the art of song is or could be. In so doing, Walker seeks to produce a similar truth effect to the one adumbrated by Foucault in his characterization of the Cynic's stance as the 'anti-sovereign sovereign'. Foucault's example is Diogenes facing Alexander, who 'by the very truth' of the [sovereignty of his bare existence] 'denounces and reveals the illusion of political kingship' (2011: 275). As he has said on many occasions, Walker's protest songs do not simply denounce and seek to expose illusion, nor do they, in any systematic way, seek to disclose, *a la* Foucault, the truth of power in its social production of docile bodies. But they come close to the practice of the *exemplars* to which Foucault turns when he suggests they put this process in reverse and speak the truth of the body's bare existence, its animality, as a form of exercise that produces its own effects of power (270). Through the discipline of song, Walker's lyrics lay bare the existence of the body from which they derive in a voice stripped of all qualities, as the one-all-alone. The truth-effect, if any, along with the power to affect and move resides in this; and the challenge it poses to the power of personality.

In light of Walker's little Christmas song that concludes *Bish Bosch*, it is perhaps possible to review the gift of the executioner Captain Ionel Boyeru, the one who did not wait for the order to fire. Boyeru confronts his sovereign and acts rather than wait for orders. Certainly, he is not

Diogenes facing Alexander. He is someone charged with carrying out the execution of a show trial that lacks state legitimacy. He is therefore, momentarily, without social being in the sense of existing between two regimes – one that has died, and one that is yet to be born. He lacks social definition, he has no authority, but he acts nevertheless in a sovereign manner precisely by not obeying orders, not waiting for 'Fire!'

An important character in Walker's oeuvre is Adolf Eichmann, the famous Nazi bureaucrat who became for Hannah Arendt the embodiment of the banality of evil. Eichmann claimed – accurately it seems – not to have killed anyone personally, even as he enabled the extermination of millions through 'obeying orders'. His crime, for Arendt, was mindlessness. He was incapable of independent thought and action, content to be a normal and compliant Nazi, a pure mouthpiece of Nazi discourse. Boyeru is the very opposite of this. He executes Nicolae and Elena Ceausescu together in defiance of the order to shoot them separately, on the basis therefore of their professed love and shared death. In doing so he spared them the indignity of the film cameras and risked his life in the process, fully expecting to be mown down by the machine gun behind him. Perhaps it was an act of romanticism – or at least that's the gift he gives himself in his self-justification – but it was also an ethical act. He takes care of them.

SWARM

Kafka and the halo of locust

According to the technique that he names successively 'tilt' and 'the drift', Walker will alight on and tilt a recognizable political event or historical fact in order to give another perspective that renders it strange. The title *Tilt* also suggests that the musical aesthetic of the album is predicated upon a fundamental imbalance. This is evident in its signature use of nameless chords that sound 'wrong'. In Kijak's documentary, Hector Zazou says memorably of the riff in 'Tilt' that, 'there's something wrong with the guitar'. A sequence of notes that form neither chords nor dis-chords, the riff twangs at the edge of tunelessness (Kijak, 2006). And just as he is keen to strike the wrong note musically, so Walker's song's lyrics are also littered with examples of literary indecorum.

In an interview with Erik Morse of *The Believer* promoting *Bish Bosch* (2012), Walker insisted on the multidimensional character of his work:

> If there's one thing I absolutely hate, it's these records that go one way. It's what they call a 'heavy' artist. The music will be dark, the singer will sound like he gargled with sulfuric acid. That's not art. It's art only when it's being balanced by lots of layers. Sometimes you have to dig for it, but it's there. (Walker in Morse, 2013)

A traditional notion of art is that it is the product of an attempt to provide an aesthetic balance to an existence that is fundamentally unbalanced, to give order to disorder, to evoke the harmony of the spheres that we cannot hear while in 'this muddy vesture of decay' (Shakespeare, *The Merchant of Venice*). With Walker, the various layers that are added to his art provide a very 'tilting' (im-)balance that is always threatening to topple over, like a game of Jenga. This is particularly the case with his use of humour and vulgarity to spice some of the bleakest subjects. In the interview, Walker's literary example is Franz Kafka, an author that he has cited frequently, particularly with regard to Kafka's use of irony and *Schwarzer humor* or black humour. 'When Kafka was reading his stories to friends, he'd become furious when they weren't laughing' (Morse, 2013). In Kafka's short story 'The Metamorphosis', for example, in which a young travelling salesman wakes up one morning to discover that he's become a giant insect, humour arises for the reader out of Gregor Samsa's misunderstanding of the nature of his condition. Flipped over on his armour-plated back, immobile, waggling his numerous 'pitifully thin' legs, Samsa's main concern is that he might miss his train and be late for work; he worries about the disapproval of his line manager the chief clerk. Samsa's mind is so saturated with concerns about train timetables and sales targets that he seems barely aware of his grotesque transformation into a giant bug.

Discussing in the same interview the development of his sound palette from *Tilt* to *Bish Bosch*, Walker described the way he likes to bind his tracks by very low, bottom-end notes through the use of baritone and bass guitars or heavy bass drum beats. By way of illustration, Walker suggests that the soundscape that he and Peter Walsh have developed is the aural equivalent of H. R. Giger's drawings for the first *Alien* movie. It's 'a combination of Pete's engineering and where I'm putting the instruments and the vocal. It's not just glossy black and grey, but it's splashes of white as well' (Morse, 2013). In Giger's drawings, the alien is depicted as an assemblage of phobic objects: both insect and serpent-like, nightmarishly genital; coiled and orthopterous, with its jowls slavering beneath the cockroach carapace of its hooded skull as it lurks in the dark, labyrinthine bowels of Nostromo's cargo deck. Revealingly, this is also the interview where Walker describes his voice as 'an alien creature', suggesting that this is its place in the bleak yet brilliant, shiny monochrome mix. A voice alien and alienated, it sounds paranoiac and threatening.

This sonic combination of bass-binding elements, along with occasional bright flashes of horns, strings or guitar higher in the mix is invariably augmented by sound objects whose origins are not always distinct and identifiable. This is the case throughout Walker's trilogy where many of the songs begin with some strange indiscernible sound: scratching on 'The Cockfighter', a machine's ignition switch and then subsequently a panoply of creaking, burbling and mechanical chirping at the beginning of 'Clara', the deep, lurching rumble that opens 'Psoriatic', the obscure high-pitch squeaking and rustling that introduces 'Phrasing', not to mention the various sudden jolts, bangs, screams and crashes that also announce and punctuate songs throughout. These sounds could also be described as Kafkaesque following Michel Chion's evocative characterization in his book *Sound: An Acoulogical Treatise* (2016). With Kafka, Chion suggests, 'every sound is referred to the interior of the human dwelling', noises that might otherwise be assumed to be innocently or indifferently ambient or environmental, 'become a persecutory nightmare in which the writer would feel himself as if perforated and disturbed by all the sounds' (Chion, 2016: 11).

A supreme example of this is Kafka's fable 'The Burrow' in which an unidentifiable noise becomes, for the rodent inhabitant of the burrow, the paranoiac basis for a multitude of speculations, delusional rationalizations and fantasies. He is disturbed and then tormented by an almost inaudible whistling noise that everywhere permeates the burrow. At first, he imagines the source as a large rival animal, a competitor, then he reasons it must be many. 'It cannot be a single animal, it must be a whole swarm that has fallen on my domain, a huge swarm of little creatures' (Kafka, 1985: 148, 153). This is also the discovery made by Nostromo's sole survivor Ripley when in the subsequent film *Aliens* she encounters the hive with its queen continuously birthing alien pupae. One-all-alone in the first movie, the alien is now one-among-many, a swarm.

The theme of the terrifying swarm runs throughout the trilogy but is first broached in 'Bouncer See Bouncer … ' from *Tilt* in the image of 'the halo of locust'. In this section, I want to look at how the figure of the swarm operates in Walker's trilogy to articulate animality with the sacred outside the purview of organized religion and the authority of the God of monotheism. One locust or many? How many make a halo? As I will argue, the swarm is precisely the name for the 'one' that is also the zero of the innumerable. It is the figure for how the innumerable functions as the one through supplanting the sovereignty of human law. With regard to the buzzing of life without being, the swarm is a different figure for an organizing and destructive power, the non-human world that has been summoned in different ways by poetry, apophatic mysticism and science.

'Bouncer See Bouncer … ' is one of Walker's most Kafkaesque songs that is given its tilting balance by many layers, including instances of indecorum. It is not 'Kafkaesque' in the usual sense of the term that indicates a satire on the imbecilic impasses of bureaucracy, but in the sense – associated with Kafka's novel *The Trial* – of an indefinable yet indelible feeling of guilt. It is the song of a speaker evidently unbalanced through having been saved from some form of calamity that he has nevertheless witnessed: the existential anguish and fathomless guilt of the survivor that is also directly related to the absurd unlikelihood and (mis)fortune of having been conceived at all.

'Bouncer See Bouncer ... ' (1995)

(N. S. Engel)

Perhaps the most terrifying song on *Tilt*, 'Bouncer See Bouncer ... ' follows 'The Cockfighter' in its disturbing if mostly suggestive conjunction of sexual transgression and violence, even mass slaughter. There are no clues in the album's lyric booklet about specific historical events, although biblical references abound from both Old and New Testaments, beginning with the reference to the trumpet of Gabriel, Angel of the Annunciation. The song is clearly written from the perspective of a traumatized witness like a small child trying to make sense, retrospectively, of his parents' 'dance' that took place in front of him. While they are said to have been dancing, the intensity of the recollection and the precise detail about the proximity of the witness suggests that the activity exceeded that of a dance. Subsequent descriptions of the physicality of the contact, its rubbing, pivoting and so on, suggests that the dance might be a confused misinterpretation: was it sex, was it a fight, was it tender, was it violent – was it forced? Was it an entertainment staged for a prison guard that ultimately resulted in their death? The repeated, anguished plea to not play a particular song again suggests that it is the source of the recollection of the dance that preceded the sexual act (if such it was) visible four feet away. The song is the musical memory of an unnamed trauma, perhaps the soundtrack to a primal scene: the impossible recollection of one's own conception or the miraculous insemination of God in woman heralded by the trumpet of Gabriel.

The song begins in an anguished exclamation about the singer's salvation, and consists largely of a litany activities, objects and people from whom he's been spared, a list that culminates in the halo of locust. The song is framed by two conjoined sound objects that run throughout as a menacing backdrop. The first is what the sleeve notes state to be 'locust sounds' made by a percussive use of Nigel Eaton's hurdy gurdy. The second is the louder and heavier sound of a ball or balls revolving around the surface of a rough or ridged bowl like a mortar or ball mill. This gives an aural sense of a halo, particularly if headphones are worn, as an effect of the sound moving from speaker to speaker. The noise of the buzzing insects, along with the revolution of the metallic ball grinding on the surface of the mortar, is painful, like a crown of sonic thorns or, indeed, a circle of chattering or buzzing insects. The idea of a grinding pestle and mortar or ball mill also supports the subsequent references to the powder on the Angel Gabriel's trumpet on the one hand, and the powder on Mary Magdalene, on the other. The bass notes of the organ of the Methodist Central Hall, played by Brian Gascoigne, signifier of the oppressive power of organized religion, binds the song together at the bottom end of the scale, while producer Peter Walsh beats out an ominous, pounding rhythm with a 'prog bass drum', as if leading a funeral procession. Other sound objects punctuate the song's various repeated sections – obscure cries and screams indiscernibly animal or human.

Lewis Williams's commentary on the song notes the pun on 'holocaust' and interprets the lyrics accordingly as another tale of survivor's guilt (like 'Jesse'), noting the references to hair and the metonymy of gold and teeth suggested by the reference to tooth fairies. Walker, however, goes further down to the biblical roots of the term. While the term 'holocaust', certainly following the extermination of Jews held in German death camps, is now synonymous with mass slaughter, it derives from the Jewish word for the immolation on a sacred altar of a sacrificial offering. The most famous – or infamous – of these was Moses's destruction of the Golden Calf that had itself been fashioned by Aaron from the gold trinkets and ornaments taken from the Jewish people while Moses was away in conference with God over the extent and enumeration of His Law (Exod. 32.4). Earlier in Exodus, God had previously inflicted a plague of locusts upon the Egyptians as a means of engineering the release of His chosen people (Exodus 10). In Moses's absence, following the idolatry of the Golden Calf, God now threatens to extend his exterminating zeal to the Jews themselves. On his return Moses, in anger, burns the Golden Calf down to a fine powder, and the Jewish people are separated between the idolaters of gold and the sons of Levi, the latter subsequently massacring three thousand of their neighbours (Exodus 20–35). Sending his Angel on before him, the 'LORD [then] plagued the people, because they made the calf' (Exod. 32.35). In the Qu'ran, it is dust from the feet of Angel Gabriel's horse that Samiri throws into the fire in order to create the Calf, an action that Moses then reverses (Qu'ran 7: 150–51). Either way, the 'powder' is not just gold dust; it is ash.

The powder associated with Mary Magdalene, who is positioned in parallel with Gabriel's trumpet in the second iteration of the first section of the song, could, according to William Henry, refer to the origin of mascara (*mufkzt*) that is also associated in both Egyptian and biblical myth with perfume and the 'vital spirit bread' that 'lifted an ordinary person to Angelic levels' (Henry, 2006: 184). Or it could simply be the ground spices that Magdalene used to perfume the oils when anointing the feet of Christ after his crucifixion and resurrection. In addition, this act and the defamation of Mary Magdalene as a prostitute have led to the naming of a sexual position which is possibly described in the child's mischaracterization of his parents' sexual act. A 'Mary Magdalene' is a 'reverse Cowgirl' position – in which a woman's long hair and hands caress her partner's feet below her. This might be the way to make sense of the reference to a 'cleft' and the description of the parents' position – where one's left hand is on the other's right foot and the right hand on the left, a position characterized in metaphors suggesting amorous combat. The combat, however, is belied by the sudden introduction of musical brightness from lighter woodwind notes and plucked strings – Walker's orphic code for the sound of love – before the pounding bass drum returns the listener back to the traumatized witness. So far as I am aware no commentator has any idea as to the meaning of the title of the song or the significance of the ellipsis. But throughout *Tilt*, Walker uses examples of literary indecorum – deliberate lapses of generic propriety, good taste, absurdity. In interviews, Walker has acknowledged the vulgarity of his title 'The Cockfighter' – its phallicism is not simply a reference to fighting cockerels – that is hugely incongruous in the context of Adolf Eichmann's testimony during his trial in Jerusalem. Perhaps the title of the song that immediately follows 'The Cockfighter' is similar, the dramatic irony of the child's misinterpretation of what he is witnessing, as his mother adopts the cowgirl position and rides on top of his father: 'bouncer see bouncer … '.

If the religious, apocalyptic imagery of 'Bouncer See Bouncer …' colours the survivor's guilt in the original sin of existence, itself disclosed in the animality of coitus, it is the strange, poetic reconfiguration of the term 'holocaust' into 'halo of locust' that really confounds. Of course, Gabriel is named in the Book of Enoch as the fifth Angel (1 En. 20: 7) whose trumpet in Revelations unleashes a cloud of locusts out of the great furnace of Hell's bottomless pit, commanded to consume the unrighteous (Rev. 9: 1–3). These locusts metamorphize into the shape of horses wearing crowns over the faces of men, the hair of women and the teeth of lions (Rev. 9: 7). But I think there is more to this evocative phrase than simply a biblical reference.

Walker's justification for his technique in songs on *Tilt* like 'The Cockfighter' and 'Bouncer See Bouncer …' is to 'work with the threads of language' in order to try and broach 'the unsayable' (*Tilt* Bonus Interview, 1995). Given the references contained in these two songs, this view would seem to both concur with but also challenge somewhat Theodor Adorno's famous injunction that 'to write poetry after Auschwitz is barbaric' (Adorno, 1981: 32). This is not just because it might be possible to suggest that Engel's lyrics are indeed barbaric in the sense that barbarism is their object; the subject matter is not what is primarily at stake. Engel's lyrics do not represent the Holocaust, they squeeze a bloody mist of poetry out of the word itself – the very means of representation. Thus, it is doubtful that they constitute the 'final stage of the dialectic of culture and barbarism' (Adorno, 1981: 32), for it is rather the case that they break the dialectic and disintegrate the system of representation altogether. Engel effects a holocaust upon the word 'holocaust'. As the signifier dissolves into a halo of locust, the one resolves itself into the zero, the ring or halo of the innumerable swarm. In this sense, Engel's writing is consistent with Philippe Lacoue-Labarthe's conception of the Holocaust as a 'caesura', the zero point or break that marks 'a silence of God more merciless than his withdrawal' (Lacoue-Labarthes, 1990: 46).

Lacoue-Labarthe adapts the meaning of the term 'caesura' from Hölderlin's reading of Greek tragedy. For Hölderlin, the term is not just the prosodic name for a pause interior to a line of poetry. It refers to a radical break in the rhythm or chain of representations that is represented in Greek drama as the tragic moment when man is separated from the gods. Or rather, it is that point of disjunction that breaks the chain of representations and discloses it *as* representation. It is the point where God definitely turns away from Man, making it thus imperative for 'man to turn back to the earth' (1990: 43). For Lacoue-Labarthe, this is what the event of Auschwitz constitutes: a radical interruption in the chain of Western history that either opens up the possibility of a different conception of history or closes history off altogether (45).

I think Engel's writing on *Tilt* and the two albums that follow is poised between these two possibilities, collapsed onto the point of the dissolution of the existential self. God may be silent, but there is noise, an invasive noise that is 'a persecutory nightmare in which the [self is] perforated and disturbed' (Chion, 2016: 11). For Hölderlin, the 'zero-moment' in which 'the sign = 0' is also the presentation of a sacred inexistence. 'The God presents himself immediately as the abyss, the *chaos* of his withdrawal' (Lacoue-Labarthe, 1990: 44). It is surely possible to see this in Engel's image of the halo of locust – and why 'locust' is singular as the signifier of the multiple.

Science and metaphysics

The chaos of God's withdrawal consists in a soundscape teeming with clouds of tumultuous life immanent yet indifferent to the house of being of human language in which it does not dwell. This becomes a major theme in some of the most important songs on *The Drift* and *Bish Bosch*, such as 'Cue', 'Buzzers', 'Psoriatic', 'Phrasing', 'Epizootics' and 'Pilgrim', the latter a satirical take on the condition of scientific knowledge.

Scientific discourse has of course fully entered the breach opened by the withdrawal of God, though without filling it. The few statements Walker has made about science – concerning the self as a transient construction of the brain, for example (Maconie interview, 2013) – suggest that he is a materialist. Certainly, he is not interested in religion or the religious beliefs of those artists he admires, such as the Jansenist Catholicism of Robert Bresson or the mysticism of Andrei Tarkovsky (Morse, 2013). At the same time, paradoxically perhaps, Engel's lyrics are full of religious imagery, and he has often spoken of trying to achieve spiritual moments in his songs. But clearly these spiritual moments occur within a lyrical soundscape that manifests the withdrawal of God and the furrows made in this destitute ground by the instruments of scientific perception.

Scientific knowledge advances, we are assured. In 2008 the Australian scientific journal *Current Biology* disclosed that desert locusts swarm and devastate land and destroy agriculture not just because their place of habitation has become depleted of food but because they are fleeing being cannibalized by their own kind. Craving protein, they attack the locusts in their immediate vicinity. The swarm's destruction of crops is a side-effect of its attempt to devour itself (*New Scientist,* 28 May 2008), itself the effect of protein imbalance. The insect swarm has thus become simply the vector of swarming protein molecules: 'A protein song howling through the meat' ('Phrasing'). In 'Phrasing', the howling song of protein as it passes through the moon and sky, fields and eye, in bodies and on the street, establishes the concealed social bond of the one-among-many that is predicated only upon pain: 'Pain is not alone.'

It is speculation upon pain that lies at the heart of Walker's most explicit meditation on science and scientific method in 'Pilgrim', the penultimate track on *Bish Bosch*.

'Pilgrim' (2012)

(Scott Walker)

'Pilgrim' revisits the conventional idea, common also to religious awe, that the origin of scientific inquiry lies with childlike wonder at the phenomena of the world. The scientist of the song is described as a 'Pilgrim', thereby designating the laboratory as a sacred site, altar to the ritual of scientific method, and its white-coated faithful. The laboratory is 'a room full of mice', a phrase repeated sixteen times throughout the song in the form of the scientist's internal monologue, delivered in a breathless whisper like a young boy's excited commentary on his play. 'Heya' he says to the little objects of his inquiry. Indeed, the lyric then shifts the site of empirical research from the room full of mice back to a childhood scene in which the child is blowing up bullfrogs with a straw to see how far they can inflate. At the point of bursting, he stares into their eyes, as if the essential guarantee of knowledge lay in the other's existential anxiety and pain. Indeed, the song's whole *mise-en-scène* stages the familiar criticism of empirical science that argues that its experiments do little other than confirm the world view of the scientist that, depending on the experiment, also offers the surplus indulgence of empathetic satisfaction. Such empathy is delusional, narcissistic, because there is an incommensurable gap between the life-world of the scientist and that of the bullfrog. It would be safe to assume that the bullfrogs have no idea what is going on. The sensation of being blown up by a straw is unlikely to be familiar to their *Umwelt* or life-world. Similarly, the laboratory is a room only for the scientist – mice have no conception of rooms, or of the little doors, bells and levers that science constructs for them out of the scientist's world of labyrinths and mazes. Walker's song concludes with a series of images suggesting vivisection or genetic manipulation that enumerate the products of the laboratory: an array of discarded eyes, ears, tails and toes.

While the goal of science may be to mathematize through measurement or formula the entirety of the world, thereby enabling its exploitation and management, Walker's song suggests that this mathematization generates both excess and deficiency. In spite of its supposed objectivity, impersonality and rational utility, science and its technological applications amass piles of waste from discarded animal body parts, oceans permeated with plastic, landfills piled up with obsolete computer hardware and a planet orbited by space junk. The irony of the drive to mathematically absorb and usefully operationalize all phenomena is that it produces ever newer forms of useless excess.

Moreover, this waste that continually poses such a problem is directly the result of how science functions as a discourse that elides and renders enigmatic the 'subjectivity [that should] remain significant ... to any sound naturalism ... a subject that is part of nature and is not afraid to speak about "reality" and to study it' (Rovelli, 2017: 161). As the scare quotes around 'reality' indicate, theoretical physicists, particularly those working in the area of quantum mechanics like Carlo Rovelli, are acutely aware not just that 'reality is not what it seems' (Rovelli, 2016), but that the scientific world view itself is constantly changing. Indeed, Rovelli's books have been popularized by the sensational idea that neither time nor space exist. Or rather, as Rovelli suggests, they exist only in Heidegger's sense that it is for an 'entity that poses the problem of existence' that 'the internal consciousness of time' can be posited as the 'horizon of being' (Rovelli, 2017: 161). Heidegger famously regarded the Newtonian idea of space and time as the metaphysical condition of empirical science. 'So long as we continue to think space and time as appearing within a space and time, we are not yet thinking of space itself or time itself' (Heidegger, 1996: 45). To do this would be to put the space and time of the 'room' necessary for scientific inquiry into the 'room' with the mice. But if space and time are not objects, neither are they, for Heidegger or Rovelli, the purely subjective effects of a representational system. Rather, as Rovelli suggests, science is a discourse that in its goal of objectivity separates subjectivity from its nature precisely by enabling it to speak and study (itself) as an object – which is to say from the 'unnatural' or exterior perspective of language or mathematics. It is the attempt – particularly by the latter – to absorb entirely the very thing it closes off that produces the excess to which it has no answer. This is because the excess *is* the very thing it closes off, the remnant that thus remains the disavowed enigma driving scientific inquiry.

In its emphasis on the fascination of the scientist of scientific inquiry, Walker's song is not suggesting that in its essence science is the sadistic activity of wanton boys who dismember flies for their sport; nor is this song simply an allegory of the scientific exploitation of the world. At the same time, neither is it a depiction of pure objectivism concerning the operative effects of space and time with regard to the maximum size a bullfrog can be made to expand and how long it takes, for example. Rather, it concerns a subject of knowledge seeking the enigma of its own nature in the eyes of the bullfrog just before it bursts.

As such, Walker's song does not attempt to provide an answer to the enigma, scientific or otherwise; he rather discloses it *as* an enigma. It is precisely in this way that it can be claimed that Walker's lyrics escape what Heidegger calls 'the metaphysical interpretation of art' (1996: 16). Science and technology are metaphysical for Heidegger because modern physics, for example, 'starts with the pure theoretical idea which sets nature up to exhibit itself as a coherence of forces calculable in advance' (Heidegger, 2009: 326). In the same way, in 'Pilgrim', Walker suggests that science arranges its room, ordering its experiments for the purpose of asking whether and how the mice and their physical bodies will respond when set up in this way. The technological applications of science are similarly metaphysical, even though they may be made of metal and wire, because they reveal and operate upon the world according to pre-established ideas and abstractions. Modern science remains for Heidegger a variety of Platonism in which the Idea precedes its physical appearance in an object.

Heidegger also maintains that a similar variety of Platonism has informed assumptions about art and poetry throughout the Western tradition. The sensuous images of art and poetry, its symbols, metaphors and allegories are not only supposed to present themselves but also point towards a higher, non-sensuous meaning: pure form, spiritual truth, moral reason and so on. The naturalism, realism and materialism of twentieth-century art of course challenged, even reversed that supposition. But such an apparent reversal remains metaphysical for Heidegger. This is also the basis of his critique of Nietzsche and Sartre. In his comment on the latter's contention that 'existence precedes essence', Heidegger states that 'the reversal of a metaphysical statement remains a metaphysical statement' (Heidegger, 2009: 232). Similarly, the indexing of a literary image of a river, say, on to a real geographical location does not for Heidegger get any closer to the essence of the river or what it does. The goal of the realist or naturalistic depiction of an actual thing, a landscape or cityscape, is to depict the 'actuality of the actual' (Heidegger, 1996: 25) – which is likewise a non-sensuous abstraction. British social realist movies of the north of England, for example, always depict the same thing: an abstract concept of (grim) 'reality'. Modern abstract art supremely illustrates this principle of the reversibility of the same: painting paint-as-paint is always ultimately the revelation of some spiritual realm of pure form, usually as conceived by Madame Blavatsky.

It seems to me that some of Walker's lyrics from *The Drift* could be described as a form of non-metaphysical poetry, following Heidegger's discussion of Hölderlin. Heidegger maintains that even as the 'essence of art' determines 'human beings as historical', the essence of art 'receives its law and structural articulation from the manner in which the world as a whole is opened up to human beings in general' (Heidegger, 1996: 23). While, for Heidegger, it is Hölderlin's poetic 'telling' of the River Ister's journeying that maintains the historical destiny of the German people, Walker's non-metaphorical, non-allegorical song of plague in 'Cue' broaches in a more equivocal manner the way in which this opening of the world also discloses, through its spatial and temporal dislocation of historical being, the possibility of a different conception of history.

I am aware of the indecorum of calling on Heidegger in this context. Indeed, Lacoue-Labarthe's book that gives a central place to Hölderlin's reading of the tragic caesura in his discussion of the significance of the Holocaust is dedicated to calling Heidegger to account not just for his brief membership of the National Socialist Party, but for his failure to offer any adequate way to confront or think this event. Notoriously, Heidegger did not comment directly on this dimension of the German catastrophe which Lacoue-Labarthe puts in biblical terms as an 'apocalyptic' 'revelation' of the essence of the West. It is not that Heidegger fails to mention it at all (as is often assumed), he does so on a number of occasions. But for him it is not a question of culture or even politics. What is called the Holocaust is for him just another phenomenon that discloses the essence of technology. This view is, for Lacoue-Labarthe, 'scandalous' (1990: 34).

Heidegger regarded the death camps as part of a process, introduced by 'modern science and the total state', in which 'Man becomes human material, which is disposed of with a view to proposed goals'. Heidegger writes, 'not only are living things technically objectivated in stockbreeding and exploitation; the attack of atomic physics on the phenomena of living matter as such is in full swing. At bottom the essence of life is supposed to yield itself to technical production' (Heidegger, 1971: 112). In the case of Auschwitz specifically, he acknowledged this was 'the production of corpses'.[1]

Heidegger's response to the death camps comes in his lectures on technology and poetry. The quotations cited above, for example, come from these essays. In one of them, 'What are poets for?' Heidegger offers a commentary on Rainer Maria Rilke. The title of the essay echoes the question posed by Friedrich Hölderlin's elegy 'Bread and Wine'. While Hölderlin's question concerning the purpose of poetry refers to a world left so destitute by the departure of the gods that not even the afterglow of their 'divine radiance' is left, Heidegger re-addresses the question in the context of the destitution as he sees it wreaked by modern science, capitalism and the total state. In the context of this destitution, the purpose of poetry, Heidegger claims, is to 'reach into the abyss' so that it may be endured (1971: 92) – until, as he would later add gnomically, the arrival of another god that might save us (Augstein and Wolff, 1966). The problem, for Heidegger, is Western metaphysics which finds its completion in technology, particularly cybernetics. This is really the catastrophe for Heidegger. In his commentary on *Nietzsche* (which he regarded as his public repudiation of Nazism, particularly its racial policies), Heidegger writes of the nascent science of cybernetics thus: 'To relegate the animated, vigorous word to the immobility of a univocal, mechanically programmed sequence of signs would mean the death of language and the petrifaction and devastation of *dasein*' (Heidegger, 1984: 1, 144).

It was Hölderlin, particularly his river poems, to whom Heidegger turned in order to find an example of non-metaphysical poetry which occupies a very different place than the dimensions of space and time of science or the geographical maps of actuality. In his book on Hölderlin's poem 'The Ister', the river is 'the locality of journeying and the journeying of locality' which provides the paradoxical or uncanny dwelling place of 'human beings as historical upon this earth' – in this case specifically German human beings (Heidegger, 1996: 33). The unhomely journeying towards dwelling in which 'coming to be at home is … a passage through the foreign' (49) could be a beautiful description of the passage of the migrant. It would even make of the (Jewish) migrant the paradigm of all peoples, of the human being generally for whom the state of 'unhomeliness' in the sphere of being is the very condition of dwelling (76). But that is not the direct concern of Heidegger in this work which he wrote in 1942 at the point of the entry of America into the Second World War. His concern is rather to unveil the essence of the 'becoming homely' of the German nation, a becoming which 'sustains the historicality of its history' and historical destiny in a poetic dialogue, via Hölderlin, with its foreign antecedents, the tragic poets of Ancient Greece (49).

Heidegger's very political reading of Hölderlin is an attempt to ground Germany in relation to Ancient Greece – 'the foreign of one's own' – in the face of what he sees as its imminent, violent uprooting or even annihilation by the nihilistic barbarism of the Americans. 'We know today that the Anglo-Saxon world of Americanism has resolved to annihilate Europe, that is, the Homeland [Heimat], and that means: the commencement of the Western world' (54). The Anglo-Saxons do not realize that they are coming to annihilate the site of their own 'commencement' in 'the ultimate act of American ahistoricality and self-devastation' (55). But, as we know, it was the Germans who committed the ultimate act of self-destruction through their own metaphysics of racial purity.

This is the view advanced by Jean-Luc Nancy in his book *The Inoperative Community* where it is suggested that the Germans' 'will to absolute immanence' in the form of racial purity guaranteed their ultimate suicide. Since it is impossible to satisfy the metaphysical criteria of purity in one's eradication of the materially impure, there can be no end to the process of eradication. And furthermore, for Nancy, the National Socialist government not only reduced Germany to ruins but also perhaps killed 'certain aspects of the spiritual reality of this nation' (Nancy, 1991: 12). Incidentally, the will to absolute immanence is not foreign to the Americans, particularly those in Silicon Valley for whom 'all of reality, including humans, is one big information system' (Lanier, 2010: 27). Integral to this information system, however, are bugs and noise, impure, inefficient, wasteful, dangerous elements. The governing assumption and concern of many in Silicon Valley in their expectation that artificial intelligence will soon be charged with finding a solution to the various existential threats facing Planet Earth is the conviction that AI's instant response will be to eradicate all human beings. The absolute immanence supposed by science (there is only the continuous identity of atoms or super strings) and technology (everything is an information system) remains a form of metaphysics.

With this context in mind, I want to turn to 'Cue', Scott Walker's epic song of devastation that deploys the German *flügelhorn* as the harbinger of plague or of forces unknown that undermine and devastate communities. At the same time, like Hölderlin's river poems, 'Cue' conjoins the 'journeying and locality' essential to historicity according to Heidegger, in a dual process of contagion and dis-locality. For Heidegger, only poetry can approach the non-metaphysical nature of things, and it is only while acknowledging the highly problematic question of Heidegger's example that I wish to deploy it in a reading of 'Cue'. I do so only in the spirit of immunology with the hope that, as Heidegger himself liked to say, again quoting Hölderlin, there 'where danger is, grows / the saving power also' (2009: 340).

Heidegger and the 'holy'

'Cue' draws from two of Walker's previous songs 'The Plague' (1967) and 'The Seventh Seal' (1969) that in turn reference, respectively, the titles and content of a novel by Albert Camus and a film by Ingmar Bergman. Both Camus's and Bergman's texts engage critically with Heidegger. Via these two texts – and in its own more oblique manner – Walker's song 'Cue' also engages with Heideggerian themes, particularly those discussed in the lecture on Hölderlin's poem 'The Ister'. Camus's novel *The Plague* is set in Algeria at much the same time as Heidegger was writing his lecture on Hölderlin, in which the military and occupying expression of the destiny of the German people is allegorized as the bubonic plague. Walker's use of the flugelhorn in 'Cue' not only identifies the plague with Germany and Austria, but also with its military. Both Bergman's movie and Walker's song that celebrates it deploy plague as a cinematic means of putting Heidegger's philosophy of being-for-death to the test. At the centre of Heidegger's lecture on Hölderlin's poem is a meditation on Sophocles in which the hidden essence of the river is correlated to the concealed essence of the 'hearth', site of the Fatherland, in the choral ode from *Antigone*. I want to argue therefore that a series of correlations can be set up, following Heidegger: the hearth = the river = the plague. For Heidegger, 'the choral ode from Sophocles and the river poems of Hölderlin poeticize the Same, and for this reason there is a poetic and historical dialogue' between them (1996: 123). I am going to suggest that Walker joins the conversation (bringing Camus and Bergman with him) and that 'Cue', indeed, 'poeticizes the Same'. The Same, of course, is not the identical for Heidegger, and it is indeed precisely in the historical differences between them that the dialogue can take place within the Same. But what is it that Walker brings to this conversation when he introduces, via Camus and Bergson, the plague into the locality of the hearth and the river?

'Cue (Flugleman)' (2006)

(Scott Walker)

In his promotional interviews for *The Drift* (2006), Walker provided various cues for listening to the songs that also pointed towards the methodological emphasis of the album's title generally. The song 'Cue', for example,

> started with that I was reading about coming plagues that we can't do anything about, we are turning a blind eye to it, all these things coming our way that we have no medicine for. And then it moved into something else, and then it became something else and at the end it becomes even something else. More of a personal song. (Weidal Interview, 2006)

Walker refused to elaborate on the 'personal' aspects any more than he did to Rob Young and others in similar interviews. 'It became something rather personal', he said to Young, 'so I'm kind of loathe to speak about it' (2006). The personal aspects of the lyrics are not evident to a general listener. Perhaps they would be to someone who knows Walker personally, and no doubt they were somewhat evident to himself. But since he claimed to never listen to his songs having recorded them, the insertion of secret personal elements into the songs is unlikely to have had any private utility for him as cues for self-reflection or *aide-mémoires*. According to interviews over the years, it is not only 'Cue' that has personal elements – many of the songs do. But for 'Cue' no anecdotal detail was forthcoming; there is just the cue itself concerning the importance of a personal dimension that is not disclosed. All that is disclosed, paradoxically, is that something important, something essential, has been concealed. While the movement 'into something else … then something else …

then something else' illustrates the drift of its compositional method, the mention of the personal dimension is also a cue for the listener to remember Heidegger's contention that the purpose of poetry concerns, 'that which in its very self-disclosure causes the appearance of that which conceals itself' (Heidegger, 1971: 132). Heidegger's contention that this disclosure of an enigma is not the unveiling of the truth of an enigma, but the disclosure that *there is* an enigma, evidently lies at the heart of Walker's lyricism. Further, it is in following the trajectory of the drift that the traces of this enigma can be discerned in the way the exterior finds itself in the intimate interior of the song.

As I have suggested, the theme of plague recurs throughout Walker's oeuvre. 'The Plague', the B-Side of the hit 'Jackie' (1967), is a slightly uncharacteristic rock song for which pestilence is the metaphor of a restless insomniac filled with anxiety about his desire and indecision. For Williams, it is an indirect retelling of Camus's novel. In contrast to the allegory of Nazi occupation, however, Williams suggests that in Camus's novel there is another metaphor of the plague that links the political to the personal that is voiced by the character Jean Tarrou. Williams says that the character is plagued 'because, through a combination of his experiences, past actions and present feelings, he has lost peace of mind – no longer capable of feeling at home in the world, self-torment replaces the innocence he remembers from childhood' (Williams, 2006: 69). This is a plausible description of Walker's character in his song, but is a slightly odd description of Tarrou, whose characterization of 'the plague' in Camus's novel is quite specific. For Tarrou, the plague is society's acceptance of the death penalty. The 'plague-stricken' are those for whom 'peace of mind is more important than a human life' because it can only be secured by the regular execution of convicted criminals (Camus, 1982: 205). It is Tarrou's refusal to 'join forces with the pestilences' that, he suggests, has doomed him to 'an exile that can never end' (207).

Walker explicitly picks up another treatment of Heidegger's philosophical theme of being-for-death in his song 'The Seventh Seal' (1969) which retells the narrative of Ingmar Bergman's classic of the same name from 1957. Here it is the Knight, Antonius Block, for whom Death – personified in the figure of the Reaper – provides the cue, in the context of a plague-ridden town, for him to question the doctrines of orthodox religion and the nature of existence. 'Cue' references both 'The Plague' and 'The Seventh Seal' in significant ways. Musically, the latter gives Bergman's movie an almost spaghetti western treatment with Ennio

Morricone's signature trumpet and lush flamenco guitar. In 'Cue' this guitar has been stripped down to two desiccated one-chord strums, and the trumpet to the five-note refrain of an eerie flugelhorn. Meanwhile, the line 'I keep pounding, pounding on the door' from 'The Plague' has been lyrically and sonically realized with the huge thumping sound of a cinder block hitting a custom built 5 × 5 wooden box. Perhaps also playing on the name of Antonius Block, the sound is repeated twenty-four times throughout the song in three batches of eight, in reference to the famous medieval call to bring out the dead and to suggest the idea of death knocking at one's door.

In interviews, Walker sometimes refers to the song as 'Flugleman', suggesting that this was the original title and noting that writing it was very difficult, taking nearly ten years. The 'Flugleman' title makes sense – the mournful sound of the flugelhorn pitched in B flat is slightly softer, lower and darker than a trumpet. Originally, a hunting instrument that developed military use before the development of the bugle, the German word *flügel* means 'flank'. In 'Cue', the flugelhorn lurks on the flanks of the plague, heralding the coming of death or, indeed, identifying the horn with the song of the plague or song-as-plague. Its suitability raises the question of why it was relegated to a subtitle and replaced with 'Cue'. As is evident from the title of the album, methodological concerns are paramount, and the title of this song is similarly indicative. What it indicates, first and foremost, is the problem of language.

The song 'Cue' begins with a little 'Q and A' concerning what the capital city of South Korea and the nation of Sudan have in common. The strange answer is that they share the same capital letter; which of course tells us nothing, or nothing other than they have nothing in common. Further, it tells us that language cannot begin to conjure up these places, underscoring the arbitrariness of language and the incommensurability between the word and its referent. Writing the Korean characters 서울 for Seoul does not improve matters. At the same time, the answer insists that these cities are nothing but language, as are all the protuberances, pits and scars of human culture upon the earth. 'Language is a virus' announced William Burroughs on numerous occasions, most notably in the novel *The Ticket That Exploded* (1962). If not a virus from outer space, language can be regarded as a disorder of nature, an artificial parasite that afflicts the human animal even as, nevertheless 'it is language that first brings man about, brings him into existence' (Heidegger, 1971: 192). It brings men and women into existence as an effect of a system of arbitrary differences that constitutes a house of being that is also a madhouse. It is the word, *logos*, that is the core of knowledge and belief in which rationality cleaves to delusion, to the certainty that everyone is delusional. 'Language *speaks*', Heidegger insists (1971: 198), 'deep as a virus', Walker concurs; men and women speak only in that they are inhabited by language (Heidegger, 1971: 210). Moreover, the intimacy between them is only 'present in the separation of the between' that is sustained by the language-virus and grounded in mortality.

In *The Drift*, Walker's compositional method often depends upon the way language brings disparate ideas and objects together around a central enigma or loss. In 'Jesse', the idea of the *twin* and its disappearance brings together the Presley brothers and the 'twin towers' of the World Trade Center. In 'Buzzers', the lengthening of the face of the horse throughout its evolution as a prairie animal is used to convey an image of time that is 'essentially a plea for love'. Walker's metaphor is both elaborate and awkward, twisting space into time. He explained to Rob Young, 'the horses' faces lengthen, [but] it's more about longing for the time a spiritual face can stay with us. ... So, it isn't actually about the lengthening in that sense, it's about lengthening of time, that you can hold that. Most of my stuff is about frustration, of being unable to hold on to a spiritual moment, always losing it' (Young, 2006). The back cover of the album tells us that the word *silver* links the song 'Buzzers' with 'Psoriatic' because it is the name of the mining town Srebrenica, and that during the Middle Ages sufferers with the skin disease psoriasis were known as the silver people. The signifier 'silver', then, denotes precious metal (money) and disease, the site of a massacre of its townspeople by the Serbians in 1995, and the bodily stigma of an auto-immune condition confused in the past with leprosy and impurity.

The word 'cue' has multiple definitions – and is a homonym for the letter 'Q'. Indeed this is the code letter (standing for 'quarantine') for the signal flag the 'Yellow Jack' that used to be flown on ships carrying plague. But 'cue' is more commonly the word for a prompt or indicator, something said offstage that directs speech or a subsequent action. It is some kind of stimulus: from the merest hint, intimation or guiding suggestion to the long tapering stick that hits a snooker ball. It can be a sensory signal that functions as a symptom of an underlying condition, provoking a particular response or memory. It can be the cue to a certain state of attunement, mood or frame of mind. As such, Walker's title indicates that his lyrics are not just to be read in a symbolic or metaphysical sense, as Heidegger would say. They are not representations of abstract, higher values, nor do they seek to describe some geographical place or historical event. They are merely indicators of something that is essentially concealed. Or, contrariwise, that which is concealed – offstage, as it were – is the 'cue' that precipitates the historical event. The cue sustains the 'historicality of history' since it is 'the law of the encounter [*Auseinandersetzung*] between the foreign and one's own [that is] the fundamental truth of history' (Heidegger, 1996: 49). To further paraphrase Heidegger, in 'Cue' the poetic essence of that which lies as deep as a virus remains concealed in the knowledge of the poet and conditions his indicative singing (1996: 19).

The journeying of the plague virus ascends lyrically from the corpses of the afflicted now done with scratching their inflammations. It is the voice, however, that is the vector of that which is virus-deep, similarly departing the body that sings. While for Sophocles it was the hearth, and for Hölderlin the river, for Walker it is the body, its suffering and death, that is the uncanny site of dis-location, as that which is concealed in the voice makes its contagious passage *through* but not simply *in* time and space. The voice, accompanied by the flugelhorn, travels from body to body – the body as a dis-located abode and site that is itself dis-located, deported, dumped, buried. The journeying of that which is concealed yet which reveals itself in signs of bodily deformity, disease and death crosses areas that are both cosmic and intimate, linking star dust with sexually transmitted disease. 'Cue' is thus an epic tale of a long (non)human history that oscillates between being and existence, death and the swarm clouds of life-without-being, evoking various plausible and implausible medical responses to plagues (there's a reference to mouse bells and the notion of 'belling the cat'). The song is twice punctuated with screaming and cries for immunity at the point where certain hygienic and biogenetic counter-measures are referenced. The implication, as with the superbugs produced by the overuse of antibiotics, is of another instance in which the progress of science is questioned as a locus of respite and remission that generates its own uncontrollable excess. The contagion goes its own way, and then stops for apparently no reason, no doubt having transformed and mutated.

Along with the fairly recognizable religious, historical and medical references in 'Cue', there is, according to Walker, the 'personal' matter and indeed the compositional impulse itself that drives the dislocating drift from one thing to the next. There is a general connection (that is not one of identification, but contagion) between the enigma of the enunciation – its event – and the enigma of those plagues that don't stop coming inspite of all the pharmacological attempts to plug the gaps in scientific understanding of the real.

For Heidegger, the openness of existence precedes the essence of art which in turn determines human beings as historical; for Walker, it is the openness to the concealed event – including the event of oneself – that underlies his art and its disclosure of the historicity – as opposed to the linear narrative – of history. For Heidegger also, poetry is not cultural in the sense of belonging to a national culture. National culture is always already only the consequence of a dwelling, which is the becoming homely of a being unhomely grounded in the poetic. 'The poetic runs counter to everything meritorious and does not fall within human merit and is nothing that exists in itself' (1996: 138). And yet, Heidegger would make of it the merit of supplying the dwelling constitutive of the destiny of the German people. In the same way, Walker's art is not cultural. It does not belong to a national culture, neither does it ground one. An American who has lived the majority of his adult life in England, there is no homeland or *heimat* for Noel Scott Engel that is not that of an exile or a migrant. He is even exiled in the name Scott Walker. Songs like 'Cue' suggest that history is nothing other than the flight of migrant and deported bodies that sing equivocal tales of massacre, survival and transformation (this is also the case with 'Scope J', the song Walker gave to Ute Lemper for her 1999 album *Punishing Kiss*). For Heidegger, finally, that which is 'poeticized in poetry' is 'the holy' (138) wherein the German people find their *heimat*, their homeliness, in the 'spirit of the river' (138). For Walker, in contrast, the spiritual moment is not found but always lost; it is precisely that loss.

From divine inexistence
to *ex-sistence*

'My work is spiritual to the core' avers Scott Walker with reference to *Bish Bosch* (Morse, 2013), the definition of which is developed over the trilogy. What does Walker mean by the term 'spiritual'? While he makes frequent use of religious imagery throughout his work – mostly negatively – it is possible to perceive a transition. God withdraws, leaving a hole, while the figure of this hole, the zero-sign at the portal of this exit, is the swarm. The divine Word, meanwhile, has become a virus whose incarnation in the flesh provides the body with a certain consistency as the fulminating site of suffering and joy, the dis-ease that provides the basis for the creation of new forms. The creation of new forms sets the work apart, exiles it from the common measure of generic conventions, and puts it on the path of ex-sistence (Miller, 2016).[2] In Walker, the path of ex-sistence is not discourse but it is indicated by an oblique exit-sign: the sound of an alienated voice proceeding from its site of enunciation to become a pure sound object resonating in silence. Neither speech nor music, the alien voice makes the link between the divine inexistence of the (absent) law of God to the outside of ex-sistence. In *Bish Bosch* (2012) this is seen supremely in the trajectory of Zercon on his path of escape, an idea encapsulated by Walker's usually strained baritone isolated in the mix, but also thematized explicitly in the demonic daffy duck/bugs bunny voice at the end of 'The Escape' from *The Drift*. On *Bish Bosch*, the path of ex-sistence will become Walker's modality for a different conception of art outside of national culture – the art of an exile – within the purview of a great, all-encompassing woman artist that denotes a space outside of the canon.

This three-part constitution of the spiritual provides the principle of construction for the song 'Psoriatic' from *The Drift*. This track references (or is infected by) nearly all of the others on the album, and pursues the path laid out by 'Cue' where it is not language that is the virus, but music and song.

'Psoriatic' (2006)

(Scott Walker)

Rather than the chess master from 'The Seventh Seal', in 'Psoriatic' Death is a thimble rigger. Thimble rigging is a conjurer or conman's game in which the dupe or mark is invited to locate a small object like a pea under one of three deftly manipulated thimbles. In the case of Death, however, rather than a thimble, the pea is hidden beneath a 'bougie', a surgical object: a small cylinder of rubber, plastic or metal that is inserted through a body passageway such as the oesophagus as a means of diagnosis or treatment. One might also lyrically suggest here that the bougie is set to release an object stuck in the throat such as the voice, or to facilitate coughing up the ghost, the breath of life. This sound object is constructed out of the elements that topologically describe the three dimensions of the spiritual: the hole, the surface flesh, sound-site of incarnation, and the miked, alienated voice. In the song it takes on nightmare proportions, as Walker related to Young. It was produced by rolling big dustbins across the same cinder box used in 'Cue', the sound amplified through a mic inside a hole drilled into the top of the crate. Sonically, 'the pea became a giant bowling ball that was slowed down' (Young, 2006). The 'bowling ball' sounds like it is grinding along a ridged surface, recalling the sonic annulus created in 'Bouncer See Bouncer ...' to suggest the halo of locusts.

'Psoriatic' has three sections, repeated twice – A-B-C, A-B-C – that are organized around this sound object. Appropriate to a song about disease and contagion, 'germs pinging on the night wind', section A has a 'catchy' rhythm derived from Arthur Field's 'Ja-Da (Ja Da, Ja Da, Jing, Jing Jing)' written by Bob Carleton in 1918 and recorded by Fields in 1923. It is one of the first examples of successful popular song recorded on phonograph. Walker's songs often contain a song-within-the-song, it being uncertain which is the host and which the parasite. 'Jesse' is based on the idea of the 'September Song' even as it deconstructs Presley's 'Jailhouse Rock'. 'Jolson and Jones' references Al Jolson and Allen Jones and quotes from the latter's 'Donkey Serenade' (1937). 'Dimple' from *Bish Bosch* contains Jimmy Durante's 'Rink-A-Dink' and, from the same album, 'Epizootics' is organized around Bing Crosby's 'Sweet Leilani' (1937). Field's version of Carleton's 'Ja-Da' reflexively thematizes both its own novelty and its catchiness. Neither 'a raggy melody', the song avers, nor opera nor classical, 'Ja-da' is intended to be 'soothing and appealing'. It quickly becomes something more: an ear worm that will 'linger, linger on your mind' so contagiously that 'ev'ry one will have it [in] their brain'.

Song-as-virus is evoked in the A section in the form of a catchy hook, riff and melody. It gives way to the more discordant section B which is rhythmically erratic, even chaotic, although punctuated by symbol crashes. This section re-iterates lyrically 'Ja-Da's implicit symbolic exchange of comfort for harm by referencing the use of poisoned blankets in the administration of Native Americans. Not only did the Europeans inadvertently bring a suite of deadly plagues and diseases to the 'New World' including bubonic plague, small pox, chicken pox, cholera and many others including a range of sexually transmitted diseases, the spreading of disease became in some parts a deliberate practice. William Trent of Fort Pitt wrote in his journal that, 'out of our regard for them we gave them two Blankets and a Handkerchief out of the Small Pox hospital. I hope it will have the desired effect' (Fenn, 2000: 30). This is germ warfare in the name of a regime of health that administers the body, that wraps it in blankets in the name of Christian charity and governance. Section B of the song ends with the announcement of the Angelus bell, yet another reference to the archangel Gabriel and the hymn to the Annunciation that will lead to the incarnation of God in human flesh. At the silence announced by the Angelus, the thimble-dustbins roll again and there is a rapid series of word associations connecting negro slaves with conned dupes and a diseased Christ that are punctuated by the phrase 'by-the-by' that repeats the 'Ja-Da' melody and rhythm. A few years before, Walker had used the phrase as a death farewell in the song about assisted suicide, 'Lullaby (By-By-By)' (1999).

The song repeats the three-part structure again, but the second iteration of section C is announced by the Angelus bell being sounded by a hammer beating on a length of lead piping, as if nails were being methodically hammered through flesh. The crucifixion is mentioned, as the second word association morphs into the evocation of the Incarnation in the form of psoriasis. Word, or rather rhythm and melody, become flesh in the symptomatic form of blistered and scaly dead skin. In this atheological metaphor, song speaks in diseased flesh, the body a field of sensations that proclaims its existence, neither alive nor dead, in the form of a glittering transformation.

Out of the hole comes the swarm. Like the one-all-alone, the swarm's one-among-many is equivocal – because essentially it has no meaning. Plagues are the sign of the disaster of the house of being designed by God's Word and in the wake of the silence of His withdrawal. Christian charity takes the form of 'swarming' tribes being treated with blankets writhing with bacteria. Songs on *The Drift* and *Bish Bosch* increasingly invoke and musically evoke forms of existence – mechanical, undead or microbiological – that problematize the biopolitical category of life. The figures of the angel and the swarm haunt and infest the work partly in order to provide metaphors for both the despotic and uncontrollable dimension of the divine apophatically conjured by the unpresentable or unexchangeable; or indeed in the notion of the innumerable or un-numberable. At the same time, the swarm is also a figure for the information (binary or genetic code, viruses) that is essentially meaningless (as Claude Shannon always insisted), that exists outside sense, having no relation to human perception or aspirations but which increasingly provides the matrix of cultural and social being, its infrastructure and the possibility of its complete de-structuration or destruction. The notion of the swarm, then, doubles as both information and its uncountable excess. The knowledge of the swarm is an effect of capitalist and scientific discourses, their means of effectivity and surplus. These discourses govern through computational, quantitative measures that establish the statistical mean governing adherence to norms that are increasingly inflected by uncontrollable viral distortions, windfalls and catastrophes. The swarm also therefore indicates the contingent mutations that produce viruses and bacteria that exist below the threshold of being measured on a human scale yet threaten, apocalyptically, to wipe it out.

The great woman artist

Bish Bosch (2012), the title of Walker's third album in the great trilogy of works from 1995 to 2012, specifically addresses the question of art in three ways that broadly correspond to the various dimensions of what he calls the spiritual. First, the title does indeed refer to the dead God (or the God of death) rendered by the famous Dutch painter Hieronymous Bosch (1450–1516), famous in particular for the strange, highly detailed triptych, *The Garden of Earthly Delights*. Completed over a twenty-year period from 1490 to 1510, the painting is a cosmic depiction of the history of the world beginning from Creation to Judgement Day, its final panel conjuring a startling and memorable fantasy of Hell. Its complexity and richly detailed yet bizarre imagery obviously provide a model for Walker's album. At the same time, the slang phrase 'bish bosh' implies the very opposite of a painstaking or highly symbolic process. It's a phrase Walker may have picked up when he worked as a painter and decorator in between the commercial failure of *Climate of Hunter* and enrolling in art college (*The Daily Telegraph*. 26 March, 2019: 31). It's 'job done', but in a perfunctory, quick and unthinking way that fine artists may also achieve after years of practice. More than art as 'techne', this is '*epimeleiac*' art-become-second-nature; art (almost) in tune with the body. The third element of the title concerns another slang term, 'bish', which is a contraction of 'bitch'. Rob Young's notes for the album on the official website record Walker's intention in conceiving of the title for the album: 'I was thinking about making the title refer to a mythological, all-encompassing, giant woman artist'. This is the dimension of art that ex-sists from the tradition of art represented by Bosch.

From the heritage of great European art to the perfunctory method of the painter and decorator, *Bish Bosch* poses a further question of art: the question of sexual difference. But what might it mean to suggest that the album is the work of a great woman artist? In Walker's description she is mythological. She does not exist, but she is nevertheless 'giant' and 'all-encompassing'. The woman is an alternative Creator, then, and therefore necessarily fictional, like the traditional one. Or perhaps it is the same one transitioning. If not the work of 'Big Louise', perhaps *Bish Bosch* might be described as a transsexual album that seeks to sustain the sexual value of 'woman' in contradistinction to its biological or anatomical reality. But this of course raises even more problems. It would be the very opposite of Simone de Beauvoir's transsexualism that would negate the specific sexual value of woman in the name of universal brotherhood. Indeed, from a certain feminist perspective, the notion of a 'woman artist' is itself problematic – particularly when it is being appropriated by a male artist. Why should the status of an artist be modified by gender? Is there a separate category of women artists, just as there are athletes or tennis players whose anatomy, biology – or even culture – sets certain essential limitations? There are after all specific literary prizes for women. But why not just an artist, an artist-who-happens-to-be-a-woman?

Walker's notion of a mythological, all-encompassing woman artist deploys the problem of sexual difference in order to posit a different conception of art than traditionally defined by national culture. 'All-encompassing', the great woman artist provides a different conception to the notion of totality, of the 'All' than the canonical conception of art that informs national culture: the pantheon of dead white men, as it has been satirically named. This traditional understanding of art is defined by a canon from which women have largely been excluded or included as a separate sub-category ('women's art' or 'women's writing') or included insofar as it stands the test of the same canonical standards. Any art of writing, therefore, that is included in this set, or that follows its model (all-women's literary prizes and so on) should be placed under the 'masculine' category of the 'All' because it is determined by the function of a universal measure defined by the law of the exception. Men and women might compete for different prizes, as they do at Wimbledon, but they are still playing the game on the same competitive basis. The drive to equalize the conditions of competitive play logically implies the erasure of women as a separate category of value or difference. Prize-winning women writers, along with the ones who lose, are a subset of the masculine 'All'.

But there is a different set of works that is 'not-All'. The 'not-All' is another conception of totality, but not the masculine or canonical one (Milner, 2010: 22). This idea draws on set theory but is well-described by Jean-Claude Milner in his essay 'Traps of the All' (2010). Although he is mostly interested in the political and historical implications of different notions of totality, universality and the limit, Milner does note how they have been, in the past, applied to different subjective conditions as 'formulas of sexuation'.[3] The two sets of the 'All' described by Milner provide a way to start to think of Walker's idea of 'an all-encompassing woman artist', outside of the 'phallic' canon of national culture. In his essay, Milner looks at these sets to enable one to think how subjects are inscribed as 'man' or 'woman' not through speculating about biological differences or modes of identification, but through an asymmetry that is produced in relation to a propositional function determining a universal measure of value. This asymmetry is an effect of the fact that the word 'all' is not univocal but depends upon logical quantifiers. 'In its first aspect', writes Milner, 'the all supposes a limit' because the operator 'for all' does not have any meaning when it is used in a single formula. 'It only takes on meaning when two formulas are correlated to each other, usually reading: for all x, Fx and There is an x such that non-Fx' (Milner, 2010: 22). The 'All' here is defined by an exception, the aspect that 'determines the inscription of the subject as man' (22). In the second aspect, 'the all is unlimited ... there is no x such that non-Fx'. Since there is no suspension of the function, it encompasses 'All' though in such a way that does not require a universal or 'phallic' measure. It is this aspect which 'determines the inscription of the subject as woman' (23). But to repeat, these signifiers 'man' and 'woman' are not markers of biological or even gender difference. They depend purely on the conventional idea of the 'phallus' as that which has traditionally set the standard for a particular system of value. The signifier 'woman', for example, can be 'phallic' in this sense as the name for a particular standard of Beauty or Truth, as is conventional in many cultures.

The idea of national culture also constitutes a totality. It is possible to think of all the culture that belongs to a nation – remembering that the idea of national culture is not necessarily limited geographically or racially. But it is limited logically. It is limited by the culture that does not belong to that nation, of course, but it is also limited internally by the notion of the exception. A canon of great literary, musical or art works is limited because it is defined by an exception, and indeed by exceptionality. Shakespeare, for example, sets the standard for a canon of English literature that is also defined by an exception in the sense of non-literature (which can also include Shakespeare), or what came before literature – the exception that defines the rule. The canon, moreover, is also comprised of a series of exceptions, exceptional works. In fact, it is because of this rule that *contemporary* art or literature is always problematic and provisional. While it remains supplementary to the canon of national culture, contemporary literature belongs to the set of the 'not-All'. While all work being produced now is contemporary literature, not all of it will be counted as part of the canon of great works. Contemporary literature refers to a set of works that cannot securely belong to the canon of literature because, on the one hand, they have not 'stood the test of time' and, on the other, the closer they cohere to canonical rules or resemble the classics, the less exceptional they are and thus cannot be categorized in the series of exceptional works. Their relation is not to the canon but to the contingency of the law that defines the genre of literature as such – which can change and thereby retrospectively redefine the canon. When this occurs, it is an effect of the new precisely bearing on the law of genre itself and for the moment contesting the very definition of art or literature or whether or not such categories should apply at all.

As a contemporary artist, Walker's work of course belongs to this category, but supremely in the way that it defies generic categorization. Hence the question that frequently arises concerning whether Walker writes songs or not. His work does not seem to belong to any genre. Is it music, poetry set to music, art, or something else entirely? Contemporary art and literature necessarily have a relation of exteriority to art and literature as institutions precisely because it is writing that exists – is in process – now. Accordingly, 'contemporary literature' is an oxymoron or, to put it another way, a placeholder for the writing or sound that does not have a name (like so many of his famous non-chords).

But this category of the 'not-All' is also limitless in another way; it is all-encompassing. It even encompasses non-art in the sense that it excludes nothing. 'Everyone is an artist', as Joseph Beuys once said, or at least for 'fifteen minutes', as Andy Warhol concurred, whether one likes it or not. As the example of Warhol suggests, at this point the example of 'celebrity', in contradistinction to fame, becomes instructive. Like national culture, fame (and infamy) is defined by a set of exceptional men and women, acts, achievements and so on, defined and recognized by the nation as part of its historical narrative if not destiny. 'Celebrity' requires none of this, it is open to all. It is multiple and evaluated by the multitude in popularity, ratings, clicks and cash – numbers essentially. Celebrity is an effect of metrics. This set is not phallic, then, as defined by a standard of Truth or Beauty, but it may be worse in all its pseudo-phallic yet limitless concern with visibility, popularity, numbers, clicks and likes.

As a member of the Walker Brothers in the 1960s Noel Scott Engel experienced directly this form of celebrity, supported as it was by the multitudinous, libidinal infatuation of screaming young women. He became a celebrity, a 'personality' with his own TV show. As suggested above, many of Walker's songs are organized around what he calls a 'fulcrum' (see Weidel Interview, 2006), such as the word 'twin' ('Jesse') or 'silver' ('Psoriatic' and 'Buzzers'). In the final track of *Bish Bosch*, 'The Day the "Conducator" Died', it is the word 'personality' that connects the notion of the personality cult and the personality questionnaire. The last question of the otherwise mostly straightforward questionnaire, printed in italics, concerns whether the subject noticed or didn't notice '*The mad dogs swarming from her groin*'. It is an enigmatic reference to the Roman version of the myth of Scylla, and the reference to Megarian's account of Scylla's transformation from girl to monster (331–2).

From Nisus his daughter stole (*furata*) that purple lock – and now fights down the mad dogs that swarm from her groin.

Perhaps this is the image of the monstrously femo-phallic, libidinal 'bish' whose 'swarm' provides the authority of the audience that determines the value of contemporary culture. The legitimacy granted by popularity was something that Walker was emphatically to reject. At the same time, he eventually eschewed the strictures of the canonical rock ballad and rock song even though, as he always insisted, it is from pop and rock music that his work and sound derive; while it includes other generic elements, it is not a form of *chanson* or *Lieder*.

There are two directions open to the contemporary artist for whom there is not (yet) any art other than the art of the past, the canon of which she necessarily cannot be a part, even though she can be popular and celebrated. In one direction there is the path determined by the prizes of generic pseudo-phallic kitsch and celebrity. The other direction requires the acknowledgement that the national canon of great works that guarantees and supports the prize-giving arbiters of pseudo-phallic kitsch is dead. More than that, it does not exist. Or at least not for her. (I would even say no longer for anyone.) There is a hole in the great tapestry of national culture where the female artist should be; but she can never fill this hole, she can only exacerbate it, unpick and unravel it. In so far as it is 'feminine', the set of the 'not-All' necessitates a relation of exteriority to the 'All' of national culture, ex-sisting at its limit of realization that is also its unravelling. It implies a relation to the contingency of the generic law of (non)art that engenders something new.

In my discussion of the examples that follow I want to look at how *Bish Bosch* engages with and renders – with intricate, comical, fascinated disgust – these three dimensions of art that are encompassed by the mythical great woman artist. However, in keeping with my method so far in which Walker's work is discussed in relation to another's work exterior to it (Sartre, Camus, Kierkegaard, Beauvoir, Arendt, Heidegger), I want to introduce an actual rather than mythical great woman artist – the writer Clarice Lispector. First, however, I shall look at a track from *The Drift* that addresses the artist-as-celebrity in thrall to the slavering, libidinal demands of the audience.

'Hand Me Ups' (2006)

(Scott Walker)

Also known as 'Audience' (Williams, 2006: 178), 'Hand Me Ups' opens with its cacophonous chorus which lyrically condenses religious and TV game show motifs over a military-tattoo drumbeat, a deep throbbing tubax and siren wail. Walker's voice howls obscurely yet plaintively, 'Mend, Amend', while lower in the mix another voice yells in the background. When this chorus repeats for the third time later in the song, following the repeated lines 'forever and ever', it becomes clear retrospectively that the word 'amen', the universal declaration of affirmation in all the Abrahamic monotheisms, is to be heard in 'amend' (the listener has to 'amend' his or her hearing). It is also perhaps possible to hear the Arabic word أذان: *adhan, athan* or *azaan* that is the Muslim call to prayer, a word which literally means 'to listen or to hear'. Indeed, as the song's mix thins a little in a later iteration of this section, the various layers of sound become more discernible such that, following the last chorus, the voice behind Walker sounds much like the Muslim call to prayer mentioned also in 'The Patriot (A Single)'.

Something is being mended and amended here, and evidently it is the function of the auditor. Authority in the form of the one Abrahamic God is being shifted to the audience, who decides on the basis of what it wants to hear. The authority of the audience is confirmed by the next line, a reference to an American Radio show from the 1940s called *Beat the Band*, broadcast on NBC. This was a musical quiz show driven by listeners who would send in musical questions designed to beat the musicians' knowledge for cash. If a musician answered an audience's question incorrectly, humiliated he would have to toss a fifty-cent piece on to a bass drum (DeLong, 2008: 70–71). This reversal of the usual relation in which members of the audience answer questions from a Quiz Master is signalled in the title 'Hand Me Ups'. The familiar phrase is 'hand-me-downs', of course, where poorer children would benefit from the clothes outgrown by their elder siblings. The idea can also be extended to the notion of tradition, culture, knowledge and wisdom handed down from generation to generation. The reversal of this top-down structure is contemporary with the reversal common to science and social science where greater wisdom is to be found in bottom-up processes. The knowledge of the hive mind is greater than that of the expert. As a recent pop science TV show on the phenomenon of the swarm pointed out, using the example of the different lifelines on 'Who Wants to Be a Millionaire', the 'Ask the Audience' lifeline is much more accurate than 'Ask a Friend', 'Fifty-Fifty', or indeed the more recent innovation 'Ask the Host' which was the most inaccurate of all (McGavin, 2018). Quiz shows are of course the paradigm of knowledge, particularly in Britain, which is why Stephen Fry and Sandi Toksvig, the hosts of the BBC quiz panel show *QI*, are regarded as that country's greatest intellectuals. But they are nothing compared to the hive mind google-swarm of Wikipedia.

'Hand Me Ups' references other game and reality shows like *Eurovision* and *Big Brother* in which success or failure is determined by the clapping 'hand' of the audience (although not mentioned is Walker's own ill-fated TV series *Scott* that ran briefly in 1969). A slow-hand clap is heard in the section that declaims the repeated, insistent demand that 'the audience is waiting'. These references are intercut with first-person evocations of the crucifixion of Christ, the experience of nails being driven into flesh and bone, and graphically violent scenes from Homer's *Iliad*. The violence and barbarism of these founding texts of Western civilization are thus emphasized, setting off the central narrative of the song that Walker explained in interviews. 'It's about a frustrated individual who'll stop at nothing including sacrificing his children on whatever altar because they steal his youth and the focus of his attention, thus preventing him from "living his dream"' (Weidel, 2006).

The narrative dramatizes the infantilization of a culture that is organized by an economy of attention-seekers and attention-givers (see Reich, 2002). In this sense, it is a 'maternal' culture rather than a 'paternal' one in which increasingly strident forms of attention-seeking are necessitated by the multiple screens that establish the competition for visibility and audibility that determines economic survival and therefore life. Life becomes an effect of the audience-function. In the online world of hyper-transparency, everyone is viewing just as they are being viewed and recorded. The demand for attention is provoked before it is met by the audience-function that gives attention and even 'care' – the 'caring professions' being the state's version of attention-givers – for the 'mental health' problems produced by the constant demand for attention. Hyper-stimulation is met by medicalization and pharmaceuticals. In Walker's song, the word 'dispensing' forms a whole line as the attention-seeker's children are drugged, mutilated and sacrificed in the space of universal childhood rendered limitless by the dream of popular celebrity.

Anamnestic soundscapes

Scott Walker was in his seventieth year by the time *Bish Bosch* (2012) was released. Given the rate at which he had been producing albums at that point, he had every reason to think it might be his last. Its frequent themes of bodily decay, rancorous reflection on the past and the prospect of impending death make this album similar in subject matter – if not in tone – to the recent valedictory albums of David Bowie's *Blackstar* (2015) and Leonard Cohen's *You Want It Darker* (2016). But then again, Walker, in Rob Young's notes for the *Bish Bosch* website, states that 'I've always thought since the late 70's, "This is my last record." Every single record has been that way'. And in fact, he followed up *Bish Bosch* quite quickly with *Soused* (2014), a collaboration with drone-metal band Sunn0))).

Nevertheless, *Bish Bosch* begins with the death of a singer, the title of the opening track, 'See You Don't Bump His Head' being a line cut from a scene in the movie *From Here to Eternity* in which Montgomery Clift cautions soldiers placing the dead Maggio, played by Frank Sinatra, in the truck. The major refrain indicates that the track is a swan song that consists of the fragments of a threadbare oeuvre, detailed by little poetic vignettes picturing instances of decline, deterioration, contamination and entropy from melting cobwebs and 'a tiny laugh' that dirties everything it touches to the drooling incontinence of characters like Donald Rumsfeld and Baron Scarpia, the once despotic now impotent Chief of Police from Puccini's *Tosca*. The song also announces one of Walker's main lyrical techniques of the album that represents a development from previous examples. Many of the songs now seem to consist entirely of details, gaps, elisions, fragments, hairs plucked from the duck's arse of history. The album is teeming with strange and grotesque details, unfamiliar words, anachronistic juxtapositions as if it were a panel on Hieronymous Bosch's famous triptych.

The life that might once have been projected, on the basis of a Sartrean existential choice and a commitment to a particular political or aesthetic Ideal, is now to be viewed retrospectively and ironically in relation to the grubby details not just of what happened, but what didn't happen or might have happened: the errors, failures and compulsive disasters. The technique might also in some ways be a parody of Sartre's notion of 'trans-factuality' that posits that facts from the past can change from the perspective of a projected future, depending upon one's (political) desire, meaning thereby becoming established retroactively with regard to that desire and its vision. For Walker's characters, as for Sartre, trans-factuality is always solipsist, is an effect of the original choice that is a pure outburst of solitary existence, the modality of a single consciousness. But on *Bish Bosch*, that choice is more often than not calamitous and oriented not around any Ideal but, on the contrary, a fascinating detail that has the status of filth and waste. The songs unfold an anamnestic soundscape of sonic and verbal fragments that recollect instances of the past, inaugural experiences of something that captivated or disgusted the heart – and usually a combination of both. The songs are full of the anamnesis of the lost Idea, or of the legacies of a medical history – the Joycean pun 'narcrotic' (narcosis and necrosis) is used twice ('Epizootics' and 'Dimple') – bodies are like 'cholesteroled mansions' ('Corps de Blah'), prayers are offered to the shit that 'pretzel[s] Christ's intestines', as if these songs were a form of immunology, a reflexive response to antigens from the past.

The second song on the album, 'Corps de Blah' is the major statement on this theme as it revisits old Nazis, characters familiar from the previous records in the trilogy.

'Corps de Blah' (2012)

(Scott Walker)

The word 'Corps' clearly refers to a body or a body of work, or even a troupe of performers (as in *corps de ballet*), but one modified by the term 'blah' suggesting that this is a body of sound: a senseless body, percussive and noisy, but also monotonous. In English 'blah, blah' is a derogatory term for speech that delivers a familiar often self-serving narrative; the same old tune. While there is clearly also the sense of an oeuvre, as in *corpus*, in English it can also be seen-heard as the word 'corpse'. Indeed, Walker's Joycean language that is both punning and percussive could be said to 'corporise' language as a fleshy surface. His lyrics embody even as they empty and mortify language as a skin-sack of flesh. Obscure, arcane and unlikely conjunctions are not about meaning so much as affect, even comic affect – or irritation – as so many critics attest. Comedy arises from strange and surprising juxtapositions, fragmentary images of fragrant beauty next to bodily deformity, unfamiliar but evocative names, technical phrases chosen for their curiosity, strangeness, exoticism and absurdity. Language does not operate here in order to subtract sensation only to promise it in the shimmering semblance of a meaning that never arrives. Verbal sensation is delivered here, directly generated in signifying excess – but that does not necessarily mean pleasure. This is usually Walker's point: to deal with unpleasant subject matter authentically is necessarily to broach the limit of aesthetic unpleasure. Throughout these albums, unsettling, even nauseating blocks of sound and noise, lurching in and out of tune, shift from one register to another, crushing sense.

Stubbornly resistant to interpretation, the 'blah blah' of song is not allowed to settle into the same old refrain but is tortured in such a way that Walker's fictions demonstrate an ability to-do-something-with the inertia of the blah blah, perhaps even disclose its essence – not through encryption but through the production of an excrescence that embodies the monstrosity of sense in the shape of an intensification that is also its enigmatic concealment.

'Corps de Blah' begins with a single cryptic adverb 'Hence' suggesting the question of origin or cause, inference, but also departure, perhaps to a place of execution. This suggestion is supported by the subsequent poetic condensation of egg, atom and atom bomb, birth and death. This opening section is also sung a cappella by Walker in a ponderous yet very simple three-note melody. It seems to be the voice of someone plunged into night, perhaps the world's night, or perhaps on a chicken farm in Nevada; the singer, like a rancid old cockfighter, groping in a henhouse after dark. The intoned melody sounds like a sepulchral lullaby, concluding with a plea to God.

The section gives way to evocations of flayed violence and boiling agony announced by high-pitched screeching, a perhaps synthesized non-tuned non-note scraped across the taut string-ends tied to the body of a violin. With *Bish Bosch*, the close tie between lyric and sound occurs on a line-by-line basis, both enhancing and undermining the line's meaning. But this sonic enhancement does not necessarily contribute to the narrative meaning of the song which is highly anachronic and multilayered with different historical characters and personae. There is a reference to an elusive 'Chiseller' that is accompanied by metallic taps evoking the sound of a chisel. Pure sound objects are also produced which function, behind the isolated vocal track, as part of the lyrical ensemble in losing any perceptible relation to their source, just as words themselves become sound objects rather than meaningful signs with obvious referents. Other sound objects in the shape of swaying reverbed electronic and industrial noise churn as if one's stomach were turning over, as waves of unpleasant affect build following the line that mentions the town of Sterzing, base camp of Nazis fleeing justice. The 'Chiseller' was one of the nicknames of Doctor Josef Mengele, 'the Angel of Death'. Mengele was the chief medical officer at Auschwitz whose role was to allocate victims for death (a 'medical matter') and who authorized the use of Zyklon B. He even deployed it personally on occasions. With his accomplice, Rottenführer Scheimetz, Mengele opened the cans and poured the contents down the small chimney into the gas chambers. According to Robert Jan van Pelt, they opened the cans with 'a special cold chisel and a hammer'; the chisel had a ring of teeth at its head (Van Pelt, 2002: 198). Mengele's grisly and horrific experiments on children, especially twins and pregnant women, undertaken without anaesthetic are well known. More recent evidence of Mengele's work, discovered in jars during renovations at the Max Planck Psychiatric Institute, include amputated body parts and excised brains.

Perhaps this is the reference to Walker's line later in the song about the room-clearing effectiveness of brain excision.

Having fled justice like Mengele via Sterzing, Erich Priebke was identified and eventually brought to trial in the 1990s. In 1998, after a number of acquittals for 'following orders' and appeals by the prosecution, Priebke was finally sentenced to life imprisonment by the Italian legal system with his old confrère Karl Hass for the Ardeatine Massacre in Italy in 1944. Priebke was 83, Hass was 86. Intercut into the main narrative of 'Corps de Blah', if there is a narrative, are two ancient, decrepit and incontinently flatulent characters who verbally joust in rancorous rivalry, threatening each other with mutually assured betrayal. They are not described as old Nazis, however, but Native American chieftains, a 'scabby Sachem' and a 'Sagmore wino'. It is as if, displaced along the chain of associations in some nightmarish dreamwork, decrepit Nazi party members morph into drunken elders of the Naz Perce, cleared from Los Alamos during the Manhattan project, but strangely or ironically adopting names from the Algonquians. Or perhaps they are veterans of the Manhattan project who have adopted the names of their victims. Walker's lyrics do indeed at this point have the appearance of free association produced out of the 'blah blah' not just of speech but everyday discourse, news items and old stories. These images and items are semblances, then, that function as indicants, references, signifiers pointing to the waste or 'wiki' basket of history's carnage.

Nevertheless, as the song heads towards its climax, a single, long extended note of strings returns to bring cinematic tension to instances of medical torture complete with more explicit Nazi references. The strings give way to a fading bass note, even as the reference to the 'Fiddler's mark' that points to the site of decapitation under the jaw. The conjunction recalls Paul Celan's canonical 'correlation of music and horror' in his poem 'Death Fugue'. The poem condenses the figure of a death camp captain onto that of a *Meister* conductor, Jewish violinists being urged to 'bow more darkly' in the digging of their own graves (Ross, 2009: 335). The song's conclusion is sung in silence, or rather to the sound of a blade being slowly sharpened. But it is not the scraping of the scythe-wielding Reaper of *The Seventh Seal*. It is not the sound of the guillotine. A medieval, double-bladed axe is the weapon of choice, evoking Anne Boleyn, Catherine Howard, Thomas Cromwell: in the care home, the undead drive of a broken body switches from atrocity to atrocity on the multiple channels of its restless remote.

Scott Walker clearly has a horror of cliché, of the 'blah blah'. But, as Walker well knows, cliché has an intimate relation to horror and therefore is also an element of his work. After all, there's nothing more clichéd than the Nazis and the Tudors, appearing every day on the History Channel, Hitler's name on the lips of every politician and political commentator who wishes to malign an opponent. Hannah Arendt encapsulated the problem in her commentary on the Eichmann trial with her phrase 'the banality of evil', a phrase that quickly became a cliché in itself, circulated by journalists as an endorsement of the idea that in the modern world evil has become ordinary or banal. But Arendt was not suggesting that there is anything banal or routine about evil, particularly the evil perpetrated by the Nazis. The banality concerned what she considered to be the emergence of a specific type of bureaucratic subjectivity that precluded intentionality and reflection. Arendt testified that Eichmann was telling the truth when he apologized that 'officialese [*Amtssprache*] is my only language'. Listening to his responses in court, Arendt confirmed that 'he was genuinely incapable of uttering a single sentence that was not a cliché' (Arendt, 2006: 48). This inability to speak in any other way also rendered Eichmann unable to think, reflect or perceive any position or perspective outside of the blah blah of officialese. It is interesting, however, how the 'shock' or *coup d'envois* of a phrase that 'strikes a chord' has to have its moment of truth erased before it can become the cliché that organizes a certain discourse.

The example of this phrase 'the banality of evil' illustrates the function of the 'one' that in the logic of set theory has to be erased to form a 'lack' or 'empty set' before it can form the basis of a numerical series. In this case, it becomes the 'truth' that sets off a series of journalistic assumptions. The discourse of journalism that, in its commentary on every atrocity, has to forget the original meaning of Arendt's phrase in order for the cliché to emerge as the trope that governs journalism's banalization of evil, crime, terrorism, disaster and suffering in the global spectacle of rolling news.

'Dimple' (2012)

(Scott Walker)

The sonic milieu of 'Dimple' sounds like it starts where Zercon ends, the character so withdrawn that he has become a brown dwarf freezing to death alone in deep space. Or he could be in the darkest most subterranean cavern. This was basically the idea that Iain Forsyth and Jane Pollard used in their performance piece for the Sydney Opera House in December 2013, *Bish Bosch: Ambisymphonic* in which the album was remixed as an immersive 3D sonic experience. Pollard explains that listeners were required first 'to take quite a long journey from the doors of the playhouse, down a darkened corridor and into a really dark chamber. Then you sit facing complete darkness, pick your feet off the floor ready for the music to start'.[4] The justification for the idea was the familiar one that darkness offers no external visual distractions so that a listener's 'mind is left to run free'. But it is also appropriate thematically given the importance of the third panel of Hieronymous Bosch's most famous painting, and that so many songs on the album concern death and the descent into one or other version of Hell. In 'Dimple', the song's persona is like a Samuel Beckett character contemplating his physical disintegration along with musical memories of old-time crooners, as if the former were somehow related to the latter. Like Zercon, the persona in 'Dimple' is frozen and suspended in night, but he spends his time making obscure references to the vicissitudes of life, a marital break-up, the partner taking the 'Dorgi' with her, along with resolutions to end one or other bad habit, determinations not to stale, stare, glare again. Sonically, the song consists almost entirely of sound objects. For the most part they are produced by keyboard FX manipulated by sound-object maestro Peter Walsh, Malloy's inventive use of percussion and intriguingly two tuned gongs played by Malloy and Mark Warman – that don't sound like gongs. Where there is the sound of recognizable musical instruments, like a strummed acoustic guitar or a drum rhythm, these occur in the section of the song that seems to consist in reflections on the past. They are memories, music being recalled as the tempo that measures out the beats of silence and shame.

Musique concrète is registered immediately as the beginning of the song is announced by a sudden, very loud thump, as if a huge block of concrete has been dropped onto a slab of metal. The reverberations of this voluble BANG! set the keynote for the soundscape. For R. Murray Schafer, who coined the term 'soundscape', a keynote is the sonic 'anchor or fundamental tone … it is in reference to this point that everything else takes on its special meaning' (Schafer, 1994: 9). Keynotes provide the 'ground' in which the 'figure' is situated. While this initial bang, seemingly produced by concrete on metal, is 'industrial', the tonal soundscape that it provides is modulated by sonic objects that sound like they have come from the BBC's Radiophonic Workshop of the 1950s and 1960s that produced space-horror science fictions like *Quatermass and the Pit*. Deep bass reverberations open up a large, cavernous, if not infinite, sense of space that is juxtaposed by higher, sharper, unidentifiable yet discrete sounds that seem to lurk or fly about the space like species of whistling mechanical birds or clicking machine-insects. Black eyes glistening like squashed insects, the Beckett-like figure lurks in the middle of the mix accompanied only by the alien noises that echo in the void.

The song has three sections, A-B-A, the first and third being for the most part another perverse courtly blazon. Rather than extolling the beauty of a beloved in metaphors of rubies, veined marble and jet, the body is described from its eyes to its lowering left-hanging testicle in various states of decrepitude: rotten teeth, sagging, crepey skin. If this is 'Narcissus in metamorphosis' then Walker has reached the point of the total de-sublimation of the self-image. Image gives way to sound, the soundscape providing the ground for the isolated and deformed figure, but also affording the tonality of a creaking body-scape; this could be inner-space as much as outer-space.

In his clue to the meaning of the song on the *Bish Bosch* website, Walker comments that 'I read somewhere no matter how much your face descends with age, the dimple remains in the same place. In this case I'm using it as a metaphor for a constant presence.' As such, a dimple is paradoxical since its presence consists in the permanence of a defining absence, a hole. At the same time, it is the mark of a singularity. Every baby is supposed to have one, as Doris Day would sing, somewhere on its knuckle or its knee, chin or cheek that pins the uniqueness of the subject to a small depression on the body: the distinction of a little corporeal 'nothing' that supplements the formality of the name. If 'Dimple' has a dimple, then accordingly it would be located in the central 'B' section of the song, sung in Danish in a high, slightly babyish voice, the Danish words for 'none' and 'nothing'. This Danish section of the song seems to consist of memories, suggesting that the mark of the dimple is also signalling the constant presence of a memory or fixation related to someone missing or to some other loss or trauma – itself signalled by the sudden dissonant crash that opens section A and its repetition at the beginning of section C. Section B begins with a rising note of alarm, and Walker's eerie sing-a-long with Jimmy Durante's novelty hit 'Ink-a-Dink-a-Do'. This song is an interesting curiosity in that it relates the changing fashions of popular song in childlike phonetic notations from the 'Fo, lo, dee, oh, do' of folk ballads, and the 'Boo, boop, ee, do' of popular jazz and swing, to the then current vogue for the 'dink, a dink a doo' of the crooners that, according to Durante's song, are even warming the cockles of the 'Eskimo belles up in Iceland'. The lyrics stress the element of 'lallation' or lullaby that underlies much of popular song.

Iceland used to be a dependency of Denmark and it is the latter that provides the location and context of the song's second section, with various Danish words being sung in a higher more sing-song register. Denmark is the home of Hans Christian Andersen, of course, the father of the modern fairy tale which supports the simple, childlike language and milieu of the Danish speech that Walker mimics. But the simulated youth of the singing also suggests the voice of another, or perhaps of a younger version of the same person, singing to a child or commenting on events. This device was used famously by Samuel Beckett in *Krapp's Last Tape*, where the character Krapp listens to tape recordings made by a younger version of himself, similarly making resolutions to drink less, not eat so many bananas and so on. He listens in particular to his younger self's account of an affair, of an obsession with a woman's eyes, 'the face she had! The eyes! Like … [*hesitates*] chrysolite!' (Beckett, 1985: 60). As at the same moment, he also recalls a dog 'yelping and pawing at me' (60). 'Dimple' begins its blazon of the face also by evoking eyes glistening in the dark, recalling, in the Denmark section, the snout of a dog (presumably the Dorgi taken in the break-up referred to in the first section) in his lap. The events incorporated into the taped recording in *Krapp's Last Tape* are usually taken to have a biographical reference, the woman being Peggy Sinclair (Knowlson, 1996: 442). But it also refers to the night 'at the end of the jetty, in the howling wind … when I suddenly saw the whole thing' (60). This was the night when Beckett had his sudden realization that, rather than attempt to suppress the darkness that dogged him, he should make it 'the source of his creative inspiration' (Bair, 1980: 298).

Walker lived in Denmark for a while in the early 1970s, initially staying with his then partner Mette Teglbjaerg (and her dog, a giant St Bernard, Woods, 2013: 137) in her flat in Copenhagen while he was writing his solo albums of the late 1960s. Walker paid tribute to this period in the song 'Copenhagen' from *Scott 3*. In August 1972, Walker and Mette had a child, Lee, born in Copenhagen. They married at the start of 1973 but divorced shortly after in 1975. It is tempting to see an autobiographical reference to 'Dimple', although what could be said or gained from doing so is not certain. It is another way of signalling a personal dimension, even as it is occluded. It can also be seen as a device, as in Beckett's play. It summons biography as another textual element – another quotation in effect – that operates to connect memory to lost love, signalled as ever in Walker's oeuvre by the child.

Immediately after the split with Teglbjaerg in 1975, Scott reunited with John Maus and Gary Leeds to re-form the Walker Brothers. He moved into a shared flat above Newton's Bistro on 517 New King's Road, Fulham, and they began writing the new material that would culminate in Engel's startling new style on *Nite Flights* (1978). Asked by Alan Bangs in a radio interview in 1984 to account for the darkly disturbing song 'The Electrician', Walker recalled, 'I wrote it in a flat in Fulham above a noisy restaurant. No one could hear me, so I could work.' In the midst of noise, Engel worked 'towards a silence' where the words would come to him, rather than 'have me force' them.

In 'Dimple', these multiple intertextual elements are flayed into fragments. The goal ultimately, as he related to Jarvis Cocker in 2013, 'is to strip everything away, all the gossip and the nonsense. At times it is a bit like a Giacometti sculpture'. Walker's voice is stripped to become both more and less than a human voice. It is an *a*-human voice, 'because it is always a question of what a self is, [one is] always asking these kinds of things' (Walker in Cocker, 2013). As a sonic construction in song, or perhaps one could say simply *as* song, the image of the self is comprised in Walker's work of the three main elements familiar from the spiritual dimensions discussed above. There is the language-flesh, the surface of sensation that provides consistency in so far as it is always changing; and second, there is the 'dimple' in the flesh that sustains a constant presence in the shape of a hole, the hole that is the mark of the self's singularity; third, there is the voice, a voice that, in relation to the self, is the locus of ex-sistence both inside and outside the body that resonates out of the hole, as it were, giving the body its particular tonality. Accompanying this voice, of course, there is also the question of the 'soul' or 'spirit' itself.

In the first section of 'Dimple', the soul is specifically referenced, but as a type of 'slurry' that lubricates the voice, enabling it to 'whistle' and 'clink' through teeth besmeared with tartare. One version of the soul is the psyche or breath, the vehicle of the voice. In the biblical tradition, the soul is interchangeable with the notion of the spirit, its ascent to heaven conventionally symbolized by birds – in the New Testament, the Holy Spirit takes the form of a dove. Prominent in the corresponding sections A and B of the song, the slurry is given as the reference to the soul in a typically a-theological manner in the form of bird spit and bird shit. Both are attributed in the song with the binding and restraining qualities essential to the anatomical and genetic consistency of the materialist idea of the self as simply body. Bones are held together by avian phlegm, while at the microbiological level 'guanine', one of the four nucleobases of DNA, is mentioned. The word 'guanine' owes its root to the word 'guano', bat or bird dung. Indeed, one meaning of the word 'guanine' is precisely the 'white amorphous substance obtained abundantly from guano, forming a constituent of the excrement of birds' (*OED*). The soul-birds in 'Dimple', then, don't ascend to heaven, they drop foul-smelling to the earth, or perhaps even lower. In the third panel of Bosch's *Garden of Earthly Delights* that depicts Hell, there is a famous detail in which a beaked, birdlike figure positioned on a latrine is consuming a naked human figure, black birds flying out of the human anus. Out of the beaked bird's own anus a big bubble-egg of blue guano births more naked figures through a shit hole into the void. Perhaps this hole leads to the cavernous, echoing space encompassing the voice in 'Dimple', a voice all-alone in the dark apart from the constant whistling and clicking of strange mechanical birds and flying insects.

Clarise Lispector and the joyful souls of insects

'Dimple's characterization of the soul as avian slurry is consistent with his use of animality and animals to figure the dimension of the spiritual. While frequently horrific, this dimension is not always constrained by orthodox religions in Walker's work, 'hunted down' by 'foreshortened' and foreshortening administrative angels ('The Escape', 2005). As the title of this song suggests, there is an escape route: joy. In 'The Escape' this is a joy before death, even a joy before the end of the world. Nevertheless, according to their composer, the main purpose of all his songs is 'joy', particularly in the play of language and in re-realizing 'the sounds in my head' (Morse, 2013). While lyrically and sonically the songs conjure visions of Hell rather than Heaven, this 'hell is not the torture of pain! It is the torture of a joy' (Lispector, 2012: 103). This description comes not from Walker but from Clarice Lispector's novel *The Passion According to G.H.* (2012). While Lispector's writing bears no stylistic resemblance to

Walker's whatsoever, the thematic and lyrical similarity – with this novel in particular – is quite uncanny. For this final brief section, then, I want to bring Walker into conjunction with Lispector for whom the 'most primary struggle for the most primary life would open with the calm, devouring ferocity of desert animals', like locusts (15), that she conceives sonically. In the words of her character G.H., her literary goal is 'contact with the supersound of the atonal [which] has an expressive joy that only flesh, in love, tolerates' (147). Flesh, like nature, is 'the exasperation of the atonal, which is [also] of deep joy' (148).

Lispector is a writer who, forty years after her premature death in 1977 at the age of fifty-seven, is entering the canon of great twentieth-century literature (much of her work has recently been translated and published in Penguin Classics), but she sits uneasily in the national culture of Brazil where she lived and worked. A Ukrainian by birth, Lispector's Portuguese does not sound Brazilian. Benjamin Moser quotes Brazilian critic Lêdo Ivo who remarked on her 'strange voice' and 'guttural diction': 'Clarice Lispector was a foreigner', her prose foreign to 'our literary history and even of the history of our language' (Moder in Lispector, 2014: xi). Rather than Brazilian writers, Lispector is frequently compared to Walker's favourite authors James Joyce and Franz Kafka. Indeed, the title of her debut novel, *Near to the Wild Heart*, is a very Scott Walker-esque line drawn from Joyce that she uses as her epigraph: 'He was alone. He was unheeded, happy, and near to the wild heart of life' (2014: 1).

Lispector is a great woman artist in the sense that her work cannot be defined by a canon of national culture. But her example also allows the consideration of a great woman artist not in a mythological sense, but in a very real, singular sense that is all-encompassing even as it is excluded from the set of the 'human' defined by 'Man'. Lispector is quite explicit about this in *The Passion According to G.H.* The novel essentially concerns her character's revelation at a horrific encounter with a giant cockroach. In some respects, the novel is a reworking of Kafka's tale 'The Metamorphosis' in which Gregor Samsa finds himself turned into a giant roach-like bug. Lispector's character does not turn into a cockroach, nor does she identify with it. On the contrary, her encounter strips her of all forms of identification, all forms of being. Rather, she discovers the principle of the swarm, the multiple, in the singular: in 'the moment in which I saw that the roach is the roach of all roaches, so do I want to find in me the woman of all women' (184). And, moreover, she discovers that this principle is precisely that of the non-human, 'faced with the living cockroach, the worst discovery was that the world is not human, and that we are not human' (65).

The Passion resembles Walker's narrative technique in its drift from the political to the existential. It begins with a political situation in which a bourgeois Brazilian woman comes to face what she believes to be the class and racial hostility of her maid, Janair, another great if solitary and unheeded woman artist. 'G.H.' discovers a drawing – a mural – that she takes to be of herself in the maid's empty, recently vacated room. In a manner that perhaps owes more to her own class guilt (we discover later that her childhood was lived in poverty) G.H. takes the drawing to be a judgement upon her, a reproach, 'a reprimand of my ... wanton ... life' (32). This discovery quickly gives way to another, however, which results in an encounter with 'something purely alive' that collapses her 'morality' and indeed her sense of self and identity. Her very being dissolves in fascinated horror as she comes face to face with a giant, ancient cockroach that in a panic she manages to jam in her wardrobe door. Oozing pus, the cockroach represents 'the hell of living matter' (65). Faced with the dying cockroach, she cannot scream lest her scream 'would awaken thousands of screaming beings who ... unleash ... the existence of the world' (58). The discovery of her common non-humanity with the insect prompts the woman to eventually eat the white roach pus in communion with its primordial insect life without Being.

The novel's displacement of Janair to the roach implies that the political search for commonality cannot take place at the ontological level of human identity. 'G.H.'s human response is immediately to assume that her way of life has been 'morally' rejected by Janair; she is 'wanton', she does not work, her maid works for her and thus is the virtuous one. This immediate response could be described as paranoid, but it is basic to social identities because it is this fear of rejection that leads immediately to a desire for protection through identification with a group whose own identity is itself founded upon the rejection of others whose mode of life and enjoyment is different. The novel implies, then, that identification take place not at the level of common humanity and its various predicates, but common non-humanity: upon non-ontological elements of commonality that do not necessarily give rise to communities segregated upon the basis of the rejection of other modes of life. Non-humanity is not the same thing as inhumanity. On the contrary – and this is what Walker's art continually exposes – politics at the non-ontological level should involve at its most elementary the common recognition and rejection of inhuman barbarism, a barbarism that also involves its naming as the senseless enjoyment of the other.

'Epizootics!' (2012)

(Scott Walker)

'A Hawaiian nightmare' (Walker in Cocker, 2013), the title of *Bish Bosch's* most rhythmic – even 'swinging' – song puns on mid-twentieth century hipster slang and a word indicating 'an unusually high rate of new infections within an epidemic', according to the *Bish Bosch* website. Indeed, many of the lyrics are coded and drawn from 'Cab Calloway's Hepsters Dictionary: language of Jive' (1939). 'Zoot' means 'exaggerated', and a 'Zoot suit' is the 'ultimate in clothes'. The song's opening line refers to 'Mamam Neigho' ('nothing doing' in Calloway's Dictionary) whose veins have either emptied or collapsed at the moment when she finds herself scared by Hawaiians. It is not clear whether the 'Hawaiian nightmare' concerns a dream had by a Hawaiian or a nightmare featuring Hawaiians, or a dream had in Hawaii. Given that the final lines of the song refer to '*Sweet Leilani, heavenly flower*', a song written by Harry Owens and made famous by Bing Crosby in the movie *Wakiki Wedding* (1937), the Hawaiians are perhaps not Hawaiians at all but frightening Hollywood actors playing Hawaiians, like Anthony Quinn ('Kimo') and Mitchell Lewis ('Koalani'). Perhaps Mama Neigho's veins are emptying or collapsing in a cinema in Harlem, the district in Manhattan named 'the land of darkness' in Calloway's dictionary, quoted in the song, where the narrative is largely set. Nightmares occur during sleep, of course, but the song sounds like the nightmare of a corpse (as with the narrative of Billy Wilder's *Sunset Boulevard*, 1950). Then again, as Pierre Schaeffer notes of *Symphonie pour un homme seul*, the sound of someone sleeping is the same as someone dying (Schaeffer, 2012: 49).

Suicide or overdose, the sleep of death has been induced or accompanied by opiates, the song referring to the 'putrid petals' of the 'narcotic leis' fallen to her ankles and feet like poppies or a pool of blood. A 'lei' is a Hawaiian garland or wreath given in honour of an arrival or departure, another form of 'halo' or 'zero' symbolically marking the passage from birth and death, even as the petals eat up the white face of her shoes. Walker's startling line uncannily echoes Lispector whose narrator in *The Passion* speaks of 'hell, where the one eating the other's living face was indulging in the joy of pain' (125).

'Epizootics!' is another 'Boschean' song about Hell – or perhaps it is purgatory, painful portal to heaven, or the sweet taste of opium. And what might be Harlem, 'land of darkness', after all, but also a garden of earthly delights? In Calloway's hepster slang, equivocation is everywhere: quoted in the final lines of the song, both 'knock me' and 'boot me' mean 'give me', the masochistic demand for violence expressed as a supplication or plea for the paradisal illusion of the amorous couple promised in the final lines taken from *Wakiki Wedding*. As Crosby croons in the movie:

> Sweet Leilani, heavenly flower
> I dreamed of paradise for two.
>
> (HARRY OWENS, 1937)

In Walker's song, though, as with Lispector, paradisal joy is indistinguishable from bodily pain and extremity. Narcosis is also necrosis; the sacred also the scatological – the word *sacer* having the double meaning of *soiled* as well as *holy*. It is where the antipodes that transcend or degrade the dignity of the human being meet up. That meeting place is more likely to be described as evil rather than good. As Lispector writes, 'The same in the stars, the same in the self – the demonic *precedes* the human' (101).

'Epizootics!' has a swinging, hand-clapping, finger-snapping, syncopated beat, lyrically evoking exotic locations, deploying striking and unusual instruments like a tubax, a rare brass instrument something like a tuba and a saxophone that can achieve very deep bass notes. The song was turned into an official, promotional but very entertaining music video produced by Suze Olbrich and Olivier Groulx. It is filmed for the most part in black and white, recalling the films from the 1930s mentioned in the song. The video also follows the narrative drift of the song, beginning with a shot of a young, lei-bedecked, grass-skirted Hawaiian woman dancing the hula in slow motion. As Walker begins to sing, this mid-range shot dissolves into a close-up of the woman's face bearing a quite demonic, or demonically innocent, grin complete with nose ring and black teeth-braces. Towards the end of the video, this woman's face further dissolves into the face of a blonde-haired woman, presumably 'Sweet Leilani'. In the final frame, it is over a close-up of the blonde woman's face that Walker sings Crosby's opening two lines, although to a George Formby ukulele, as maggot-petals fall in slow motion in front of her face before the screen finally turns black.

The video lasts for 10 minutes and I do not wish to do a frame-by-frame analysis, but other notable scenes implicitly relate this song to others on *Bish Bosch* and elsewhere, notably 'Bouncer See Bouncer ...'. A sharp-pitched reveille from Gabriel's trumpet announces the most rhythmic 'Harlem' sections of the song, where, in the video, slowed-down and speeded-up shots show a couple in 1940s outfits jiving (no more than four feet away) to lyrics that evoke the street-hassle life on Lexington above 110th Street. As with 'Bouncer', the dance described here is conflated with sex and fighting, the dactyl-trochee combination of the phrases hitting the beat on the 'one', as in funk. The only scene shot in colour during one of the song's 'light relief' sections, familiar also from 'Bouncer' and 'The Electrician', announced with a 'SHHHHHH ...', depicts a pastoral, tree-lined sunlit glade in which a naked, beaten and bloodied corpse writhes undead, again in slow motion to a quietly sustained synthesized string note and machined buzzing sounds. Another 'SHHHHHHH' and the video instantly cuts to the 'souls of insects' section and the close-up of a spindly tropical spider atop a naked human torso on the cusp of its navel (or conceivably a large dimple). Once again, insects (and the image of an arachnid) ambiguously signify the locus of the sacred and life without Being.

The video certainly does justice to the demonic dimension of the song – there are even clouds of sulphurous smoke billowing in the darkness, as Walker voices Satan in an a cappella sequence, politely apologizing for the clumsiness of the beatings that he inflicts as he processes the damned, newly arrived on Hell's Ellis Island. But the video doesn't explore the direct and indirect allusions to the history of migrations that provide the song with its historical and political dimension. The Hawaiian lei garland was itself introduced to the islands by Polynesian voyagers from Tahiti, navigating by the stars, and in her nightmare, Maman Neigho hitches a ride on the Spanish galleon *Cacafuego*, famously seized with all its treasure by English pirate Sir Francis Drake off the coast of Ecuador in 1579. *Cacafuego* (which means literally 'shitfire', or 'fireshitter') was the nickname of *Nuestra Señora de la Concepción* one of the largest galleons in the Spanish fleet. The conjunction of the names reinforces the sacred connection between the scatological and the holy in a manner consistent with Walker's lyrical conceptions elsewhere on the album. The conflict between the Spanish and the English is also, of course, symbolic of the European colonization of large parts of the world, causing further migrations and displacements through the spread of war and disease. But ultimately in the song there is the history of New York as the focal point of European migration generally, and Harlem in particular as the refuge for African American economic migrants fleeing the South from 1905. Known as the 'Great Migration', a mass movement of people that reached its peak in the middle decades of the twentieth century, this ultimately accounted for the movement of nearly 6 million former slaves and their descendants. It has been described as 'one of the largest and most rapid mass internal movements in history – perhaps the greatest not caused by the immediate threat of execution or starvation' (Lemann, 1991: 20).

The theme is signalled by the title 'Epizootics!', particularly in the context of Walker's oeuvre where epidemics are the figure for and of migratory displacements, exile and death, the instance of the one-all-alone and the one-among-many. Indeed, a certain view of history could be echoed here that, contra Heidegger, does not regard history as the property of a settled people like the German nation that defines itself in poetic and philosophical contemplation of its intellectual origins in Ancient Greece. Heracles may have travelled down the Danube, as Hölderlin hopes and believes, but only mythically. He did not migrate to the Ruhr looking for work. As Jean-Claude Milner states, echoing Jacques Lacan following James Joyce, 'history [is] nothing more than a flight, of which only exoduses are told' (Milner, 2016: 263).

A migrant and exile himself, maintaining that he does not feel any strong sense of identity (Maconie, 2013), Walker's situation is similar to Lispector's in Brazil and to that of James Joyce, their shared source of inspiration. Joyce's famous quotation from *A Portrait of the Artist as a Young Man* still stands as a kind of manifesto for the artist of displacement:

I will tell you what I will do and what I will not do. I will not serve that in which I no longer believe, whether it calls itself my home, my fatherland, or my church: and I will try to express myself in some mode of life or art as freely as I can and as wholly as I can, using for my defense the only arms I allow myself to use – silence, exile, and cunning. (Joyce, 2000: 269)

It is not often noted that this statement announces a new kind of political subject, even a subject of rights. This subject would not be the citizen (home and Fatherland) for whom the migrant is a foreigner and therefore without rights, at least in the first instance. Nor would these rights be guaranteed by the Church. Joyce's subject is not a creation of God, but nor is he or she a Cartesian or philosophical inference, an effect of thought or reason. In his book *Relire la Révolution* (2016), Jean-Claude Milner echoes these words of Joyce in his re-reading of the French revolution and the declaration of the Rights of Man. He asserts that in contrast to the rights of the citizen, which always implies signifiers of cultural identity held in common, the ground of the rights of man should be simply the body – the body that is established by the fact of birth and of death. The fact of existence is the sole reality and 'he who in declaring his rights derives his authority from himself alone' (Milner, 2016: 263; see also Milner, 2017: 13). Perhaps we can avoid the universalization of 'Man' in this formulation and the problem of the masculine pronoun (not to mention the 'traps of the all') if we take Milner's suggestion as an invitation to substitute the perspective of the One to that of Man. From the Rights of Man to those of the one-all-alone.[5]

ONE-ALL-ALONE

Fatal audition

Apart from the soundtrack for *The Childhood of the Leader*, Scott Walker's most recent album is *Soused* (2014), a collaboration with Stephen O'Malley, Greg Anderson and Tos Nieuwenhuizen of the drone-metal band Sunn0))). In an interview with John Doran for online music magazine *The Quietus* (Doran, 2014), Walker provided an explanation for the choice of the title. 'I had two potential names ... "Ronronner" which is the French word for purr. You know, like the noise a big cat would make [but the designer of the album cover] said that [the] French would read that as too cute. So I came up with *Soused*' (Doran, 2014). Upon further inquiry about whether this alternative title related to an affection for alcohol, Walker acknowledged that the title has a number of meanings, but that their preferred meaning was the sense of 'being submersed in water'. On the one hand, then, there is a sense of the sonorous noise of the body of a large cat that is conveyed by a French onomatopoeia, 'ronronner', that sounds nothing like the English equivalent of 'purr'. This disjunction highlights the incommensurability even at the level of onomatopoeia between sound and language. On the other hand, the alternative title describes a state of submersion that could signal either prenatal immersion in amniotic fluid or drowning. Certainly, the relation between birth and death is a major theme of the album. It seems to take as its motto the famous lines about the duration of life from Samuel Beckett's *Waiting for Godot*: 'Astride of a grave and a difficult birth. Down in the hole, lingeringly, the grave-digger puts on the forceps' (Beckett, 1981: 90–1). Walker's rendition of a similar idea is more brutal, conjuring the long arm of a 'vet ape', a henchman of 'Herod 2014', reaching into the womb to pull on the legs of the foetus.

Birth and death are two states in which the human body is *in extremis* at its most animal, divested of thought and, one assumes, consciousness.

But as the feline's purr suggests, this animal body remains sonorous. What Walker was looking for, as the keynote for the sound world for *Soused*, was 'a really primal noise' without harmony for which he looked to the drone-metal of Sunn0))) because 'the basic in music is the drone' (Doran, 2014). Given the French register of 'ronronner', the human animal is not so much a *corps de blah*, as a *corps sonore*. Sunn0))) are notorious for producing drones so loud, deep and rumbling that they are not heard as much as felt. Walker recalls that 'when we recorded them [laughs] it was shockingly loud. … But you can feel it right up through your knees, it's such a weird thing'. During gigs, great pulverizing soundwaves pulse through the body from the knees to the solar plexus, threatening to disassemble the body's bones and sinews. From foetal to fatal audition, *Soused* is sonically and lyrically concerned to evoke the production of singular bodies of sound that resonate from the years of birth to death. It attempts through the drone to attune the body to what Clarice Lispector calls the 'exasperation' of the atonal. 'Nature is the exasperated atonal, that was how the worlds formed: the atonal got exasperated' (Lispector, 2012: 148).

'Lullaby (By-By-By)' (1999)

(N. S. Engel)

Soused seems to have had quite a long gestation period, as do most of Walker's albums. A collaboration with Sunn0))) was first mooted in 2009 when O'Malley and Anderson approached Walker about contributing a song to their album *Monoliths + Dimensions*. Walker couldn't do it at the time, but he did immerse himself in their work and was enthused. If there is a lyrical continuity to *Soused*, it is set by an older song from 1999, 'Lullaby (By-By-By)', originally written along with 'Scope J' for Ute Lemper's album *Punishing Kiss* (2000). In the Doran interview, Walker says that the genesis of the song began with the vexed issue of assisted suicide and the various technologies that enable it. He states: 'I'm very frightened about the idea of people engineering our deaths in a technological way', adding that the reason the song contains extended quotations from William Byrd's 'My Sweet Little Darling' 'is because the English language is considered to be the technological language' (Doran, 2014). It might seem strange to think of a lullaby as a piece of technology, but it is certainly possible to think of a lullaby as a device to lull someone to sleep. In that sense it is an apt metaphor for a fatal soporific, the word itself containing, as the parenthesis in his title emphasizes, the farewell 'bye-bye'. How the English language – and Byrd's sixteenth-century English – is supposed to convey the idea of technological language (and also perhaps language as a particular form of technology) is a little more oblique. But certainly, Byrd's song is central both to 'Lullaby (By-By-By)', its companion piece 'Herod 2014', and much else on *Soused*. Byrd's song might be considered the album's 'urtext'.

Written in 1588, Byrd's 'My Sweet Little Darling' is not a lullaby as such, although it does use the word in the refrain. It is a consort song that combines the dramatic lament with the cradle song. Indeed, this conjunction makes it seem rather macabre and eminently suited to *Soused*. It is worth quoting the first verse and refrain:

My sweet little Baby, what meanest Thou to cry?
Be still, my blessed Babe, though cause Thou hast to mourn,
Whose blood most innocent to shed the cruel king has sworn;
And lo, alas! behold what slaughter he doth make,
Shedding the blood of infants all, sweet Saviour, for Thy sake.
A King, a King is born, they say, which King this king would kill.

O woe and woeful heavy day when wretches have their will!
Lulla, la-lulla, lulla, lullaby.

(**WILLIAM BYRD**, 'My Sweet Little Darling', 1588)

Ostensibly sung by Mary to her infant son Jesus, it would be a strange parent, I would think, who would these days seek to sing her child to sleep with a lullaby that suggested that the king's men were out to slit his throat and proceeded to evoke the blood and slaughter of infanticide and Herod's massacre of the innocents in quite such graphic terms. Sweet dreams! An ordinary child might well happily consent to the identification with the baby Jesus that is offered in the lyric and take satisfaction at the prospect of the massacre of these other children who are, after all, rivals for the affections of his mother. And he might also suppose that in this respect there is in the song a clear correlation between the Christ and Herod, the king that kills kings, the children that die for our sake and so on. There is a condensation that brings Christ, Herod and the child-listener of the lullaby together around the secret enjoyment and guilt of the 'wretched will' that slaughters its innocent rivals in compensation for the loss of the maternal object. For Freud, the traumatic loss of the maternal object is the model for all other traumas, and maternal voice is the compensatory, leftover or re-found part of that object that provides the parcel of attachment upon which all the other libidinal representations are based. Walker's songs on *Soused* clearly illustrate this but with the difference, characteristic of obsessional neurosis, that the object does not belong to the mother but to the subject. And here, the subject suffers from the voice that afflicts him. 'It's absolutely brutal', as Walker describes his singing of the sections from Byrd. 'I'm absolutely screaming it so there's no vocal quality at all in it. It's not a quiet lullaby it's an absurd lullaby because I'm shouting it' (Doran, 2014). Walker sings – or rather screeches – Byrd's words 'My sweet little darling / My comfort and joy. … In beauty surpassing the princes of Troy', with a sharp atonal intensity, belying their meaning with a bitter irony. Walker doubles the voice of the mother or singing parent, infusing it with the wretchedness of the will as it follows Herod's sinister threats and promises. This process will be pursued in more imaginative detail in 'Herod 2014'. But even in 'Lullaby (By-By-By)', Byrd's lines are intercut with those of another mimicking them, and lines citing other historical child murderers as well as others promising the torture of infantile foot binding and the extinguishing of the light of life, even as his assistant sings songs that will expose one's most intimate details. In 'Herod 2014', the voice obsessively pursues a mother who has tried to conceal her children from the rapacious king, evoking numerous threats to the newborn: cannibalism, disease-bearing insects, the brutal action of secret police and security forces, infestation, plague – even colic. In Walker's performance of psychopathic obsession in 'Herod 2014', there is the suggestion that some central trauma has become embodied and purified in the sound of the maternal voice.

Walker's use of the lullaby in 'Herod' and 'Lullaby' as a form and metaphor for pathological obsession and a technologized, bureaucratic death by fatal soporific drug is interesting in that it chimes with Friedrich Kittler's description of the use and development of the lullaby alongside the origins of bureaucracy in Germany in the late eighteenth and early nineteenth centuries. In his major work, *Discourse Networks 1800/1900* (1990), Kittler shows that the discourse networks of 1800 establish the conditions for the rise of the classic Freudian neuroses, obsession and hysteria, when traditional German (and by extension European) child-rearing practices gave way to the imperative that infants be instructed by 'the loving voice of the mother singing lullabies' (Winthrop-Young, 2011: 32). Kittler argues that the role of maternal voice, reduced to its function as pure sound and sonority was part of the 'methodological purification of speech' (Kittler, 1990: 37) designed to enable the German language to become a 'general, purified, homogeneous medium' for national culture (Kittler, 1990: 36). So, while the working life of the modern, essentially bureaucratic subject would accordingly be determined by various technologies of writing, reading, storing and processing information, the libidinal core of this activity remained tied to the demand of a pure voice enjoining the bureaucrat to express his inner nature in great thoughts and poetry. Or, as Walker's song illustrates, enjoining those possessed by the voice to obsessive thoughts of sex and death. Walker's work fits this model to the degree that the thoughts and images that populate the songs of his mature work, the torturers, chiefs of police and perverted bureaucrats, are automata and have significance as marionettes giving local colour to a more profound experience tied to the singular sonority of a voice that seeks to plumb and emerge from the depths of enunciation beyond itself, beyond any specific identity or even voice, as it strips song of all personality in its attempt to perform impersonal horror.

The a-tone-all-alone

The opening of 'Herod 2014' deploys two interesting sound objects. At the very beginning, there is the pure sound of a bell which, Walker states, is the 'representation of the female in the song' (Doran, 2014). The bell is a figure for the maternal voice that remains throughout the song 'submerged', but 'keeping a pulse and hiding away'. By contrast, there is another noise at the beginning, 'a kind of wah wah wah noise – that's taken from a recording that gets played to babies in the womb. It's a white noise sound that's meant to keep them tranquil … but the fucking thing is really loud, I don't know how it works! It's a scary noise' (Doran, 2014). While he does not say that this sound is the representation of 'Herod', the device has the same ambivalence of the lullaby that is deployed with malevolence by the voice of Herod. At the very least it is the intimation, in utero, of a threatening outside.

Apparently, all babies are born with absolute or perfect pitch (AP), but this 'best voice' is lost (Karpf, 2006: 105 and Kessen, 1979: 99). The initial ability to identify a tone-all-alone, that is without reference to a supporting scale, becomes the means for imitating pitched tones and thus provides a basis for musical identification. However, once possessed of a polymorphous (if not perverse) 'panoply of vocal and auditory talents', the post-natal abilities enabled by AP diminish, even as they map the sonic ground for the comprehension of words, to 'enable us to learn our mother tongue' (Karpf, 2006: 106). The tone-all-alone is by definition not music, since it does not yet have its supporting scale, or a discourse to name it as such which, when acquired, dissolves it. For a baby, what we understand as music does not pre-exist language, of course, it is part of the sonority of the world in which the relative consistency represented by voice, language and music provides the familiarity that both shapes the body in utero and provides part of the sound world, the sonic milieu into which the baby is born.

When asked in 2006 if he thinks there is any continuity between his early and later work, Walker conceded that his mature work is 'a lot harder and shaved down, but the mood is probably the same. The mood is shaved down as well, but if you go back there you can find who that very young guy was' (Graham-Dixon, 2006). It is mood, then, a certain tonal affect or feeling that provides continuity not just across the oeuvre, but between the work and the man. For an artist like Walker, music is not just art as *techne*, but art as *epimeleia*, in Heidegger's understanding of these Greek words. It is an acquired ability that has become 'second nature and basic to *Dasein*' (Heidegger, 1984: 164). *Epimeleia* is a modality of care for oneself and one's being-in-the-world in the context of *Dasein*'s most basic *having-to-be-open* to the Other. This is closely related to the notion of a 'basic attunement', which also resonates throughout Heidegger's work. 'Attunement' (*die stimmung*) is basic to the constitution of *Dasein* and correlative to a certain distinctive mood (*Gestimmtheit*) (2010: 133–5).

How far is this mood or attunement that forms the basis of *epimeleia* the effect of a tonality distinct from language or, rather, bound to those tones that provided the sonic ground for the comprehension of words? This sonic ground is conventionally given the name lallation which 'comes from the Latin *lallare*, which … designates the act of singing' (Soler, 2014: 25). It refers also to the so-called mother tongue that produces the affective boundaries of the body of the infant through its correlation of sound and sense: 'The first things heard, parallel the first forms of bodily care' (Soler, 2014: 25). Care implies a prior precarity, an apprehension of the precariousness of existence that is sensed especially in one's vulnerability to sound that is an effect of the perpetual openness of the ear. Sound is always in excess since ears don't have a muscle like a sphincter that can close or regulate its reception. Unlocalizable sounds from the earliest instances of foetal audition, intimations of an outside, to sounds that go bump in the night, can produce anxiety. Indeed, as with Sartre in his novel *Nausea*, sound is pre-eminently if not paradigmatically the force that produces the body-event that is traumatic in so far as its reverberations can be perceived in repetitions of dissonance around which a chaotic world may be oriented for better or worse. The incursion of sound results in the production of a sonic body that is not simply an effect of an image. Rather, this sonic body is produced in the event of a sensation that reverberates in a way that is both intimate and strange to language and the body-image. Just as everyone is a speaking body, so, in a different way, is everyone a sonic, musical body.

Evolutionary musicologist Gary Tomlinson maintains that music is both universal and developed independently of, although in conjunction with, language. He writes,

> Making music, considered from a cognitive and psychological vantage, is the province of all who perceive and experience what is made. We are, almost all of us, musicians – everyone who can entrain (not necessarily dance) to a beat, who can recognize a repeated tune (not necessarily sing it), who can distinguish one instrument or one singing voice from another. (Tomlinson, 2015: 23)

In accounts of the lallation that is usually assumed to form the basis of the lullaby, it is conventionally regarded as being a primitive form of speech or a proto-language. The idea that there is a progression from motherese to language proper, along with the idea that music is a kind of pre- or proto-language, has been a common assumption across disciplines for very many years, informing discussions about the evolution of language. But, as Tomlinson writes, 'we can imagine a sing-song comforting of an infant even during the protodiscursive stages of hominim evolution – protomotherese, so to speak' (268). And yet, he adds significantly, 'a full lullaby is inconceivable until discrete pitch perception was formed and linked to the temporal hierarchies we call metre' (268). The 'la, la, las' of lallation may seem meaningless but they are not unstructured.

Music has its own rules in which distinct pitches and tones function in combinations that are very different from language, on the one hand, and from gesture-calls such as a laugh, a sigh, or a grunt on the other. Unlike language or music, gesture-calls are entirely indexical, they cannot be recombined, recomposed or modulated into something like a sentence or a tune. Tomlinson's book argues convincingly that music evolved in parallel to language in a complex, dual process in which the sounds of gesture-calls gradually became socialized, assembled into chants accompanying collectivized behaviour and shared tasks. Ultimately, these utterances and sounds became differentiated from accompanying gestures and abstracted to the point where they constituted self-referential systems. Discrete pitches and notes became organized into hierarchies that characterize tonality, nested rhythmic periodicity and meter that, Tomlinson speculates, paralleled and perhaps even enabled the role of hierarchy in social structures in the form of a sonic system.

Tomlinson points out that even the simplest lullaby requires the virtual presence of a complex sonic symbolic system of interchangeable discrete elements. However, it is only in this structural sense that music is symbolic since it carries no semantic or syntactical meaning. Nevertheless, organized sound that is distinct from indexical gesture-calls remain necessarily correlated to bodily sensation and affects, even when sense is produced in differential relations where certain tones are further indexed to other tones or sounds in the system. Even before a baby is born, a body is being shaped in sound by the pitch, volume, rhythm and melody of the mother's voice and her sonic environment which, even if it is not recognized as speech as such, directly connects the foetus to its milieu – indeed, it even renders its milieu musical in an extended sense (Karpf, 2006: 64. See also Fifer and Moore, 1994). In utero, sound vibrations are experienced as direct contact, making impressions on the body and its various perceptual systems even as they develop (Niederland, 1958). So perhaps this, or the loss of absolute pitch, is what accounts for the emergence of the notion of attunement that is so important to Heidegger. The motherese of the mother tongue has the double function of attuning the sensations that it broaches in the body to sound, a broaching that produces a split in a now essentially *a*-tonal body where the '*a*' marks the place of the lost continuity between speech and song, language and music. It could be named 'Orpheus', the perfect voice born of separation and darkness, the sundering that produces a specific sound, a remnant in place of the lost unary pitch, that is the basis of a fundamental attunement that always bears with it the discord born of the initial cut of separation in the sound of the sonic body.

The discordant sound of this cut pulses through the five songs of *Soused* from 'Brando' to 'Lullaby'. Indeed, in the former it is even thematized in the shape of all the beatings that the American actor has taken throughout his movie career. Walker fancifully supposes that the masochistic Brando must have had it written into his contract that he gets a beating at some point in all his films. 'Brando' provides a list, culminating in the movie *Reflections in a Golden Eye*, where he gets repeatedly beaten across the face with a riding crop by Elizabeth Taylor. Sonically, the bull whip is cracked in the section of the song where the first Sunn0))) drone is introduced, driven by a drum-machined pulse and Walker's discordant yet sing-song three-note lullaby melody 'whip-poor-will'. This gives way to a high crying sound like a baby. 'Bull', described by Walker as a 'crusade against existence itself', is driven phonetically by a pumping labial refrain, 'Bump the beaky', that again emphasizes a traumatic 'bump' sound that compulsively repeats. The recorded voice of a child, Peter Walsh's young son Mark, recites Latin phrases describing both this movement of repetition and the unquiet, restless pain that it bears. 'Fetish', as the title suggests, is a commentary on the perverse disavowal and enjoyment of the cut of sonic castration, of an insistent sound 'lopping off all interruption', as Walker states in his interview with Doran (2014). It has three main sections in which an infantile polymorphous perverse pornutopia of 'bescumbered' drive objects is flanked by a phallic 'Choo-choo Mama', on the one hand, and a scene of bodily scarification on the other, in which the body including the face is shaped. The flesh of the body is produced as a 'naked intaglio', the sign that claws, ploughs, carves and stilettos the body, fleshing it out as a surface of inscription – and indeed audition, again without interruption. Soused in sound, the immersed body is moulded in the drones and pulses of a fundamental noise that provides the base note for the particularities of its sound world. 'People say there's a certain sound in the early stuff that runs through everything. There probably is', reiterates Walker in an interview with Alex Clark of *The Guardian* (2018) promoting *Sundog* (2018), the Faber collection of his lyrics.

Heidegger suggests that among the chain of notes and frequencies, a body becomes attuned to a certain tonality that is particularly resonant. Sound attunes the body through sensations that are not just sensible in the sense that feeling is correlated with meaning, but sensational in the sense of an event of something surprising, pleasurable or un-pleasurable that produces the body as a sensitive surface and substance. For Heidegger, this is the '*Ek-static*' production of 'man' as a substance of attunement. In his 'Letter on Humanism', Heidegger states that 'the "substance" of man is ek-sistence'. That is to say he is oriented by or attuned to an outside of both being and existence. He states that this means that the way 'man in his proper essence becomes present to Being is ecstatic inherence to the truth of Being' (233). Ek-sistence is related to ecstasy, of course, the rapturous or joyful transportation to an outside, often associated with poetic inspiration or contemplation of the divine. The truth of being, therefore, is outside being, its substance precisely this surface open to the outside. Thus, for Heidegger, 'ecstatic existence is experienced as "care"' (234).

Heidegger develops the notion in his book on Nietzsche's aesthetics of the body, where consistency of mood is an effect of the attunement to *rausch*. As David Farrell Krell in his translation notes,

> no single English word – rapture, frenzy, ecstasy, transport, intoxication, delirium – can capture all the sense of *rausch*. Our word 'rush' is related to it: something 'rushes over' us and sweeps us away. Heidegger writes, 'Rapture [*rausch*] is feeling, an embodying attunement, an embodied being that is contained in attunement, attunement woven into embodiment.' (1984: 104)

Attunement defines a mood and therefore a sensibility or sensation that suggests that the substance of the body does not simply resonate with its own singular tonality, but also *reasonates* even if the particulate system may lack the semantic meaning of language. Somatic knowledge therefore can be presupposed through the correlation of sound and sense in an attunement of bodily sensations; this knowledge is apprehended sonically in the experience of the body's *reasonation* that is separate from, even if in conjunction with, the acquisition of language. The body sings – or is rather sung – through what it receives of the music of its sonic environment having hollowed itself out like a reed in order to resonate with its own basic tonality or fundamental attunement (*die Grund-stimmung*) that tunes the mode of being-in-the-world. As Heidegger writes, *rausch* (rapture, ecstasy or joy) is an experience of the outside, feeling or mood (*Gestimmtheit*) that 'is the mode of the embodying, attuned stance toward beings as a whole, beings which for their part determine the pitch of attunement' (1984: 106).

But, as the example of Heidegger highlights, there is a social and political danger in his notion of attunement, particularly where its pitch is supposed to be determined by social being. This is evident in the early 1930s when Heidegger is attempting to correlate his ideas to the project for National Socialism. Aware of part of the danger, Heidegger rejects the idea that attunement should be understood as a mode of tuning-in to the popular mood of the *Volk*; Heidegger is generally hostile to German romantic folkish appeals to communal essence. Yet in his notorious 'Black Notebooks', Heidegger does set out to define the imperative to retune them. 'Finally: incorporated into creative joint-responsibility of the truth of folkish [*völkisch*] *Dasein*. Basic attunement' (82). This basic attunement, incorporated as the immanent passion of 'the spiritual-historical destiny' of the German people, is the necessary condition and principle force for the 'productive recreation of Dasein' and the means for National Socialism to 'accomplish itself' through 'struggle' (Heidegger, 2016: 303).

The mood of Walker's work, by contrast, is never in step with such a force of political 'accomplishment', even as it is clearly fascinated by its potential for morbid violence. Walker's songs de-tune and de-ontologize the political assumption of Heidegger's notion of the 'basic attunement' (*die Grundstimmung*) of *Dasein* to its being-in-the-world. Walkerian *ek-stasis* does not provide the *rausch* of a collective ecstasy, but a continual, ascetic exacerbation of one's discordance with one's sonic reality. This can be heard everywhere in Walker's oeuvre, but perhaps most specifically in the relation he has with his voice which, from the beginning, has been regarded as contingent and strange. John Maus was initially the lead singer of the Walker Brothers, and Williams reports the anecdote from the recording of the Mann and Weil song 'Lover Her' that 'one of the greatest voices in popular music' came 'out of nowhere' when producer Nick Venet asked if anyone in the band would like to try to sing in a baritone (Williams, 2006: 20). As it becomes honed and extended throughout his career, the tonality of Walker's voice, as described by Alison Goldfrapp in Kijak's documentary, is both 'beautiful and unpleasant' (2006). The aesthetic of the voice negates itself in an ugliness beautifully attuned to the trauma of existence. Elsewhere, Walker has described his voice as 'a beast all on its own'; 'I think of it as another thing' (Thorn, 2015: 196). Walker's voice 'calls the alien as that to which the invisible imparts itself in order to remain what it is – unknown' (Heidegger, 1971: 225).

Is Scott Walker a poet in a destitute time?

A cursory listen to any of Walker's later albums would certainly lead one to believe that the current time is a destitute one, devoid not only of the gods but any form of constraint that didn't precisely drive the barbarism of the world to greater feats of depravity. But his songs also suggest that there has never been any other time than this. Furthermore, Walker isn't a poet. He's a lyricist and, according to Don Paterson, author of the latest attempt to define the parameters of poetry, poems are not songs and lyricists necessarily make bad poets. This is because the 'musicality' inherent to poetic speech has to be stripped out in order to be enhanced by actual music (Paterson, 2018: 10). Poetry is the product of 'natural human speech' (70) not the sound of a baritone straining at the limit of its range. Incidentally, Paterson's conception of poetry is both highly canonical and exemplary of the mimetic tradition of aesthetics from Plato and Aristotle, that Heidegger calls metaphysical (1996: 18). Indeed, Paterson seeks to ground and justify poetry, or at least the poetry that he likes and values, in the science of acoustics and the way that sound is processed in the brain (Paterson, 2018: 48–9). The problem with this form of justification, as the physicist Heisenberg stated in the mid-twentieth century, is that scientific descriptions of nature do not describe nature but the scientific relationship with nature (Heisenberg, 1958: 28–9). For Heisenberg, famously, 'the scientific method of analysing, explaining and classifying … has become conscious of its own limitations, which arise out of the fact that by its intervention science alters and refashions the object of investigation' (1958: 29). The supposed objectivity of the correlation that would ground the language of the poem in the scientific description of nature erases the blind spot that is the position of (scientific) deformation; it is this position, this hole, from which poetry precisely proceeds.

From Paterson's critical perspective, that is metaphysical in both its aesthetics and its scientism, Walker writes not only bad poetry but also bad lyrics because they are frequently too similar to poetry. They can be difficult and full of techniques more suited to poetry than lyrics. He starts songs *in media res*, making them 'from fragments'; he introduces 'ellipsis, lacunae, discontinuous leaps', unfamiliar diction, he works particularly with the 'half-said' that requires 'each reader to meet the poem half-way' (Paterson, 2018: 17). As such, these are bad lyrics to very bad songs. You can't sing along or dance to them. They are unlikely to form the backdrop to a love affair or dinner party. Eimear McBride, in her introduction to *Sundog*, suggests that in literary terms Walker's work answers Ezra Pound's rallying cry 'Make it New!' (2018: xx). But not as a modernist like Pound, or even a postmodernist or ironic artist-as-object. Walker's work summons the outside; it is the conduit of the spiritual because, as he suggests, his sound resonates in 'the world's night' (Heidegger, 1971: 94).

Walker's late work does not offer an experience of listening pleasure by most people's standards, nor of the pleasures normally associated with song. It poses many problems, not least of lyrical comprehension which, given that the words are supposed to provide the music with its principle of organization, means that the fragmented nature of the music likewise compounds the lack of formal structure and orientation. Along with the strangeness of Walker's voice, another consistent aspect of his work's mood that takes on a more formal, constitutive role in the later work is his signature use of tone which is poised uncertainly between a chord and a dis-chord, a major and a minor, that is frequently sustained over an extended period. Walker's orchestral arranger Brian Gascoigne, speaking in *30th Century Man* at the time of *The Drift*, comments that 'the strings are mostly one note for 16 bars. He gets them to do it again and again until he gets the "emotion" [that he says he wants], but in fact in the case of the string players, when he hears the difference, its irritation' (Kijak, 2006). This comment has the unfortunate effect of suggesting that Gascoigne thinks that Walker is an idiot and doesn't know or appreciate the difference. I think it is likely that the sound produced by stretched, stressed and 'irritated' musicians is precisely the sound that Walker wants; irritation provides the existential grounding of the musicians' technical simulation of emotion. In many of his songs, no doubt, the irritated semblance of emotion is iterated at various intervals, heightening the sense of edginess and tension. Similarly, Walker's baritone voice is pushed to the top of its range, straining at a vertiginous point to produce an uneasy listening experience, forcing listeners to attend to words that barely make sense. According to the same film, Walker's producer Peter Walsh says that the vocal melody is kept from the musicians until the point of recording in order to prevent 'the band' interpreting (or 'rocking') it in their own way. Walker's songs must not swing, they must not bear a military beat or a mindless groove.

Formally, Walker's *a*-tonal string drones and vertiginously pitched baritone seek precisely to mark the point of differentiation between existence and being. The songs pre-suppose a pre-ontological existence of a one-all-alone that is out of tune with being. There is no communal essence to them, no folky concern, no group improvisation. Which is no doubt why they are unpopular. If the pleasure of song, of singing and listening, provides a sense of well-being to the social bond that the individual has to his or her community, Walker's songs do the opposite. They produce friction between this individual and its community. They are not concerned with the individual. They aren't going to console, galvanize, celebrate or commemorate any community. While they clearly have a political dimension, they are neither folk nor protest songs. In McBride's introduction to Walker's lyrics, which she says is not so much about the songs as 'their extraordinary effect', this is the experience that they convey: 'He is alone in it and then you are alone in it. At times, listening to a Scott Walker record is like listening to the very distillation of solitude' (McBride, 2018: ix.). Indeed, this is the very kernel of the political potential of his records in which 'the revolt of a singular subject … meets resonances in other subjects (Caroz, 2018: 111). Alone, Walker's songs enjoin us to care for ourselves, and therefore for others, limitlessly because fathomless solitude is the very basis of that care. This is part of their efficacy as a form of *epimeileia* in which the care-for-oneself is the pre-condition for an openness to the world in all its otherness. It can perhaps be summed up by Nietzsche in *Thus Spake Zarathustra*:

> The thought most difficult to bear, as the convalescent's conquering thought, must first of all be *sung*; … such singing … must itself become the convalescence; [moreover] such singing must be *singular* … it dare not become a popular tune.
>
> **(NIETZSCHE IN HEIDEGGER**, 1984: II: 58)

Rejecting the path of popularity in an age where it is becoming the only form of legitimacy implies destitution, but it does not mean that the unpopular does not remain open to the world. On the contrary, it is on the basis of the singular know-how of his art, and his exclusive fidelity to it, that Walker continued to engage with the world even as that necessitated rebelling against generic conformity, political clichés, external authorities and common ideals – including those that had become common to his own practice. Of course, Walker worked with other people, often the same people, and the songs are offered to a listener; to all listeners alive and yet to be born. Acknowledging his relative unpopularity, Walker allowed that in the first instance 'I am writing for myself, but I'm writing for everyone else too … I feel I'm writing for everyone. Just they haven't discovered it yet', laughing that by that time, he'll be 'six feet under' (Clark, 2018). Only Walker's writing, then, and its destiny among the in-existent, can answer the question of whether or not he is 'a poet in a destitute time' or what might remain 'fateful' in his song (Heidegger, 1971: 142).

'A Lover Loves' (2006)

(Scott Walker)

In a number of interviews Walker has drawn attention to the way his albums tend 'to end with whimpers' (Young, 2013: 255). The last tracks of *Climate of Hunter, Tilt, The Drift* and *Bish Bosch* end with relatively simple songs in which Walker is accompanied by a single instrument – acoustic guitar or piano – which he usually plays himself. This is the case with 'A Lover Loves', *The Drift*'s closer. In his interview with Rob Young, Walker does not confirm Young's suggestion that it is a deathbed song, but he does acknowledge that it is addressed to inexistence, to people who are dead or who, because they are fictional, have never existed (255). The song has an A-B-A structure, and the middle 'B' section consists of a list of dances (waltz, samba, gavotte) offered to a series of named figures who represent a characteristic set of Walker's personae: extinct and cartoon animals, the Kaiser, Joseph Beuys, the socialist revolutionary Rosa Luxembourg and Tintin, an amusing example of European culture. The lover loves them all? The important thing, it seems, is that none of them exist – anymore than the dances, said to be dedicated to them, are musically represented in the song. For the most part, 'A Lover Loves' consists of a very simple two-note refrain plucked, as if by an absolute beginner, from the bass 'E' and 'A' strings of an acoustic guitar. The notes are at least tuneful through the first section of the song until it reaches the list of the dead and fictional when an upstroke on the 'D' string produces a typical Walkerian non-note, a minimal (dis)chord that introduces a third element to disrupt the couple.

Another couple, also apparently dead or indifferent – 'one cold hand in another colder' – are the subject of the first and third sections of the song. The image recalls Philip Larkin's medieval earl and countess, sculpted in memorial stone, in 'An Arundel Tomb', the last poem of his collection *The Whitsun Weddings* (1964). The poet, ghosting around churches and cathedrals as was Larkin's custom, experiences a 'sharp, tender shock' as he notices that the couple, otherwise conventionally attired in knightly and ceremonial garb, are shown hand in hand. This reference is supported by the opening line of Walker's song where 'corneas misted' echo the 'blurred faces' in Larkin's poem. Both works convey a sense of scepticism to the idea of eternal love, however. 'Time has transfigured them into untruth', declares Larkin philosophically, making him sound almost like Heidegger, who writes in his essay on 'What Are Poets For?' that 'what is presumed to be eternal merely conceals a suspended transiency' (Heidegger, 1971: 142). Larkin's scepticism, however, is shaped by his idea of Englishness. His poem paints a typically equivocal picture that is poised between regret for the passing of Chivalric romance and the disenchantment of an atheistic scientism: love is an 'almost-instinct almost true'. In Walker's song, the love that might amount to everything, if only for a moment, if only the lover could reach it, appears to be countermanded by the dis-chord of the unattuned string, the *a*-tone of the one-all-alone, unless this dis-chord is precisely the symptom of their idiosyncratic coupling. Indeed, counter-pointed to both words and music, almost redeeming, almost ruining the song is an insistent sound object, '*Psst*': the plosive vocative commonly used to attract attention, often indicating a secret message or intimate connection. It sounds like one of Walker's rare, direct appeals to the listener, his singular partner, perhaps dead or inexistent, but left with an enigmatic promise that from *a* hand to *one* hand, no matter how cold, everything is within reach.

'Song is existence', writes Heidegger, quoting from Rainer Maria Rilke's *Sonnets to Orpheus* (Heidegger, 1971: 138). While for the god Orpheus, 'who lives in-finitely in the Open', song is easy, for mortals it is hard because 'the singing may no longer be a solicitation, but must be existence' (138–9). Walker's song calls us enigmatically into existence in the form of a solicitation. *Psst!* 'Song is the awareness of time', writes Rovelli, following Heidegger, 'it *is* time'. The songwriter is thus the conduit of the destitution brought by time. But as such the songwriter or poet is also a conduit to the future, from where he or she arrives in the song of a once-present existence; a one-all-alone, suspending time 'in the void of a durationless now' (Heidegger, 1971: 142): a hand holding on to the sound in which one can hear everything.

NOTES

Introduction

1 The interpretative commentaries are often quite detailed, but because of copyright restrictions it is not possible to quote many examples of the lyrics. Therefore to get the full benefit of this book, it is important to have access to the songs in the form of records or CDs and to consult the lyrics printed on the record sleeve or CD booklet.

2 See for example Pierre-Gilles Guéguen on the role Georges Dyer played for Francis Bacon. (Guéguen, 2016).

3 Lewis Williams in his track-by-track account of Walker's songs writes that it is unclear exactly what Semel's contribution to the songs were, suggesting that 'Walker had already written the tunes and most of the lyrics before working on them with Semel, and part of the latter's contribution was to strike out words "likely to offend old ladies"'. (2006: 94).

4 That existence or the 'there is' is something of the One is the defining call of the henology of Jacques Lacan's late seminars. First announced in Seminar XIX, titled ... or Worse (2018), Lacan develops his notion of the One independent from Being from a reading of Plato's *Parmenides* and set theory in a logic that is also based in the absence of a sexual relation (Lacan's other keynote declaration of the time). With regard to the *Parmenides*, the question of whether there is One, or whether there is not One, is the fundamental point around which the question of existence revolves. The question of the One is thus outside and prior to the realm of Platonic Ideas from which Being is formed. What *is* can only be defined in its (non)relation to that which is not, deriving its very support, moreover, 'from an *out there* that is not'. What is at issue with the One, Lacan writes, 'arises from a *point* that for Plato [is] the *instant*, the *sudden*, and it's the only point at which he can make it subsist' (Lacan, 2018: 117). In this work on Scott Walker, I am concerned with the example of psychoanalysis only in the sense, following my previous book, that the real of this 'instant' or 'suddenness' is always announced by sound, that is to say in non-sense. (Wilson, 2015).

One

1   At the time of writing, this configuration of traits is being applied to US president Donald Trump. '100% of Trump's aides say he's childlike' claims Michael Wolff in his exposé, describing his leadership style in *Fire and Fury: Inside the Trump White House* as 'chaotic' (Wolff, 2018: 111, 113). No doubt the incredulous alarm triggered by the 'gruesomely fascinating' Donald Trump is a tacit recognition of this common quality. In his review of the book for the *New Statesman*, John Gray also seems to confirm Foucault's suggestion that Trump's buffoonery and childishness is a useful 'distraction' to the real exercise of power in the American state which is rapidly turning into 'an oligarchical and illiberal democracy not unlike the kinds that have emerged in post-communist Europe', for whom Vladimir Putin, another sinister figure whose narcissism frequently verges on the risible, is the model (John Gray, 2018).

2   Foucault describes the connection in a slightly different way: 'From Nero, perhaps the founding figure of the despicable sovereign, down to the little man with trembling hands crowned with forty million deaths who, from deep in his bunker, asks for only two things, that everything else above him be destroyed and that he is given chocolate cakes until he bursts, you have the whole outrageous functioning of the despicable sovereign' (Foucault, 2003: 12).

Swarm

1   This quotation is from one of the four lectures delivered at Bremen on the subject of technology. This is the one comment that is cited by Lacoue-Labarthe: 'Agriculture is now a motorized food industry, the same thing in its essence as the production of corpses in the gas chambers and the extermination camps, the same thing as blockades and the reduction of countries to famine, the same thing as the manufacture of hydrogen bombs' (1990: 34).

2   In his essay on 'Ex-sistence' (2016) Jacques-Alain Miller notes first that psychoanalysis has to set itself apart from the discourse of common sense, since the latter is the product of repression, but also second, that in spite of all efforts to engage with and develop the science of linguistics, the analysis of rhetoric, logic and mathematization, psychoanalysis remains proscribed from the university. Tillers in the cybernetic furrows of university discourse are compelled 'to act as if Lacan's teaching had never existed' (17–18). With this acknowledgement, I continue on this ironic path.

3   These formulas are also from Jacques Lacan, formulated initially in Seminar XIX (2018) and XX (1998), the Seminar entitled 'Encore: On Feminine

Sexuality, The Limits of Love and Knowledge'. Jean-Claude Milner's account is authoritative (he was invited by Lacan to contribute to Seminar XX, see 101–2) and allows me both to extend Lacan's logic to cultural and political matters and to conform to the prohibition mentioned above in note 2.

4   See the installation on this website: www.iainandjane.com/work/installation/ bish-bosch-ambisymphonic

5   This is the 'invitation' that Jacques-Alain Miller takes from the final seminars of Jacques Lacan in the 1970s. '*Je la prend ici au niveau clinique comme une invitation à sacrifier le totalitarisme de l'universel à la singularité de l'Un.*' '*Être et l'Un*', 4 avril 2011.

REFERENCES

Adorno, T. W. (1981) 'Cultural Criticism and Society'. In *Prisms*, translated by
  S. S. Weber. Cambridge, MA: MIT Press.
Alden, Ginger (2014) *Elvis & Ginger: Elvis Presley's Fiancée and Last Love Finally
  Tells Her Story*. New York: The Berkeley Publishing Group.
Altham, Keith (1966) 'Walker Hostility on the Wane'. *NME*, 15.04.66.
Ansermet, Francois (2019) 'Inventions vs Certainties'. *The Lacanian Review
  Online*, http://www.thelacanianreviews.com/inventions vs-certainties/
  (Accessed 05.04.19).
Arendt, Hannah (2006) *Eichmann in Jerusalem: A Report on the Banality of Evil*.
  Harmondsworth: Penguin.
Arendt, Hannah (2017) *The Origins of Totalitarianism*. London: Penguin.
Augstein, Rudolf and Georg Wolff (1966) 'Martin Heidegger'. *Der Spiegel*
  23.09.66; published 31 May 1976.
Anonymous (2019) *The Times*, 26.3.2019.
Bair, Deirdre (1980) *Samuel Beckett*. London: Picador.
Bakewell, Sarah (2016) *At the Existentialist Café*. London: Chatto and Windus.
Bangs, Alan (1984) 'Interview with Scott Walker'. *Night Flights*, German Radio.
Bataille, Georges (1986 [1957]) *Erotism: Death & Sensuality*, translated by Mary
  Dalwood. San Francisco, CA: City Lights.
Bataille, Georges (1988) *Inner Experience*. New York: SUNY Press.
Bataille, Georges (1991) *The Accursed Share*, Vols. II, The History of Eroticism &
  III Sovereignty [1976], translated by Robert Hurley. New York: Zone Books.
Baudrillard, Jean (2002) *The Spirit of Terrorism*. London: Verso.
Beaumont Thomas, Ben (2019) 'Scott Walker, experimental pop hero, dies
  aged 76' *The Guardian*, 25.3.2019. 10.11 GMT. https://www.theguardian.c
  om/music/2019/mar/25/scott-walker-experimental-pop-hero-dies-aged-76
  (Accessed 25.03.19).
De Beauvoir, Simone (2009) *The Second Sex*, translated by Constance Borde and
  Sheila Malovany-Chevallier. London: Cape.
Beckett, Samuel (1981) *Waiting for Godot*. London: Faber.
Beckett, Samuel (1985) 'Krapp's Last Tape'. *Collected Shorter Plays of Samuel
  Beckett*. London: Faber.
Biers, Katherine (2015) 'The Typewriter's Truth'. In Stephen Sale and Laura
  Salisbury (eds), *Kittler Now: Current Perspectives in Kittler Studies*. London:
  Polity, 132–54.
Blanchot, Maurice (1981) *The Gaze of Orpheus*. New York: Station Hill Press.
Blanchot, Maurice (1982) *The Space of Literature*. Lincoln: University of Nebrska
  Press.

Blanchot, Maurice (2007) *The Last Man*, translated by Lydia Davis. New York: Ubueditions.

Blum, William (2003) *Killing Hope: US Military and CIA Interventions since WWII*.

Bosworth, R. J. B. (2017) *Claretta: Mussolini's Last Lover*. New Haven, CT: Yale University Press.

Breton, Andre (1930) *Manifestoes of Surrealism*, Ann Arbor Paperbacks. Ann Arbor: University of Michigan Press.

Butler, Judith (1990) *Gender Trouble*. London: Routledge.

Camus, Albert (1977a) *The Myth of Sisyphus*. Harmondsworth: Penguin.

Camus, Albert (1977b) *The Rebel*. Harmondsworth: Penguin.

Camus, Albert (1982) *The Plague*. London: Penguin.

Camus, Albert (2012) *The Outsider*. London: Penguin.

Caroz, Gil (2018) 'Why Does Politics Need to Be Enlightened by Psychoanalysis Today?' In Bogdan Wolf (ed), *Psychoanalytic Notebooks* 32. London: The London Society of the New Lacanian School, pp. 105–14.

Chion, Michel (2016) *Sound: An Acoulogical Treatise*. Durham, NC: Duke University Press.

Churchland, P. M. and P. S. Churchland (1998) *On the Contrary: Critical Essays 1987-1997*. Cambridge, MA: The MIT Press.

Clark, Alex (2018) 'Interview with Scott Walker'. *The Guardian*, 15.01.18. www.theguardian.com/music/2018/jan/15/scott-walker-sundog-book-lyrics-interview (Accessed 03.02.18).

Cobb, Noel (1992) *Archetypal Imagination*. Hudson, New York: Lindisfarne Press.

Cocker, Jarvis (2013) 'Interview with Scott Walker'. *Sunday Service*, BBC6 Music.

Coleman, Nick (2017) *Voices: How a Great Singer Can Change Your Life*. London: Jonathan Cape.

DeLong, Thomas A. (2008) *Quiz Craze: America's Infatuation with Game Shows*. New York: Praeger.

Devin, William Daniels (2012) 'Tracing the Footsteps of Scott Walker'. *The Bomber Jacket*, 07.08.12. http://thebomberjacket.com/2012/08/07/tracing-the-footsteps-of-scott-walker/ (Accessed 06.0618).

Dennis, Jon (2014) 'Scott Walker's Top Ten Best Songs'. *The Guardian*, 05.03.14.

Derrida, Jacques (1981) *Positions*. Chicago, IL: University of Chicago Press.

Dillon, Michael and Julian Reid (2009) *The Liberal Way of War*. London: Routledge.

Dolar, Mladan and Slavoj Zizek (2002) *Opera's Second Death*. London: Routledge.

Doran, John (2014) 'Interview with Scott Walker', *The Quietus*, 08.10.14.

Dostoevsky, Fyodor (1994) *Demons*. New York: Vintage.

Doyle, Tom (2013) 'Peter Walsh & Scott Walker Producing Bish Bosch'. *Sound on Sound*, 08.01.13. www.soundonsound.com/people/peter-walsh-scott-walker (Accessed 05.05.19).

Fenn, Elizabeth A. (2000) 'Biological Warfare in Eighteenth-Century North America'. *The Journal of American History*, 86.4: 23–42.

Ferrara, Abel (2014) *Pasolini*. BFI. BFIV2058.

Fifer, W. P. and C. M. Moore (1994) 'The Role of the Mother's Voice in the Organization of Brain Function in the Newborn'. *Acta Paediatric Supplement*, 397: 380–405.

Foucault Michel (1978) *The History of Sexuality: An Introduction*. Harmondsworth: Penguin.

Foucault, Michel (1983) *Discipline and Punish*. London: Penguin.

Foucault, Michel (1989) *Foucault Live*. New York: Semiotext(e).

Foucault, Michel (2003) *Abnormal: Lectures at the Collège de France, 1974–75*. London: Verso.

Foucault, Michel (2011) *The Courage of Truth: Lectures at the Collège de France, 1983–84*. London: Palgrave Macmillan.

Freud, Sigmund (1989) *Civilization and Its Discontents*. New York: Norton Press.

Freud, Sigmund (2001a) 'On Narcissism'. In James Strachey (ed), *Standard Edition*, Vol. XIV (1914–16), London: Vintage, 73–105.

Freud, Sigmund (2001b) 'Group Psychology and the Ego'. In James Strachey (ed), *Standard Edition*, London: Vintage, 67–144.

Fukuyama, Francis (1989) 'The End of History?' *The National Interest*, 16 (summer): 3–18.

Fukuyama, Francis (1992) *The End of History and the Last Man*. Harmondsworth: Penguin.

Gillespie, Nancy (2018) 'Posthuman Desire: The One-All-Alone in *Her, Ex Machina* ...' In Svitlana Matviyenko and Judith Roof (eds), *Lacan and the Posthuman*. London: Palgrave, 153–69.

Graham-Dixon, Andrew (2006) *The Culture Show*. BBC TV.

Graham-Harrison, Emma (2014) '"I'm Still Nervous," Says Soldier Who Shot Nicolae Ceausescu'. *The Guardian*, 07.12.14. www.theguardian.com/world/2014/dec/07/nicolae-ceausescu-execution-anniversary-romania (Accessed 09.06.17).

Gray, John (2016) 'The Shifting Shaman of the Modern Age'. *The New Statesman*, 18.01.16.

Gray, John (2018) 'Inside the Madhouse: Why American Oligarchy Won't Let Trump Fail Yet'. www.newstatesman.com/culture/books/2018/01/inside-madhouse-why-american-oligarchy-won-t-let-trump-fail-yet (Accessed 03.04.18).

Griffiths, Trevor (1980) *Comedians*. London: Faber.

Guéguen, Pierre-Gilles (2016) 'Manipulation of the Imaginary in a Homosexual Couple'. In M.-H. Brousse (ed), *The Lacanian Review* 2 (2017), 30–42.

Hainge, Greg (2013) *Noise Matters: Towards an Ontology of Noise*. London: Bloomsbury.

Halberstam, Jack and Marie-Hélène Brousse (2016) 'The Dialogue'. *The Lacanian Review*, 2: 21–9.

Heidegger, Martin (1971) *Poetry, Language, Thought*. London: Harper & Row.

Heidegger, Martin (1984) *Nietzsche: Volumes One and Two*. London: Harper Collins.

Heidegger, Martin (1996) *Hölderlin's hymn 'The Ister'*. Bloomington: Indiana University Press.

Heidegger, Martin (2000) *Elucidations of Hölderlin's Poetry*. New York: Humanity Press.

Heidegger, Martin (2009) 'The Question Concerning Technology'. In *Basic Writings*. London: Routledge.

Heidegger, Martin (2010) *Being and Time*. Albany, NY: SUNY Press.

Heidegger, Martin (2016) *Ponderings* II–IV Black Notebooks 1931–38. Bloomington: Indiana University Press.

Heisenberg, Werner (1958) *The Physicist's Conception of Nature*. London: Hutchinson Scientific and Technical, pp. 28–29.

Henry, William (2006) *Mary Magdalene: The Illuminator*. Adventures Unlimited Press, p. 184.

Hoare, Philip (2016) 'Lighting Up a Blacked-Out Britain'. *The New Statesman*, 15–21.01.16.

Hoffmam, Frank and Michael Pitts (2002) *The Rise of the Crooners*. The Scarecrow Press.

Joyce, James (2000) *Portrait of the Artist as a Young Man*. London: Penguin.

Kafka, Franz (1985) *Metamorphosis and Other Stories*. London: Penguin.

Karpf, Anne (2006) *The Human Voice: The Story of a Remarkable Talent*. London: Bloomsbury, p. 105.

Kessen, William et al. (1979) 'The Imitation of Pitch in Infants'. *Infant Behaviour and Development*, 2.1: 99.

Kierkegaard, Søren (2004) *Either/Or*. London: Penguin.

Kierkegaard, Søren (2012) *Fear and Trembling*. London: Merchant Books.

Kijak, Stephen (2006) *30th Century Man*. Verve Pictures.

Kittler, Friedrich (1990) *Discourse Networks*. Stanford, CA: Stanford University Press.

Kittler, Friedrich (1997) *Literature, Media, Information Systems*, edited and introduced by John Johnston. London: G&B Arts.

Knowlson, James (1996) *Damned to Fame: The Life of Samuel Beckett*. London: Bloomsbury.

Kojève, Alexandre (1968) *Essaid'une histor*.

Kray, Reginald (1991) *Born Fighter*. London: Arrow.

Lacan, Jacques (1998) *Encore: On Feminine Sexuality. The Limits of Love and Knowledge*. The Seminar of Jacques Lacan Book XX edited by Jacques-Alain Miller, translated by Bruce Fink. New York: Norton.

Lacan, Jacques (2018) *... or Worse*. The Seminar of Jacques Lacan Book XIX edited by Jacques-Alain Miller, translated by A. R. Price. London: Polity.

Laclau, Ernesto (2007) *On Populist Reason*. London: Verso.

Lacoue-Labarthe, Philippe (1990) *Heidegger, Art and Politics*. Oxford: Blackwell.

Lanier, Jared (2010) *You Are Not a Gadget*. London: Penguin.

Le Guin, Ursula (2010) *Lavinia*. London: Phoenix.

Lemann, Nicholas (1991). *The Promised Land: The Great Black Migration and How It Changed America*. New York: Vintage.

Lispector, Clarice (2012) *The Passion of G.H.* London: Penguin.

Lispector, Clarice (2014) *Near to the Wild Heart.* London: Penguin.

Love, Jeff (2018) *The Black Circle: A Life of Alexandre Kojève.* New York: University of Columbia Press.

Luke, Hugh J. (1965) 'Introduction'. *The Last Man* by Mary Shelley. Lincoln: University of Nebraska Press.

Maconie, Stuart (2013) 'Interview with Scott Walker'. *The Freak Zone*, BBC Radio 6.

McCormick, Neil (2014) 'Scott Walker & Sunn O))), Soused, Review'. *The Daily Telegraph*, 24.10.14. www.telegraph.co.uk/culture/music/cdreviews/111700 93/Scott-Walker-and-Sunn-O-Soused-review-self-absorbed.html (Accessed 08.08.18).

McGavin, George (2018) *Swarms.* BBC4; BBC Animal/Plant Co-production.

Metzinger, Thomas (2003) *Being No One: The Self-Model Theory of Subjectivity.* Cambridge, MA: The MIT Press.

Metzinger, Thomas (2009) *The Ego Tunnel: The Science of the Mind and the Myth of the Self.* New York: Basic Books.

Miller, Jacques-Alain (2016) 'Ex-sistence'. *Lacanian Ink* 48. New York: Wooster Press, pp. 14–47.

Miller, Jacques-Alain (2018) 'The Space of a Hallucination'. In *The Lacanian Review* 6: 83–108.

Miller, James (1993) *The Passion of Michel Foucault.* London: Harper Collins.

Milner, Jean-Claude (2016) *Relire la Révolution.* Paris: Verdier.

Milner, Jean-Claude (2017) 'An Interview with Jean-Claude Milner'. In Brousse, Marie-Hélène (ed), *The Lacanian Review* 3: pp. 12–19.

Milner, Jean-Claude Milner (2010) 'The Traps of the All'. *Journal of the Jan van Eyck Circle for Lacanian Ideology Critique*, 3: 22–39.

Moder, Benjamin (2014) in Clarice Lispector, *Near to the Wild Heart.* London: Penguin.

Moi, Toril (2010) 'The Adulteress Wife', *London Review of Books*, 32.3: 3–6.

Morse, Erik, (2013) 'An Interview with Scott Walker' *The Believer*. Issue 100. 1st July.

Nancy, Jean-Luc Nancy (1991) *The Inoperable Community.* Minneapolis: University of Minnesota Press.

Niederland, William G. (1958) 'Early Auditory Experiences, Beating Fantasies and Primal Scene', *Psychoanalytic Study of the Child.* (in Karpf, p. 65.)

Nietzsche, Friedrich (1968) *Twilight of the Idols.* London: Penguin.

Nietzsche, Friedrich (1974) *The Gay Science.* Harmondsworth: Penguin.

Pasolini, Pier Paolo (1976) 'The Cinema of Poetry'. In Bill Nichols (ed), *Movies and Methods* I Berkeley: University of California Press.

Paterson, Don (2018) *The Poem: Lyric, Sign, Metre.* London: Faber.

Petridis, Alexis (2012) 'Scott Walker's *Bish Bosch*'. *The Guardian*, 29.11.12. www.theguardian.com/music/2012/nov/29/scott-walker-bish-bosch-review (Accessed 08.08.18).

Pitts, Michael and Frank Hoffman (2001) *The Rise of the Crooners.* Lanham, MD: Scarecrow Press.

Plato (1985) *The Symposium*. London: Penguin.

Pudovkin, V. I. (1985) 'Asynchronism as a Principle of Sound Film'. In Elisabeth Weis and John Belton (eds), *Film Sound: Theory and Practice*. Columbia University Press, 86–91.

Reich, Robert (2002) *The Future of Success*. London: Vintage.

Rejali, Darius (1994) 'The History of Electric Torture'. http://www.reed.edu/poli_sci/faculty/rejali/articles/History_of_Electric_Torture.html (Accessed 13.08.16).

Roberts, Mike (2018) *How Art Made Pop and Pop Became Art*. London: Tate Publishing.

Ross, Alex (2009) *The Rest Is Noise*. New York: Harper Perennial.

Rovelli, Carlo (2016) *Reality Is Not What You Think It Is*. London: Penguin.

Rovelli, Carlo (2017) *The Order of Time*. London: Allen Lane, Penguin.

Sandall, Robert (1995) 'Interview with Scott Walker'. *BBC Radio*, 3.

Sartre, Jean-Paul (1966) 'Jean-Paul Sartre Répond'. *Arc*, 30: 87–96.

Sartre, Jean-Paul (1975) 'The Childhood of the Leader'. In *The Wall*. London: New Directions, 84–144.

Sartre, Jean-Paul (1976) *Critique of Dialectical Reason*. London: New Left Books.

Sartre, Jean-Paul (2000) *Nausea*. London: Penguin Modern Classics.

Sartre, Jean-Paul (2003) *Being and Nothingness*. London: Penguin Classics.

Sartre, Jean-Paul (2007) *Existentialism Is a Humanism*. Oxford: Blackwell.

Sartrelli, Stephen (2014) *The Selected Poetry of Pier Paolo Pasolini: A Bilingual Edition*. Chicago University Press, 387, 389.

Schaeffer, Pierre (2012) *In Search of a Concrete Music*. Oakland: University of California Press.

Schaeffer, Pierre (2017) *Treatise on Musical Objects*. Oakland: University of California Press.

Schafer, R. Murrey (1994) *Our Sonic Environment and the Soundscape*. Rochester, Vermont: Destiny Books.

Schwartz, Barth David (2017) *Pasolini Requiem*. Chicago, IL: University of Chicago Press.

Scott, George (2015) *Je t'aime: The Story of French Song with Petula Clark*. BBC4 Documentaries.

Shelley, Mary (1965) *The Last Man*. London: Penguin.

Soler, Colette (2014) *Lacan – The Unconscious Reinvented*. London: Karnac.

Soler, Colette (2018) *Lacan Reading Joyce*. London: Routledge.

Thompson, EP (1967) *Time, Work, Discipline and Industrial Capitalism*. London: Penguin.

Thorn, Tracey (2015) *Naked at the Albert Hall: The Inside Story of Singing*. London: Virago.

Tomlinson, Gary (2015) *A Million Years of Music*. New York: Zone Books.

Turkle, Sherry (2010) *Alone Together: Why We Expect More from Technology and Less from Each Other*. New York: Basic Books.

Turkle, Sherry (2015) *Reclaiming Conversation*. New York: Basic Books.

Van Pelt, Robert Jan (2002) *The Case for Auschwitz: Evidence from the Irving Trial*. Indiana University Press.

Walker, Scott (2018) *Sundog: Selected Lyrics* with an Introduction by Eimear McBride. London: Faber.

Webb, Stanley (1988) 'The Organs of Winchester Cathedral'. *The Musical Times* 129: 369–72.

Weidel, Stefan (2006) 'Interview mit Scott Walker'. *Frankfurter Allgemeinen Sonntagszeitung*, 23.04.2006, Nr. 16 / Seite 27.

Williams, Lewis (2006) *Scott Walker: The Rhymes of Goodbye*. London: Plexus.

Williamson, Joel (2014) *Elvis Presley: A Southern Life*. Oxford: Oxford University Press.

Wilson, Scott (2015) *Stop Making Sense: Music from the Perspective of the Real*. London: Karnac.

Winthrop-Young (2011) *Kittler and the Media*. London: Polity.

Wire, *The* (2012), 'Scott' issue 346, December 2012, https://www.thewire.co.uk/about/artists/scott-walker (Accessed 5.3.17).

Wolff, Michael (2018) *Fire and Fury: Inside the Trump White House*. Little, Brown.

Woods, Paul (2013) *The Curious Life and Work of Scott Walker*. London: Omnibus Press.

Young, Rob (2006) 'Interview with Scott Walker' Unedited transcript. *The Wire* 267, 23.05.06. http://forum.index.hu/Article/showArticle?t=9115509 (Accessed 5.3.17).

Young, Rob (2013) *No Regrets: Writings on Scott Walker*. London: Wire.

SELECT DISCOGRAPHY

The Walker Brothers – singles:

(1964)   *Pretty Girls Everywhere / Doin' The Jerk.* Philips BF1401
(1965)   *Love Her / The Seventh Dawn.* Philips BFR1409
(1965)   *Make it Easy on Yourself / But I Do.* Philips BF1454
(1965)   *My Ship is Coming In / You're All Around Me.* Philips BF1454
(1966)   *The Sun Ain't Gonna Shine Anymore / After the Lights Go Out.*
        Philips BF1473
(1966)   *(Baby) You Don't Have to Tell Me / My Love is Growing.* Philips 1514
(1966)   *Another Tear Falls / Saddest Night in the World.* Philips BF1514
(1966)   *Deadlier than the Male / Archangel.* Philips BF1548
(1967)   *Stay with me Baby / Turn Out the Moon.* Philips BF1548
(1967)   *Walking in the Rain / Baby Make it the Last Time.* Philips
        BF1576
(1975)   *No Regrets / Remember Me.* GTO GT42
(1976)   *Lines / First Day.* GTO GT67
(1976)   *We're All Alone / Have You Seen My Baby.* GTO GT78
(1978)   *The Electrician / Den Haague.* GTO GT230

The Walker Brothers – albums:

(1965)   *Take it Easy with the Walker Brothers.* Philips BL7691
(1966)   *Portrait.* Philips BL7732
(1967)   *Images.* Philips BL7770
(1975)   *No Regrets.* GTO GTLP007
(1976)   *Lines.* GTO GTLP014
(1978)   *Nite Flights.* GTO GTLP 033.

Scott Walker – singles:

(1967)	*Jackie/The Plague*. Philips 1628
(1968)	*Joanna / Always Coming Back To You*. Philips 1662
(1969)	*The Lights of Cincinnati / Two Weeks Since You've Gone*. Philips 1793
(1971)	*I Still See You / My Way Home*. Philips 6006-168
(1973)	*The Me I Never Knew / This Way Mary*. Philips 6006-311
(1973)	*A Woman Left Lonely / Where Love Has Died*. CBS 1795
(1974)	*Delta Dawn / We Had it All*. CBS 2521
(1984)	*Track Three / Blanket Roll Blues*. Virgin VS 666
(1993)	*Man From Reno / Indecent Sacrifice*. Fontana CD 682382-2 (France)

Scott Walker – EPs:

(1967)	*Great Scott*. Philips Cassette. MCP-1006
(2007)	*And Who Shall Go to the Ball? And What Shall Go to the Ball?*. Instrumental Music written by Scott Walker for the dance piece performed by CandoCo Dance Company. Choreography by Rafael Bonachela. 4AD limited edition.

Scott Walker – albums:

(1967)	*Scott*. Philips 7816. Reissued on Fontana CD 510 879-2, 1992.
(1968)	*Scott 2*. Philips 7840. Reissued on Fontana CD 510 880-2, 1992.
(1969)	*Scott 3*. Philips 7882. Reissued on Fontana CD 510 881-2, 1992.
(1969)	*Scott: Scott Walker Sings Songs from his TV Series*. Philips 7900.
(1969)	*Scott 4*. (credited to Noel Scott Engel) Philips 7913. Reissued by Fontana CD 510 882-2, 2000 – credited to Scott Walker.
(1970)	*'Til the Band Comes In*. Philips 6308 035. Reissued by Water Music CD226, 2006.
(1973)	*The Moviegoer*. Philips 6308 120
(1973)	*Any Day Now*. Philips 6308 148
(1973)	*Stretch*. CBS 65725
(1974)	*We Had it All*. CBS 80254
(1984)	*Climate of Hunter*. Virgin V2303. Reissued on Virgin CDV 2303, 2006.
(1995)	*Tilt*. Fontana vinyl 526 859-1/Fontana CD 526 859-2

(2006)   *The Drift*. 4AD vinyl CAD 2603/4AD CD CAD 2603
(2012)   *Bish Bosch*. 4AD vinyl CAD 3220 / CAD 3220CD
(2014) + Sunn0)))   *Soused*. 4AD vinyl CAD3428 / CAD3428CD

Scott Walker – soundtracks:

(1999)   *Pola X*. Bande original du film de Leos Carax composée
              Scott Walker. Barclay 547 608-2
(2016)   *The Childhood of the Leader: Original Soundtrack by Scott
              Walker*. 4AD CAD3620CD

Scott Walker – selected compilations:

(1981)   *Fire Escape in the Sky: The Godlike Genius of Scott Walker*. Zoo 2.
(1981)   *Scott Walker Sings Jacques Brel*. Phonogram 6359 090. Reissued
              on Fontana CD 838 212-2, 1990.
(1990)   *Boy Child – the Best of 1967–70*. Fontana 8428323-1
(1992)   *No Regrets: The Best of Scott Walker and the Walker Brothers
              1965–1976*. Fontana 510 831-1

INDEX